First World War
and Army of Occupation
War Diary
France, Belgium and Germany

1 DIVISION
Divisional Troops
13 Sanitary Section
8 April 1915 - 31 March 1917

WO95/1259/3

The Naval & Military Press Ltd
www.nmarchive.com
Published in association with The National Archives

Published by

The Naval & Military Press Ltd

Unit 10 Ridgewood Industrial Park,

Uckfield, East Sussex,

TN22 5QE England

Tel: +44 (0) 1825 749494

www.naval-military-press.com

www.nmarchive.com

This diary has been reprinted in facsimile from the original. Any imperfections are inevitably reproduced and the quality may fall short of modern type and cartographic standards.

Contents

War Diary	Cours St Vaast	21/04/1915	21/04/1915
War Diary	Locon	21/04/1915	22/04/1915
War Diary	Les Harrisoirs	22/04/1915	22/04/1915
War Diary	Locon	22/04/1915	23/04/1915
War Diary	Cours St Vaast	23/04/1915	23/04/1915
War Diary	Locon	23/04/1915	23/04/1915
War Diary	Allouange	24/04/1915	24/04/1915
War Diary	Cours St Vaast	24/04/1915	24/04/1915
War Diary	Locon	25/04/1915	25/04/1915
War Diary	Locon	25/04/1915	26/04/1915
War Diary	Lours St Vaast	25/04/1915	25/04/1915
War Diary	Locon	24/04/1915	24/04/1915
War Diary	Lacouture Cours St Vaast	25/04/1915	25/04/1915
War Diary	Locon	25/04/1915	26/04/1915
War Diary	Long Cornet	26/04/1915	26/04/1915
War Diary	Rue Des Chevattes	26/04/1915	26/04/1915
War Diary	Lucon	26/04/1915	27/04/1915
War Diary	Long Cornet	27/04/1915	27/04/1915
War Diary	Locon	28/04/1915	28/04/1915
War Diary	Long Cornet	28/04/1915	28/04/1915
Miscellaneous	Richebourg	29/04/1915	29/04/1915
War Diary	Long Cornet	29/04/1915	29/04/1915
War Diary	Locon	29/04/1915	29/04/1915
War Diary	Richebourg	30/04/1915	30/04/1915
War Diary	Pont Davelette	30/04/1915	30/04/1915
War Diary	Allouagne	30/04/1915	30/04/1915
War Diary	Lacouture	30/04/1915	30/04/1915
War Diary	Locon	30/04/1915	30/04/1915
War Diary	Circular Memorandum-Sanitation.		
War Diary	Conviction Quashed		
War Diary	R.A.M.C. Orders		
Miscellaneous	1st Division Summarised but not Copied No 13. Sanitary Section May 1915 Vol I		
Miscellaneous	Lacouture	01/05/1915	01/05/1915
War Diary	Richebourg	01/05/1915	01/05/1915
War Diary	Le Touret	01/05/1915	01/05/1915
War Diary	Locon	01/05/1915	01/05/1915
War Diary	Vendin	02/05/1915	02/05/1915
War Diary	Locon	02/05/1915	02/05/1915
War Diary	Richebourg	02/05/1915	02/05/1915
War Diary	Richebourg	03/05/1915	03/05/1915
War Diary	Hinges	03/05/1915	03/05/1915
War Diary	Locon	03/05/1915	03/05/1915
War Diary	Richebourg	04/05/1915	04/05/1915
War Diary	Locon	04/05/1915	04/05/1915
War Diary	Richebourg	05/05/1915	05/05/1915
War Diary	Mesplaux Farm	05/05/1915	05/05/1915
War Diary	Les Facons	05/05/1915	05/05/1915
War Diary	Rue Des Chevattes	05/05/1915	05/05/1915
War Diary	Mesplaux Farm	05/05/1915	05/05/1915
War Diary	Les Facons	05/05/1915	05/05/1915
War Diary	Le Touret	05/05/1915	05/05/1915
War Diary	Locon	05/05/1915	05/05/1915
War Diary	Richebourg	06/05/1915	06/05/1915
War Diary	Cornet Malo	06/05/1915	06/05/1915
War Diary	Locon	06/05/1915	07/05/1915

War Diary	Cornet Malo	07/05/1915	07/05/1915
War Diary	Mesplaux Farm	07/05/1915	07/05/1915
War Diary	Locon	07/05/1915	07/05/1915
War Diary	Cornet Malo	08/05/1915	08/05/1915
War Diary	Mesplaux Farm	08/05/1915	08/05/1915
War Diary	Bethune	08/05/1915	08/05/1915
War Diary	Hinges	08/05/1915	08/05/1915
War Diary	Locon	08/05/1915	09/05/1915
War Diary	Locon	09/05/1915	09/05/1915
War Diary	Bethune	09/05/1915	09/05/1915
War Diary	Locon	09/05/1915	09/05/1915
War Diary	Locon	10/05/1915	10/05/1915
War Diary	Hinges Vendin	10/05/1915	10/05/1915
War Diary	Locon	11/05/1915	11/05/1915
War Diary	Bethune	11/05/1915	11/05/1915
War Diary	Hinges	12/05/1915	12/05/1915
War Diary	Locon	12/05/1915	12/05/1915
War Diary	Bethune	12/05/1915	17/05/1915
War Diary	Beuvry	17/05/1915	17/05/1915
War Diary	Cambrin	17/05/1915	17/05/1915
War Diary	Beuvry	18/05/1915	18/05/1915
War Diary	Cambrin	18/05/1915	18/05/1915
War Diary	Bethune	18/05/1915	18/05/1915
War Diary	Beuvry Cambrin	18/05/1915	18/05/1915
War Diary	Bethune	18/05/1915	18/05/1915
War Diary	Cambrin	18/05/1915	18/05/1915
War Diary	Beuvry	19/05/1915	19/05/1915
War Diary	Cambrin	19/05/1915	19/05/1915
War Diary	Sailly Labourse	19/05/1915	19/05/1915
War Diary	Bethune	19/05/1915	19/05/1915
War Diary	Beuvry	20/05/1915	20/05/1915
War Diary	Sailly Labourse	20/05/1915	20/05/1915
War Diary	Noyeau Les Vermelles	20/05/1915	20/05/1915
War Diary	Cambrin	20/05/1915	20/05/1915
War Diary	Annequin	20/05/1915	20/05/1915
War Diary	Bethune	20/05/1915	20/05/1915
War Diary	Sailly Labourse	21/05/1915	21/05/1915
War Diary	Bethune	21/05/1915	21/05/1915
War Diary	Sailly Labourse	22/05/1915	22/05/1915
War Diary	Labourse	22/05/1915	22/05/1915
War Diary	Bethune	22/05/1915	22/05/1915
War Diary	Sailly Labourse	23/05/1915	23/05/1915
War Diary	Bethune	23/05/1915	23/05/1915
War Diary	Labourse	23/05/1915	23/05/1915
War Diary	Bethune	23/05/1915	23/05/1915
War Diary	Sailly Labourse	24/05/1915	24/05/1915
War Diary	Labourse	24/05/1915	24/05/1915
War Diary	Beuvry	24/05/1915	24/05/1915
War Diary	Labourse	24/05/1915	25/05/1915
War Diary	Verquin	25/05/1915	25/05/1915
War Diary	Sailly Labourse	25/05/1915	26/05/1915
War Diary	Verquin	26/05/1915	26/05/1915
War Diary	Labourse	26/05/1915	26/05/1915
War Diary	Sailly Labourse	27/05/1915	27/05/1915
War Diary	Verquin	27/05/1915	27/05/1915
War Diary	Bethune	27/05/1915	27/05/1915

Type	Place	From	To
War Diary	Labourse	27/05/1915	28/05/1915
War Diary	Sailly Labourse	28/05/1915	28/05/1915
War Diary	Verquin	29/05/1915	29/05/1915
War Diary	Labourse	29/05/1915	29/05/1915
War Diary	Sailly Labourse	29/05/1915	29/05/1915
War Diary	Fouquieres	29/05/1915	29/05/1915
War Diary	Verquin	29/05/1915	30/05/1915
War Diary	Labourse	30/05/1915	30/05/1915
War Diary	Verquin	30/05/1915	31/05/1915
War Diary	Labourse	31/05/1915	31/05/1915
War Diary	Verquigneul	31/05/1915	31/05/1915
War Diary	Bethune	31/05/1915	31/05/1915
War Diary	Verquin	31/05/1915	31/05/1915
Heading	121/6135 June 1915 1st Division No 13. Sanitary Section Vol II June 1915		
Heading	War Diary of Lieut G. Q. Lennane RAMCT O C No 13 Sanitary Section From June 1st 1915 To June 30 1915 (Volume 2)		
War Diary	Verquin	01/06/1915	01/06/1915
War Diary	Pithead (N.R) Prieure St Pry	01/06/1915	01/06/1915
War Diary	Vaudricourt	01/06/1915	01/06/1915
War Diary	Pithead Prieure St Pry.	01/06/1915	01/06/1915
War Diary	Bethune	02/06/1915	02/06/1915
War Diary	Pithead (Prieure St Pry)	02/06/1915	02/06/1915
War Diary	Vaudricourt	02/06/1915	03/06/1915
War Diary	Bethune	03/06/1915	03/06/1915
War Diary	Pithead Near Prieure St. Pry	03/06/1915	03/06/1915
War Diary	Bethune	04/06/1915	04/06/1915
War Diary	Pithead Near Prieure St Pry	04/06/1915	04/06/1915
War Diary	Pithead	04/06/1915	04/06/1915
War Diary	Bethune	05/06/1915	05/06/1915
War Diary	Pithead	06/06/1915	06/06/1915
War Diary	Bethune	06/06/1915	06/06/1915
War Diary	Fouquereul	06/06/1915	06/06/1915
War Diary	Annezin	06/06/1915	06/06/1915
War Diary	Vaudricourt	06/06/1915	06/06/1915
War Diary	Pithead Prieure St Pry	06/06/1915	06/06/1915
War Diary	Bethune	07/06/1915	07/06/1915
War Diary	Annezin	07/06/1915	07/06/1915
War Diary	Font Nelle Farm	07/06/1915	07/06/1915
War Diary	Pithead Prieure St Pry	07/06/1915	07/06/1915
War Diary	Bethune	08/06/1915	08/06/1915
War Diary	Fontnelle Farm	08/06/1915	08/06/1915
War Diary	Annezin	08/06/1915	08/06/1915
War Diary	Pithead Prieure St Pry.	08/06/1915	08/06/1915
War Diary	Bethune	09/06/1915	09/06/1915
War Diary	Fontnelle Farm	09/06/1915	09/06/1915
War Diary	Annezin	09/06/1915	09/06/1915
War Diary	Pithead Prieure St Pry	09/06/1915	09/06/1915
War Diary	Bethune	10/06/1915	10/06/1915
War Diary	Vaudricourt	10/06/1915	10/06/1915
War Diary	Labeuvriere Lapugnoy	10/06/1915	10/06/1915
War Diary	Pithead Prieure St Pry	10/06/1915	10/06/1915
War Diary	Bethune	11/06/1915	11/06/1915
War Diary	Annezin	11/06/1915	11/06/1915
War Diary	Pithead Prieure St Pry	11/06/1915	11/06/1915

War Diary	Vaudricourt	11/06/1915	11/06/1915
War Diary	Bethune	12/06/1915	12/06/1915
War Diary	Annezin	12/06/1915	12/06/1915
War Diary	Vaudricourt	12/06/1915	12/06/1915
War Diary	Labeuvriere	12/06/1915	12/06/1915
War Diary	Labuissiere	12/06/1915	12/06/1915
War Diary	Pithead Prieure St Pry	12/06/1915	12/06/1915
War Diary	Labeuvriere	13/06/1915	13/06/1915
War Diary	Annezin	13/06/1915	13/06/1915
War Diary	Vaudricourt	13/06/1915	13/06/1915
War Diary	Fontenelle Farm	13/06/1915	13/06/1915
War Diary	Bethune	13/06/1915	13/06/1915
War Diary	Pithead Prieure St Pry	13/06/1915	13/06/1915
War Diary	Labeuvriere	14/06/1915	14/06/1915
War Diary	Bethune	14/06/1915	14/06/1915
War Diary	Pithead Prieure St Pry	14/06/1915	14/06/1915
War Diary	Labeuvriere	15/06/1915	15/06/1915
War Diary	Bethune	15/06/1915	15/06/1915
War Diary	Pithead Prieure St Pry	15/06/1915	15/06/1915
War Diary	Bethune	16/06/1915	16/06/1915
War Diary	Labeuvriere	16/06/1915	16/06/1915
War Diary	Pithead Prieure St Pry	16/06/1915	16/06/1915
War Diary	Labeuvriere	17/06/1915	17/06/1915
War Diary	Bethune	17/06/1915	17/06/1915
War Diary	Fouquieres	17/06/1915	17/06/1915
War Diary	Pithead Prieure St Pry	17/06/1915	17/06/1915
War Diary	Labeuvriere	18/06/1915	18/06/1915
War Diary	Fouquieres	18/06/1915	18/06/1915
War Diary	Bethune	18/06/1915	18/06/1915
War Diary	Pithead Prieure St Pry	18/06/1915	18/06/1915
War Diary	Bethune	19/06/1915	19/06/1915
War Diary	Beuvry	19/06/1915	19/06/1915
War Diary	Pithead Prieure St Pry	19/06/1915	19/06/1915
War Diary	Pithead	20/06/1915	20/06/1915
War Diary	Bethune	20/06/1915	20/06/1915
War Diary	Verquin	20/06/1915	20/06/1915
War Diary	Vaudricourt	20/06/1915	20/06/1915
War Diary	Verquin	21/06/1915	21/06/1915
War Diary	Bethune	21/06/1915	21/06/1915
War Diary	Bois De Montagnes	21/06/1915	21/06/1915
War Diary	Pithead Prieure St Pry	21/06/1915	21/06/1915
War Diary	Verquin	22/06/1915	22/06/1915
War Diary	Bethune	22/06/1915	22/06/1915
War Diary	Pithead Prieure St Pry	22/06/1915	22/06/1915
War Diary	Beuvry	23/06/1915	23/06/1915
War Diary	Bethune	23/06/1915	23/06/1915
War Diary	Pithead Prieure St Pry	23/06/1915	23/06/1915
War Diary	Bethune	24/06/1915	24/06/1915
War Diary	Pithead Prieure St Pry	24/06/1915	24/06/1915
War Diary	Marles Les Mines	25/06/1915	25/06/1915
War Diary	Bethune	24/06/1915	25/06/1915
War Diary	Lapugnoy	26/06/1915	26/06/1915
War Diary	Marles Les Mines	27/06/1915	27/06/1915
War Diary	Lozinghem	27/06/1915	27/06/1915
War Diary	Burbure	27/06/1915	27/06/1915
War Diary	Marles Les Mines	28/06/1915	28/06/1915

War Diary	Verquin	29/06/1915	29/06/1915
War Diary	Vermelles	29/06/1915	29/06/1915
War Diary	Bethune	29/06/1915	29/06/1915
War Diary	Pithead Prieure St Pry	29/06/1915	29/06/1915
War Diary	Verquin	30/06/1915	30/06/1915
War Diary	Labourse	30/06/1915	30/06/1915
War Diary	Novelles Les Vermelles	30/06/1915	30/06/1915
War Diary	Verquigneul	30/06/1915	30/06/1915
War Diary	Pithead Prieure St Pry	30/06/1915	30/06/1915
Heading	121/6401 1st Divisions No 13 Sanitary Section July 1915 Vol III		
Heading	War Diary of Lieut G. Q. Lennane RAMCT O.C. No 13 Sanitary Section 1st Div From 1st July 1915 To 31st July 15 (Volume 4)		
War Diary	Verquin	01/07/1915	01/07/1915
War Diary	Labourse	01/07/1915	01/07/1915
War Diary	Novelles Lez Vermelles	01/07/1915	01/07/1915
War Diary	Vermelles	01/07/1915	01/07/1915
War Diary	Le Routoire	01/07/1915	01/07/1915
War Diary	Sailly Labourse	01/07/1915	01/07/1915
War Diary	Pithead Prieure St Pry	01/07/1915	01/07/1915
War Diary	Verquin	02/07/1915	02/07/1915
War Diary	Labourse	02/07/1915	02/07/1915
War Diary	Novelles Lez Vermelles	02/07/1915	02/07/1915
War Diary	Sailly Labourse	02/07/1915	02/07/1915
War Diary	Pithead Prieure St Pry	02/07/1915	02/07/1915
War Diary	Verquin	03/07/1915	03/07/1915
War Diary	Labourse	03/07/1915	03/07/1915
War Diary	Sailly Labourse	03/07/1915	03/07/1915
War Diary	Novelles Lez Vermelles	03/07/1915	03/07/1915
War Diary	Pithead Prieure St Pry	03/07/1915	03/07/1915
War Diary	Novelles Lez Vermelles	04/07/1915	04/07/1915
War Diary	Sailly Labourse	04/07/1915	04/07/1915
War Diary	Labourse	04/07/1915	04/07/1915
War Diary	Pithead Prieure St Pry	04/07/1915	05/07/1915
War Diary	Sailly Labourse	05/07/1915	05/07/1915
War Diary	Labourse	05/07/1915	05/07/1915
War Diary	Verquin	05/07/1915	05/07/1915
War Diary	Labourse	05/07/1915	05/07/1915
War Diary	Sailly Labourse	05/07/1915	05/07/1915
War Diary	Novelles	05/07/1915	05/07/1915
War Diary	Pithead Prieure St Pry	05/07/1915	05/07/1915
War Diary	Pithead	06/07/1915	06/07/1915
War Diary	Sailly Labourse	06/07/1915	06/07/1915
War Diary	Labourse	06/07/1915	06/07/1915
War Diary	Pithead Prieure St Pry	06/07/1915	06/07/1915
War Diary	Labourse	07/07/1915	07/07/1915
War Diary	Sailly Labourse	07/07/1915	07/07/1915
War Diary	Novelles	07/07/1915	08/07/1915
War Diary	Sailly Labourse	08/07/1915	08/07/1915
War Diary	Labourse	08/07/1915	08/07/1915
War Diary	Fouquereuil	08/07/1915	08/07/1915
War Diary	Verquin	09/07/1915	09/07/1915
War Diary	Pithead Prieure St Pry	09/07/1915	09/07/1915
War Diary	Verquin	10/07/1915	10/07/1915
War Diary	Novelles	10/07/1915	10/07/1915

War Diary	Sailly Labourse	10/07/1915	10/07/1915
War Diary	Labourse	10/07/1915	10/07/1915
War Diary	Hesdigneul	10/07/1915	10/07/1915
War Diary	Pithead Prieure St Pry	10/07/1915	10/07/1915
War Diary	Hesdigneul	11/07/1915	12/07/1915
War Diary	Bethune	12/07/1915	12/07/1915
War Diary	Vaudricourt	12/07/1915	12/07/1915
War Diary	Fouquieres	12/07/1915	12/07/1915
War Diary	Pithead Prieure St Pry	13/07/1915	13/07/1915
War Diary	Fouquieres	13/07/1915	13/07/1915
War Diary	Vaudricourt	13/07/1915	13/07/1915
War Diary	Pithead Prieure St Pry	13/07/1915	13/07/1915
War Diary	Fouquieres	14/07/1915	14/07/1915
War Diary	Vaudricourt	14/07/1915	14/07/1915
War Diary	Bethune	14/07/1915	14/07/1915
War Diary	Fouquieres	15/07/1915	15/07/1915
War Diary	Bethune	15/07/1915	15/07/1915
War Diary	Verquigneul	16/07/1915	16/07/1915
War Diary	Fouquieres	16/07/1915	16/07/1915
War Diary	Bethune	16/07/1915	16/07/1915
War Diary	Pithead Prieure St Pry	16/07/1915	16/07/1915
War Diary	Verquigneul	17/07/1915	17/07/1915
War Diary	Sailly Labourse	17/07/1915	17/07/1915
War Diary	Labourse	17/07/1915	17/07/1915
War Diary	Fouquieres	17/07/1915	17/07/1915
War Diary	Pithead Prieure St Pry	17/07/1915	17/07/1915
War Diary	Pithead	17/07/1915	17/07/1915
War Diary	Sailly Labourse	18/07/1915	18/07/1915
War Diary	Labourse	18/07/1915	18/07/1915
War Diary	Fouquieres	18/07/1915	18/07/1915
War Diary	Verquin	18/07/1915	18/07/1915
War Diary	Labeuvriere	18/07/1915	18/07/1915
War Diary	Verquigneul	18/07/1915	18/07/1915
War Diary	Labourse	18/07/1915	18/07/1915
War Diary	Pithead	18/07/1915	18/07/1915
War Diary	Sailly Labourse	19/07/1915	19/07/1915
War Diary	Fouquieres	19/07/1915	19/07/1915
War Diary	Bethune	19/07/1915	19/07/1915
War Diary	Pithead Prieure St Pry	19/07/1915	19/07/1915
War Diary	Sailly Labourse	20/07/1915	20/07/1915
War Diary	Labourse	20/07/1915	20/07/1915
War Diary	Bethune	20/07/1915	20/07/1915
War Diary	Fouquieres	20/07/1915	20/07/1915
War Diary	Vaudricourt	20/07/1915	20/07/1915
War Diary	Pithead Prieure St Pry	20/07/1915	20/07/1915
War Diary	Novelles	21/07/1915	21/07/1915
War Diary	Sailly Labourse	21/07/1915	21/07/1915
War Diary	Bethune	21/07/1915	21/07/1915
War Diary	Pithead	21/07/1915	21/07/1915
War Diary	Novelles-Lez-Vermelles	22/07/1915	22/07/1915
War Diary	Sailly Labourse	22/07/1915	22/07/1915
War Diary	Annezin	22/07/1915	22/07/1915
War Diary	Bethune	22/07/1915	22/07/1915
War Diary	Fouquieres	22/07/1915	22/07/1915
War Diary	Fouquereuil	22/07/1915	22/07/1915
War Diary	Pithead	22/07/1915	22/07/1915

War Diary	Novelles	23/07/1915	23/07/1915
War Diary	Annezin	23/07/1915	23/07/1915
War Diary	Bethune	23/07/1915	23/07/1915
War Diary	Pithead	23/07/1915	23/07/1915
War Diary	Novelles	24/07/1915	24/07/1915
War Diary	Annezin	24/07/1915	24/07/1915
War Diary	Labourse	24/07/1915	24/07/1915
War Diary	Bethune	24/07/1915	24/07/1915
War Diary	Pithead Prieure St Pry	24/07/1915	24/07/1915
War Diary	Pithead	25/07/1915	25/07/1915
War Diary	Fontinelle Farm	25/07/1915	25/07/1915
War Diary	Fouquieres	25/07/1915	25/07/1915
War Diary	Annezin	26/07/1915	26/07/1915
War Diary	Labourse	26/07/1915	26/07/1915
War Diary	Bethune	26/07/1915	26/07/1915
War Diary	Pithead	26/07/1915	26/07/1915
War Diary	Labourse	27/07/1915	27/07/1915
War Diary	Annequin	27/07/1915	27/07/1915
War Diary	Bethune	27/07/1915	27/07/1915
War Diary	Labuissiere	27/07/1915	27/07/1915
War Diary	Pithead Prieure St Pry	27/07/1915	27/07/1915
War Diary	Labourse	28/07/1915	28/07/1915
War Diary	Annezin	28/07/1915	28/07/1915
War Diary	Bethune	28/07/1915	28/07/1915
War Diary	Pithead	28/07/1915	28/07/1915
War Diary	Labourse	29/07/1915	29/07/1915
War Diary	Annezin	29/07/1915	29/07/1915
War Diary	Bethune	29/07/1915	29/07/1915
War Diary	Pithead	29/07/1915	29/07/1915
War Diary	Labourse	30/07/1915	30/07/1915
War Diary	Annezin	30/07/1915	30/07/1915
War Diary	Fouquereuil	30/07/1915	30/07/1915
War Diary	Bethune	30/07/1915	30/07/1915
War Diary	Pithead	30/07/1915	30/07/1915
War Diary	Annezin	31/07/1915	31/07/1915
War Diary	Brette River Camp	31/07/1915	31/07/1915
War Diary	Fouquereuil	31/07/1915	31/07/1915
War Diary	Bethune	31/07/1915	31/07/1915
War Diary	Pithead Prieure St Pry	31/07/1915	31/07/1915
Heading	August 1915 121/6807 1st Division No 13 Sanitary Section Vol IV August 15		
Heading	War Diary of Lieut G Q Lennane RAMCT O.C No 13 Sanitary Section From 1 August 1915 To 31 August 1915 (Volume 5)		
War Diary	Brette River Camp	01/08/1915	01/08/1915
War Diary	Verquin	01/08/1915	01/08/1915
War Diary	Brette River Camp Garden City Camp	02/08/1915	02/08/1915
War Diary	Garden City Camp	02/08/1915	02/08/1915
War Diary	Annezin	02/08/1915	02/08/1915
War Diary	Bethune	02/08/1915	02/08/1915
War Diary	Vermelles	02/08/1915	02/08/1915
War Diary	Pithead Prieure St Pry	02/08/1915	02/08/1915
War Diary	Annezin	03/08/1915	03/08/1915
War Diary	Bethune	03/08/1915	03/08/1915
War Diary	Pithead (Prieure St Pry)	03/08/1915	03/08/1915
War Diary	Bethune	04/08/1915	04/08/1915

War Diary	Annezin	04/08/1915	04/08/1915
War Diary	Pithead (Prieure St Pry)	04/08/1915	04/08/1915
War Diary	Annezin	05/08/1915	05/08/1915
War Diary	Bethune	05/08/1915	05/08/1915
War Diary	Pithead Prieure St Pry	05/08/1915	05/08/1915
War Diary	Verquin	06/08/1915	06/08/1915
War Diary	Bethune	06/08/1915	06/08/1915
War Diary	Vermelles	06/08/1915	06/08/1915
War Diary	Annezin	06/08/1915	06/08/1915
War Diary	Pithead Prieure St Pry	06/08/1915	06/08/1915
War Diary	Vermelles	07/08/1915	07/08/1915
War Diary	Verquin	07/08/1915	07/08/1915
War Diary	Annezin	07/08/1915	07/08/1915
War Diary	Verquigneul	07/08/1915	07/08/1915
War Diary	Labourse	07/08/1915	07/08/1915
War Diary	Verquin	08/08/1915	08/08/1915
War Diary	Novelles	08/08/1915	08/08/1915
War Diary	Labourse	08/08/1915	08/08/1915
War Diary	Pithead Prieure St Pry	08/08/1915	08/08/1915
War Diary	Verquin	09/08/1915	09/08/1915
War Diary	Bethune	09/08/1915	09/08/1915
War Diary	Pithead (Prieure St Pry)	09/08/1915	09/08/1915
War Diary	Verquin	10/08/1915	10/08/1915
War Diary	Verquigneul	10/08/1915	10/08/1915
War Diary	Bethune	10/08/1915	10/08/1915
War Diary	Garden City	10/08/1915	10/08/1915
War Diary	Pithead (Prieure St Pry)	10/08/1915	10/08/1915
War Diary	Verquin	11/08/1915	11/08/1915
War Diary	Bethune	11/08/1915	11/08/1915
War Diary	Bethune And Annezin	11/08/1915	11/08/1915
War Diary	Fouquieres	11/08/1915	11/08/1915
War Diary	Garden City	11/08/1915	11/08/1915
War Diary	Pithead (Prieure St Pry)	11/08/1915	11/08/1915
War Diary	Verquin	12/08/1915	12/08/1915
War Diary	Bethune	12/08/1915	12/08/1915
War Diary	Annezin	12/08/1915	12/08/1915
War Diary	Fontenelle Farm	12/08/1915	12/08/1915
War Diary	Pithead	12/08/1915	12/08/1915
War Diary	Verquin	13/08/1915	13/08/1915
War Diary	Bethune And Annezin	13/08/1915	13/08/1915
War Diary	Fouquiers Garden City	13/08/1915	13/08/1915
War Diary	Novelles	13/08/1915	13/08/1915
War Diary	Verquigneul	13/08/1915	13/08/1915
War Diary	Pithead (Prieure St Pry)	13/08/1915	13/08/1915
War Diary	Verquin	14/08/1915	14/08/1915
War Diary	Vermelles	14/08/1915	14/08/1915
War Diary	Fouquieres Bethune	14/08/1915	14/08/1915
War Diary	Annezin	14/08/1915	14/08/1915
War Diary	Fouquieres Garden City	14/08/1915	14/08/1915
War Diary	Pithead	14/08/1915	14/08/1915
War Diary	Verquin	15/08/1915	15/08/1915
War Diary	Cambrin & Vermelles	15/08/1915	15/08/1915
War Diary	Pithead	15/08/1915	15/08/1915
War Diary	Verquin	16/08/1915	16/08/1915
War Diary	Bethune	16/08/1915	16/08/1915
War Diary	Fouquieres	16/08/1915	16/08/1915

War Diary	Labourse	16/08/1915	16/08/1915
War Diary	Pithead	16/08/1915	16/08/1915
War Diary	Verquin	17/08/1915	17/08/1915
War Diary	Bethune Annezin	17/08/1915	17/08/1915
War Diary	Fouquieres	17/08/1915	17/08/1915
War Diary	Labourse	17/08/1915	17/08/1915
War Diary	Annequin	17/08/1915	17/08/1915
War Diary	Novelles	17/08/1915	17/08/1915
War Diary	Pithead	17/08/1915	17/08/1915
War Diary	Verquin	18/08/1915	18/08/1915
War Diary	Bethune	18/08/1915	18/08/1915
War Diary	Fouquieres Garden City	18/08/1915	18/08/1915
War Diary	Annequin Cambrin	18/08/1915	18/08/1915
War Diary	Labourse	18/08/1915	18/08/1915
War Diary	Pithead	18/08/1915	18/08/1915
War Diary	Verquin	19/08/1915	19/08/1915
War Diary	Bethune Annezin	19/08/1915	19/08/1915
War Diary	Fouquieres Garden City	19/08/1915	19/08/1915
War Diary	Labourse	19/08/1915	19/08/1915
War Diary	Verquin	20/08/1915	20/08/1915
War Diary	Bethune And Annezin	20/08/1915	20/08/1915
War Diary	Garden City	20/08/1915	20/08/1915
War Diary	Labourse	20/08/1915	20/08/1915
War Diary	Sailly Labourse	20/08/1915	20/08/1915
War Diary	Verquin	20/08/1915	20/08/1915
War Diary	Sailly Labourse	20/08/1915	20/08/1915
War Diary	Pithead	20/08/1915	20/08/1915
War Diary	Bethune	21/08/1915	21/08/1915
War Diary	Annezin	21/08/1915	21/08/1915
War Diary	Fouquieres	21/08/1915	21/08/1915
War Diary	Verquin	21/08/1915	21/08/1915
War Diary	Labourse	21/08/1915	21/08/1915
War Diary	Sailly Labourse	21/08/1915	21/08/1915
War Diary	Labourse	21/08/1915	21/08/1915
War Diary	Bethune	21/08/1915	21/08/1915
War Diary	Pithead	21/08/1915	21/08/1915
War Diary	Verquin	22/08/1915	22/08/1915
War Diary	Labourse	22/08/1915	22/08/1915
War Diary	Annezin	22/08/1915	22/08/1915
War Diary	Vermelles	22/08/1915	22/08/1915
War Diary	Sailly Labourse	22/08/1915	22/08/1915
War Diary	Pithead	22/08/1915	22/08/1915
War Diary	Verquin	23/08/1915	23/08/1915
War Diary	Labourse	23/08/1915	23/08/1915
War Diary	Garden City	23/08/1915	23/08/1915
War Diary	Bethune	23/08/1915	23/08/1915
War Diary	Annezin	23/08/1915	23/08/1915
War Diary	Pithead	23/08/1915	23/08/1915
War Diary	Verquin	24/08/1915	24/08/1915
War Diary	Labourse	24/08/1915	24/08/1915
War Diary	Annezin	24/08/1915	24/08/1915
War Diary	Garden City Camp	24/08/1915	24/08/1915
War Diary	Sailly Labourse	24/08/1915	24/08/1915
War Diary	Pithead	24/08/1915	24/08/1915
War Diary	Verquin	25/08/1915	25/08/1915
War Diary	Bethune	25/08/1915	25/08/1915

War Diary	Annezin	25/08/1915	25/08/1915
War Diary	Garden City and Fouquieres	25/08/1915	25/08/1915
War Diary	Labourse	25/08/1915	25/08/1915
War Diary	Vermelles	25/08/1915	25/08/1915
War Diary	Pithead	25/08/1915	25/08/1915
War Diary	Verquin	26/08/1915	26/08/1915
War Diary	Labourse	26/08/1915	26/08/1915
War Diary	Bethune Annezin	26/08/1915	26/08/1915
War Diary	Garden City Camp	26/08/1915	26/08/1915
War Diary	Bethune	26/08/1915	26/08/1915
War Diary	Pithead	26/08/1915	26/08/1915
War Diary	Verquin	27/08/1915	27/08/1915
War Diary	Labourse	27/08/1915	27/08/1915
War Diary	Bethune Annezin	27/08/1915	27/08/1915
War Diary	Garden City Camp	27/08/1915	27/08/1915
War Diary	Bethune Fouquieres	27/08/1915	27/08/1915
War Diary	Verquin	28/08/1915	28/08/1915
War Diary	Labourse	28/08/1915	28/08/1915
War Diary	Bethune Annezin	28/08/1915	28/08/1915
War Diary	Fouquieres Garden City Camp	28/08/1915	28/08/1915
War Diary	Vermelles	28/08/1915	28/08/1915
War Diary	Pithead	28/08/1915	28/08/1915
War Diary	Annequin	29/08/1915	29/08/1915
War Diary	Verquin	29/08/1915	29/08/1915
War Diary	Annezin Bethune	29/08/1915	29/08/1915
War Diary	Labourse	29/08/1915	29/08/1915
War Diary	Fouquieres Garden City Camp	29/08/1915	29/08/1915
War Diary	Sailly Labourse	29/08/1915	29/08/1915
War Diary	Pithead	29/08/1915	29/08/1915
War Diary	Verquin	30/08/1915	30/08/1915
War Diary	Bethune Annezin	30/08/1915	30/08/1915
War Diary	Fouquieres Garden City	30/08/1915	30/08/1915
War Diary	Pithead	30/08/1915	30/08/1915
War Diary	Verquin	31/08/1915	31/08/1915
War Diary	Labourse	31/08/1915	31/08/1915
War Diary	Annezin	31/08/1915	31/08/1915
War Diary	Bethune Prieure St. Pry	31/08/1915	31/08/1915
Heading	121/7082 1st Division No 13. Sanitary Section Vol V Sep 1.15		
Heading	War Diary of Capt G Q Lennane RAMCT O.C No 13 Sanitary Section From September 1st To September 30th (Volume 6)		
War Diary	Auchel	01/09/1915	01/09/1915
War Diary	Verquin	01/09/1915	01/09/1915
War Diary	Labourse	01/09/1915	01/09/1915
War Diary	Annezin	01/09/1915	01/09/1915
War Diary	Garden City Camp	01/09/1915	01/09/1915
War Diary	Pithead	01/09/1915	01/09/1915
War Diary	Annezin	02/09/1915	02/09/1915
War Diary	Labourse	02/09/1915	02/09/1915
War Diary	Pithead	02/09/1915	02/09/1915
War Diary	Prieure St Pry	03/09/1915	03/09/1915
War Diary	Marles. Les. Mines	03/09/1915	03/09/1915
War Diary	Verquin	03/09/1915	03/09/1915
War Diary	Fouquieres Garden City Camp	03/09/1915	03/09/1915
War Diary	Annezin Bethune	03/09/1915	03/09/1915

War Diary	Labourse	03/09/1915	03/09/1915
War Diary	Marles-Les-Mines	04/09/1915	05/09/1915
War Diary	Gosnay	05/09/1915	05/09/1915
War Diary	Ferfay	06/09/1915	06/09/1915
War Diary	Ames	06/09/1915	06/09/1915
War Diary	Lieres	06/09/1915	06/09/1915
War Diary	Lespresses	06/09/1915	06/09/1915
War Diary	Auchel	06/09/1915	06/09/1915
War Diary	Marles-Les-Mines	06/09/1915	06/09/1915
War Diary	Allouagne	07/09/1915	07/09/1915
War Diary	Lozinghem	07/09/1915	07/09/1915
War Diary	Marles-Les-Mines	07/09/1915	07/09/1915
War Diary	Ferfay	08/09/1915	08/09/1915
War Diary	Lieres	08/09/1915	08/09/1915
War Diary	Allouagne	08/09/1915	08/09/1915
War Diary	Marles-Les-Mines	08/09/1915	08/09/1915
War Diary	Allouagne	09/09/1915	09/09/1915
War Diary	Marles-Les-Mines	09/09/1915	09/09/1915
War Diary	Philosophe	10/09/1915	10/09/1915
War Diary	Marles-Les-Mines	10/09/1915	11/09/1915
War Diary	Lieres	12/09/1915	12/09/1915
War Diary	Mazingarbe	12/09/1915	12/09/1915
War Diary	Philosophe	12/09/1915	12/09/1915
War Diary	Marles-Les-Mines	12/09/1915	12/09/1915
War Diary	Gosnay	13/09/1915	13/09/1915
War Diary	Marles-Les-Mines	13/09/1915	13/09/1915
War Diary	Ecquesdecques	14/09/1915	14/09/1915
War Diary	Lapugnoy	14/09/1915	14/09/1915
War Diary	Lozinghem	14/09/1915	14/09/1915
War Diary	Marles-Les-Mines	13/09/1915	13/09/1915
War Diary	Philosophe	15/09/1915	15/09/1915
War Diary	Marles-Les-Mines	15/09/1915	16/09/1915
War Diary	Philosophe	17/09/1915	17/09/1915
War Diary	Marles-Les-Mines	17/09/1915	17/09/1915
War Diary	Philosophe	18/09/1915	18/09/1915
War Diary	Ferfay and Bellery	18/09/1915	18/09/1915
War Diary	Marles-Les-Mines	18/09/1915	18/09/1915
War Diary	Ferfay	19/09/1915	19/09/1915
War Diary	Bellery	19/09/1915	19/09/1915
War Diary	Auchel	19/09/1915	19/09/1915
War Diary	Marles-Les-Mines	19/09/1915	19/09/1915
War Diary	Ferfay And Bellery	20/09/1915	20/09/1915
War Diary	Lapugnoy	20/09/1915	20/09/1915
War Diary	Marles-Les-Mines	20/09/1915	20/09/1915
War Diary	Lapugnoy	21/09/1915	21/09/1915
War Diary	Marles-Les-Mines	21/09/1915	21/09/1915
War Diary	Gosnay	22/09/1915	22/09/1915
War Diary	Vaudricourt	22/09/1915	22/09/1915
War Diary	Verquin	22/09/1915	22/09/1915
War Diary	Lapugnoy	22/09/1915	24/09/1915
War Diary	Marles-Les-Mines	22/09/1915	22/09/1915
War Diary	Lapugnoy	23/09/1915	23/09/1915
War Diary	Marles-Les-Mines	23/09/1915	23/09/1915
War Diary	Verquin	23/09/1915	24/09/1915
War Diary	Noeux-Les-Mines Mazing Arbe Philosophe	25/09/1915	25/09/1915
War Diary	Verquin	25/09/1915	25/09/1915

War Diary	Noeux-Les-Mines	25/09/1915	25/09/1915
War Diary	Verquin	25/09/1915	25/09/1915
War Diary	Philosophe	26/09/1915	26/09/1915
War Diary	Verquin	26/09/1915	26/09/1915
War Diary	Noeux-Les-Mines	26/09/1915	26/09/1915
War Diary	Philosophe	27/09/1915	27/09/1915
War Diary	Verquin	27/09/1915	27/09/1915
War Diary	Gosnay	27/09/1915	27/09/1915
War Diary	Philosophe	28/09/1915	28/09/1915
War Diary	Verquin	28/09/1915	29/09/1915
War Diary	Noeux-Les-Mines	28/09/1915	29/09/1915
War Diary	Verquin	29/09/1915	29/09/1915
War Diary	Noeux-Les-Mines	30/09/1915	30/09/1915
Heading	No. 13 Sanitary Section Oct. 1915-Dec.		
War Diary	Noeux-Les-Mines	01/10/1915	06/10/1915
War Diary	Mazingarbe	07/10/1915	08/10/1915
War Diary	Noeux-Les-Mines & Mazingarbe	09/10/1915	15/10/1915
War Diary	Allouagne	16/10/1915	18/10/1915
War Diary	Burbure	19/10/1915	19/10/1915
War Diary	Auchel	20/10/1915	31/10/1915
War Diary	Auchel	01/11/1915	05/11/1915
War Diary	Marles-Les-Mines	06/11/1915	15/11/1915
War Diary	Noeux-Les-Mines	16/11/1916	31/12/1916
Heading	No. 13 Sanitary Section Jan-May 1916		
War Diary	Noeux Les Mines	01/01/1916	15/01/1916
War Diary	Lillers	16/01/1916	31/01/1916
War Diary	Lillers	01/02/1916	15/02/1916
War Diary	Bracquemont Noeux-Les-Mines	16/02/1916	29/02/1916
War Diary	Bracquemont Noeux-Les-Mines	01/03/1916	31/05/1916
Heading	Vol 6 to 15 War Diary of Capt G.Q. Lennane RAMCT O c No 13 Section 1st Division 1916 to 31st July 1916		
War Diary	Bracquemont Noeux-Les-Mines	01/06/1916	30/06/1916
War Diary	Bracquemont	01/07/1916	03/07/1916
War Diary	Bruay	04/07/1916	05/07/1916
War Diary	Lillers	06/07/1916	06/07/1916
War Diary	Flesselles	07/07/1916	07/07/1916
War Diary	St Cratien	08/07/1916	08/07/1916
War Diary	Dernancourt	10/07/1916	10/07/1916
War Diary	Albert	20/07/1916	20/07/1916
War Diary	St Gratien	26/07/1916	26/07/1916
War Diary	Montigny	29/07/1916	31/07/1916
Heading	1st Div. No. 13 Sanitary Section Aug 1916		
Heading	Vol 16 War Diary of Capt G.Q. Lennane. R.A.M.C.T O.C No 13 Sanitary Section 1st Division 1st To 31st August 1916 Volume		
War Diary	Montigny	01/08/1916	14/08/1916
War Diary	Albert	15/08/1916	31/08/1916
Heading	Vol 17 War Diary of Captain G. Q. Lennane R.A.M.C.T. O.C No. 13 Sanitary Section-1st Division From 1st To 30th September 1916 Volume IX		
War Diary	Albert	01/09/1916	11/09/1916
War Diary	Montigny	12/09/1916	30/09/1916
War Diary	140/1788 War Diary of Cari G Q Lennane. R.A.M.C. T. O.C. No 13 Sanitary Section-1st Division From 1st To 31st October 1916 Volume		
War Diary	Montigny	01/10/1916	02/10/1916

War Diary	Moyenneville	03/10/1916	31/10/1916
Heading	140/1246 War Diary of Capt C Yates Ford-R.A.M.C. O.C. No 13 Sanitary Section 1st Division From 1st To 30th Novr 1916 Volume		
Heading	Baizieux	01/11/1916	04/11/1916
Heading	Fricourt	05/11/1916	30/11/1916
Heading	Vol 20 140/1900 War Diary of Capt C Yates Ford-R. A. M. C O.C. No-13 Sanitary Section 1st Division From 1st To 31st December. 1916 Volume XII		
War Diary	Fricourt	01/12/1916	31/12/1916
Heading	Vol 21 140/1941 War Diary of Capt L R Tosswill-R.A.M.C.T. O.C. No-13 Sanitary Section 1st Division From 1st to 31st January 1917 Volume		
War Diary	Fricourt	01/01/1917	23/01/1917
War Diary	Baizieux	24/01/1917	26/01/1917
War Diary	Chuignolles	27/01/1917	31/01/1917
Heading	140/1994 Vol 23 War Diary of O. C No. 13 Sanitary Section 1st Division From 1st to 28th February 1917 Volume XIV		
War Diary	Chuignolles	01/02/1917	28/02/1917
War Diary	Vol 23 140/243 War Diary of Marles-Les-MineO C No 13 Sanitary Section 1st Division From 1st to 31st March 1917 Volume XV		
War Diary	Chuignolles	01/03/1917	31/03/1917

WO 95/1259 (3)

13 Sanitary Section

Apr '15 – Mar '17

1st Division

Medical

13th Sanitary Section

~~April 1915~~ DEC 1915

1915 APL — 1917 MAR

TO 2 ARMY

121/561Y

april 1915

CONFIDENTIAL

WAR DIARY

of

Lieutenant. G. Q. Lennane R.A.M.C. T. O.C.

No 13 SANITARY SECTION. 1st DIV.

FROM APRIL. 8TH 1915 TO. ~~APRIL. 30TH 1915~~ May 30th 1915

(VOLUME I)

Instructions regarding War Diaries and Intelligence Summaries are contained in F. S. Regs., Part II. and the Staff Manual respectively. Title pages will be prepared in manuscript.

WAR DIARY
or
INTELLIGENCE SUMMARY

(Erase heading not required.)

Army Form C. 2118.

Hour, Date, Place	Summary of Events and Information	Remarks and references to Appendices
6.45 am April 8 1915 CHOCQUES	Arrived	
9 am do BETHUNE	Arrived from CHOCQUES in Motor Lorry	
11 am do LOCON	Arrived by car from BETHUNE and reported to A.D.M.S. [illegible] at 1st Div Hdqrs. G.L.	
April 9 1915 LOCON		
LATOMBE WILLOT	Inspected billets of 2nd Bn R Munster Fusiliers with Captain A.C.S. Irwine RAMC	Captain Irwine [illegible] Sanitary Officer 1st Division
April 9 1915 CORNET MALO, LES CHOCQUAX, AVELETTE, HINGETTE, HINGE, LONG CORNET, MESPLAUX FARM	Billeting areas of 1st Division units visited in company with Captain A.C.S. Irwine G.L.	
April 10 1915 LOCON	Took over command of No 13 Sanitary Section attached 1st Division from Capt A.C.S. Irwine RAMC	
LE TOURET	Visited and inspected billets finding them generally very insanitary. Arranged for squad from Sanitary Section, assisted by fatigue party of 50 men from 1st Bn CAMERON HIGHLANDERS and 6 prisoners, to clean up the various billets on the following day	
LES FACONS, MESPLAUX FARM	Inspected Headquarters and billets of 39th BRIGADE R.F.A. G.L.	
April 11 1915 LOCON	1607 Acting Lce Cpl [illegible] of Sanitary Section, 1269 Pte Lewis 4th R Welch Fus, 10405 Pte Brand, 11668 Pte Hobbs, 11415 Pte Warrington of the 1st Bn [illegible] Bor[derers], 4527 Pte Sullivan of the R Munster Fusiliers, 2712 Pte Richards 2nd Bn Welch Regt, 2705 Pte Fenton and [illegible] Pte [illegible] reported [illegible] [illegible] [illegible] to the Medical Officer 1st Division [illegible] for Sanitary duties	The men from various units had previously been attached to the Sanitary Section

1247 W 3299 200,000 (E) 8/14 J.B.C. & A. Forms/C. 2118/11.

Instructions regarding War Diaries and Intelligence Summaries are contained in F. S. Regs., Part II. and the Staff Manual respectively. Title pages will be prepared in manuscript.

WAR DIARY
or
INTELLIGENCE SUMMARY
(Erase heading not required.)

Army Form C. 2118.

Hour, Date, Place	Summary of Events and Information	Remarks and references to Appendices
April 11 1915 LE TOURET	Visited this village and directed work of Sanitary Squad assisted by fatigue party and prisoners as arranged yesterday	Fatigue party of 50 men from 1st BN CAMERON HIGHLANDERS 6 Prisoners Sanitary Squad 1 NCO 7 men
LOCON	Strength 4717 Pte Kelsey 4923 Pte Keogh 5070 Pte Mahoney reported for duty from the 2nd Bn R MUNSTER FUSILIERS. [initials]	
April 12 1915 LE TOURET	Squad at work cleaning billets and surroundings assisted by fatigue party and prisoners	Fatigue party of 50 men from 1st Bn SCOTS GUARDS 6 prisoners Sanitary Squad 1 NCO 7 men
	Inspected billets of 39th Brigade Ammunition Column (R.F.A.) finding same in fair sanitary condition	
LES CHOCQUEAUX [illegible]	Visited and inspected billets in this area. Arranged for large quantity of refuse etc to be burned or buried	
LOCON	Strength 11894 Pte Edwards and 4281 Pte Deacon of 1st Bn SOUTH WALES BORDERERS reported for duty with Section. [initials]	
April 13 1915 LE TOURET	Squad at work in [illegible] cleaning up [illegible] Squad was assisted by fatigue party and prisoners.	Fatigue party 50 Men 1st Bn SCOTS GDS 5 prisoners Sanitary Squad 2 NCOs 13 men
	Inspected Headquarters 28th BDE R.F.A. finding same in [illegible] sanitary condition	
BETHUNE	Purchased implements required for completing work at LE TOURET	4 forks 2 [illegible]
LOCON	1 Motor Ambulance disinfected.	
	Strength 13165 L/Cpl Howes & 13478 Pte [illegible] of 1st Bn SOUTH WALES BORDERERS 4729 Pte Poer and 7376 Pte [illegible]gan of 2nd Bn R MUNSTER FUSILIERS reported for duty with Section [initials]	

Instructions regarding War Diaries and Intelligence Summaries are contained in F. S. Regs., Part II. and the Staff Manual respectively. Title pages will be prepared in manuscript.

WAR DIARY
or
INTELLIGENCE SUMMARY

(Erase heading not required.)

Army Form C. 2118.

Hour, Date, Place	Summary of Events and Information	Remarks and references to Appendices
9am April 14 1915 LE TOURET	Sanitary squad assisted by prisoners continued work [illegible]. Arranged with O.C. 113th BATTERY R.F.A. for loan of horses to draw cart required for carting manure away from [illegible] of billets. Arranged with [illegible] LOWLAND FIELD Co. [illegible] to have [illegible] regulation latrines in the billets replaced by regulation latrines ([illegible]).	[illegible] 1 N.C.O. [illegible] men 6 prisoners
10.30am April 14 1915	Visited with A.P.M. 1st Div. Hdqrs [illegible] BRIGADE. Discussed with Staff Captain matters concerning Sanitary conditions of billets in [illegible] BRIGADE area.	
VENDIN	Inspected billets of 2nd K.R.R. CORPS	
OBLINGHEM	Inspected billets of 5th Bn Royal SUSSEX [illegible]. These were generally speaking in good condition with the exception of a few manure [illegible] which [illegible] attention. The M.O. promised to attend to these details.	
LOCON	Two officers of L.N.C. [illegible] called [illegible] for information concerning the working of the Sanitary Section. Discussed with [illegible] the question of [illegible] [illegible] should be taken in regard to these. A.D.M.S. [illegible] [illegible] [illegible] [illegible] [illegible] [illegible] [illegible] [illegible] [illegible] [illegible] [illegible]. [signature]	
April 15 1915 LE TOURET	Sanitary squad and prisoners continued work. The squad had one cart and 2 horses (lent by the 113 BATTERY R.F.A.) at work. [illegible] and [illegible] work.	Sanitary squad 4 N.C.O. [illegible] 3 prisoners

1247 W 3299 200,000 (E) 8/14 J.B.C. & A. Forms/C. 2118/11.

Instructions regarding War Diaries and Intelligence Summaries are contained in F. S. Regs., Part II. and the Staff Manual respectively. Title pages will be prepared in manuscript.

WAR DIARY
or
INTELLIGENCE SUMMARY
(Erase heading not required.)

Army Form C. 2118.

Hour, Date, Place	Summary of Events and Information	Remarks and references to Appendices
April 15 1915 LOCON	2209 Acting L/Cpl Lawrence [illegible] to the Section from 4th Bn Royal Welsh Fusiliers. [initials]	
April 16 1915 LE TOURET	Sanitary Squad [illegible] work here	[illegible]
9.15 am do do	Drove out with ADMS 1st Div and inspected the [illegible] of the work which had occupied one week.	[illegible]
	Inspected lines of LOWLAND [illegible] for RE [illegible] in [illegible] measures in accordance with * G 150 order were discussed with Adjutant of latter unit.	* Appendix No 1.
LES FACONS MESPLAUX FARM	Inspected billets of 1st Bn BLACK WATCH. At LES FACONS one billet was found to be in a very unsatisfactory condition owing to an accumulation of water from the washing of clothes lying around a large manure heap upon which had been dumped a considerable quantity of [illegible]. Saw Company officer and MO in regard to this. Afterwards visited MESPLAUX FARM and saw [illegible] 1st Bn BLACK WATCH.	
2.15pm	Went with ADMS to 2nd BRIGADE HDQRS where matters regarding [illegible] measures in Brigade area were discussed.	
VENDIN	Inspected and found condition of 2nd Bn KRR billets much improved.	
LOCON	Complaint received, regarding unsatisfactory condition of 114th Battery Heavy Artillery billets, by ADMS who passed complaint on to me. [initials]	

Army Form C. 2118.

WAR DIARY
or
INTELLIGENCE SUMMARY

(Erase heading not required.)

Instructions regarding War Diaries and Intelligence Summaries are contained in F. S. Regs., Part II. and the Staff Manual respectively. Title pages will be prepared in manuscript.

Hour, Date, Place	Summary of Events and Information	Remarks and references to Appendices
April 17 1915 KUCCHA RD. NR LACOUTURE	Visited this district with regard to complaint received yesterday. Found billets now occupied by 5th BATTERY RFA and HEAVY HOWITZER BTY CANADIAN ARTILLERY [illegible] [illegible] condition [illegible] [illegible] [illegible] paper [illegible] strewn [illegible] about [illegible] remained uncovered [illegible] [illegible] [illegible] [illegible] [illegible] [illegible] [illegible] [illegible] [illegible] [illegible] [illegible] [illegible] [illegible] of HEAVY BATTERY [illegible] [illegible] [illegible] [illegible] [illegible] be [illegible] at once. Reported immediately condition of things in writing to ADMS	
RUE DES CHEVATTES	Inspected billets of the Batteries in this area and found them in fair sanitary condition	
LOCON	Sanitary Section at work covering in middens around Headquarters 1st Div. Section was assisted by prisoners.	6 prisoners.
	Billet of 39th BRIGADE AMMUNITION COLUMN [illegible]	G.J.
April 18 1915 LE TOURET	Billet occupied by 3 officers of 2nd Bn ROYAL MUNSTER FUSILIERS disinfected after case of diphtheria. Visited billet and enquired into case.	
LOCON	Sanitary Section carried out routine duties.	G.J.
April 19 1915	Visited billeting area of 40th Battery RFA and discussed with OC steps to be taken for covering manure middens.	
RICHEBOURG	Arranged with OC 51st BATTERY for fatigue party to assist Sanitary [illegible] in clearing up lines tomorrow	

1247 W 3299 200,000 (E) 8/14 J.B.C. & A. Forms/C. 2118/11.

Instructions regarding War Diaries and Intelligence Summaries are contained in F. S. Regs., Part II. and the Staff Manual respectively. Title pages will be prepared in manuscript.

WAR DIARY
or
INTELLIGENCE SUMMARY
(Erase heading not required.)

Army Form C. 2118.

Hour, Date, Place	Summary of Events and Information	Remarks and references to Appendices
April 19 1915 RICHEBOURG	Visited and found billets of 51st BATTERY and CANADIAN HEAVY BTTY in an improved condition	
LE TOURET / LES FACONS	Visited billeting areas in these districts and found that the billets occupied by 1st Bn SOUTH WALES BORDERERS and 2nd Bn ROYAL MUNSTER FUSILIERS no steps had been taken to cover manure middens	
RUE DES BOIS	Midden at billets of 113th BATTERY R.F.A. not covered but steps were being taken to have the midden covered	
LOCON	Routine work carried on by Sanitary Section. G.J. [illegible]	
April 20 1915 LACOUTURE	Sanitary squad at work on billets of 51st BATTERY and CANADIAN HEAVY BTTY visited and inspected work	Squad - 10 men & 1 NCO
COURS St VAAST	Visited billets of 26th FIELD Co RE and arranged with OC to let me have tomorrow fatigue party to assist in covering very large manure middens. Discussed with MO & OC steps to be taken for covering the middens	
	Arranged with OC 26th BRIGADE R.F.A. AMM COL to discontinue [illegible] dumping [illegible] on manure midden in a farm in the lines at once & [illegible] to cart away contents at once.	
LOCON	Sanitary section continued routine work and covering of middens. 7644 Pte Love 4th R. WELSH FUSILIERS was admitted to Hospital. 13177 Pte Prytherch, 13390 Pte Kilroy of 1st Bn SOUTH WALES BORDERERS, 10267 Pte Nolan, 1353 Pte Smith and 12014 Pte Stokes of the 2nd WELCH REGT reported for duty with the section. G.J. [illegible]	

1247 W 3299 200,000 (E) 8/14 J.B.C. & A. Forms/C. 2118/11.

Instructions regarding War Diaries and Intelligence Summaries are contained in F. S. Regs., Part II. and the Staff Manual respectively. Title pages will be prepared in manuscript.

WAR DIARY
or
INTELLIGENCE SUMMARY
(Erase heading not required.)

Army Form C. 2118.

Hour, Date, Place	Summary of Events and Information	Remarks and references to Appendices
April 21st 1915 CORNET MALO / LE TOUQUE WILLOT	Visited and inspected billets in these areas. Interviewed Staff Captain [illegible] Coldstream Guards Headquarters re question of manure middens. Visited Hdqrs 1st Bn CAMERON HIGHLANDERS and found large manure midden being dealt with, [illegible] informed that all middens in regimental area would be dealt with. Visited billets of SCOTS GUARDS 1st Bn and found burning midden at which [illegible] serious attempt was made at covering. Reported to ADMS	
LACOUTURE (RUE [illegible] ROAD)	Sanitary Squad at work here completing cleaning up.	
COURS ST. VAAST	[illegible] after finishing work at LACOUTURE proceeded here and was assisted by party from 26th F[illegible] Co. R.E. in cleaning up lines and filling in middens.	
LOCON	Remainder of Sanitary Section continued routine work at LOCON covering in middens. G. [illegible]	
April 22nd 1915. LOCON	Inspected Headquarter billets and lines of 4th SIEGE BATTERY found sanitary condition very unsatisfactory. Found long deep trench latrines in use, refuse, manure, tins and excreta lying about. Saw O.C. and arranged for lines to be cleaned and short trench latrines dug. Arranged for squad from Sanitary Section to erect an incinerator.	
LES HARRISOIRS.	Inspected billets of 1st NORTHAMPTONS here. Found that no steps had hardly been taken for covering in of manure middens and that sanitary conditions were unsatisfactory. Unsatisfactory incinerators, pits not deep enough and human excreta [illegible] uncovered. Saw M.O. & O.C. with	

1247 W 3299 200,000 (E) 8/14 J.B.C. & A. Forms/C. 2118/11.

Instructions regarding War Diaries and Intelligence Summaries are contained in F. S. Regs., Part II. and the Staff Manual respectively. Title pages will be prepared in manuscript.

Army Form C. 2118.

WAR DIARY
or
INTELLIGENCE SUMMARY
(Erase heading not required.)

Hour, Date, Place	Summary of Events and Information	Remarks and references to Appendices
April 22. LES HARISOIRES	references to this and suggested a better provision of the Sanitary Squad with equipment	
LOCON	Saw Captain of Gendarmerie and asked for loan of cart for removal of liquid refuse from middens. Cart promised for today.	
	Routine work continued by Section	
	G.H.	
April 23 1915 LOCON	Inspected billets of 1st Div. ARTILLERY HORSES with special reference to cleaning of middens. Visited lines of 1st SIEGE BATTERY and found conditions much improved. Incinerator built by Squad from Section	
COURS ST VAAST	Party from Section cleaning up lines of 26th FIELD Co. R.E.	Party of 1 NCO & 10 men
LOCON	Inspected billets and horse lines of NORTHUMBERLAND HUSSARS found conditions unsatisfactory and arranged with OC for a fatigue party. Lent a Squad from Section to put matters straight.	
	Men of Section paid out	
	Routine work continued	
	G.H.	
April 24 1915 LOCON	Accompanied A.D.M.S. in his inspection of billets in and near locality	
ALLOUAGNE	Discussed steps with OCs and MOs of 1st Bn BLACK WATCH and LONDON SCOTTISH for prevention of spread of MEASLES infection	

Instructions regarding War Diaries and Intelligence Summaries are contained in F. S. Regs., Part II. and the Staff Manual respectively. Title pages will be prepared in manuscript.

WAR DIARY
or
INTELLIGENCE SUMMARY

(Erase heading not required.)

Army Form C. 2118.

Hour, Date, Place	Summary of Events and Information	Remarks and references to Appendices
April 24 1915 COURS ST VAAST	Squad from Section continued work of cleaning up [illegible]	Squad 1 NCO + 10 men
LOCON	Party from Section assisted in clearing lines of NORTHUMBERLAND HUSSARS	Squad 1 NCO + 4 men
	Routine work continued by remainder of section clearing middens etc.	
	Billets of 1st DIV CYCLISTS cleaned. Urinals and latrines dug. G.H.	
April 25 1915 LACOUTURE	Accompanied A.D.M.S. on his inspection of billets in these districts	Squad 1 NCO 10 men
COURS ST VAAST	At latter place Squad from Section continued work of cleaning up. Squad were assisted by prisoners	5 prisoners
LOCON	Routine work carried on by remainder of Section.	
	5096 Pte Mahoney was yesterday admitted to Hospital G.H.	Pte Mahoney attached to Section from 2nd Bn R. MUNSTER FUSILIERS
April 26 1915 LOCON	Visited billets of 21st C of LONDON BTTY 1st BDE R.F.A. arranged with OC to deal with certain insanitary conditions obtaining in his lines and arranged to send a squad from Section tomorrow morning to assist	
LONG CORNET	Accompanied A.D.M.S. who inspected billets of 1st BN L NORTH LANCASHIRE Regt and 5th BN R. SUSSEX REGT. Saw M.O. & O.C. of these units and discussed steps to be taken with regard to middens & other insanitary conditions obtaining. Condemned one billet occupied by men of 5th SUSSEX and arranged for Squad from Section to clean up billets and surroundings today	

Instructions regarding War Diaries and Intelligence Summaries are contained in F. S. Regs., Part II. and the Staff Manual respectively. Title pages will be prepared in manuscript.

WAR DIARY
or
INTELLIGENCE SUMMARY
(Erase heading not required.)

Army Form C. 2118.

Hour, Date, Place	Summary of Events and Information	Remarks and references to Appendices
April 26 1915 LONG CORNET	Squad from section at work in afternoon on billets of 5 ROYAL SUSSEX REGT	Squad 1 NCO [illegible]
RUE DES CHEVATTES	Visited billets of 7th MOUNTAIN BATTY R.F.A. Found area in bad conditions saw O.C. with regard to sanitary matters and discussed steps as to remedying them. Instructed Bombardier as to best method of dealing with insanitary conditions.	
LOCON	Routine work carried out by Section. G.H.	
April 27 1915	Visited billets of 25th BDE R.F.A. AMM COL and found several middens requiring to be filled in or otherwise dealt with. Conditions otherwise satisfactory	
LOCON	Visited lines of 2nd Co of LONDON BATTY where squad from section was at work	
	Visited lines and billets of NORTHUMBERLAND HUSSARS where party from from Sanitary Section was at work assisting fatigue party of unit	
	Arranged with Captain of Gendarmerie for cleaning ditch around General's House	
	Arranged to send party to 25th BDE RFA to deal with midden near canal which I inspected with the MO of the unit	
	Routine work carried out by Section	
	Enquired into charge against acting L/Cpl [illegible] of Conduct prejudicial to good order and conduct in [illegible] endeavouring [illegible]	L Cpl Evans attached to Section from 1st Bn SOUTH WALES BORDERERS

Instructions regarding War Diaries and Intelligence Summaries are contained in F. S. Regs., Part II. and the Staff Manual respectively. Title pages will be prepared in manuscript.

WAR DIARY
or
INTELLIGENCE SUMMARY
(Erase heading not required.)

Army Form C. 2118.

Hour, Date, Place	Summary of Events and Information	Remarks and references to Appendices
April 27 1915 LOCON	been without sufficient payment and (2) Striking a woman LCpl Evans was remanded till tomorrow for the attendance of a material witness.	
	1667 Acting LCpl Martin reported for duty with section returning from 1st DIVISIONAL TRAIN	
LONG CORNET	Visited 2nd BDE Headquarters and billets of 5th ROYAL SUSSEX Regt	G.J.
April 28 1915 LOCON	Visited and found lines of 1st DIV. HDQRS. in an indifferent sanitary condition. Instructed NCO in charge to put matters in order.	
	Inspected with ADMS lines of NORTHUMBERLAND HUSSARS and found them, with exception of middens, in good condition	
	Routine work continued by section.	
	—	
	Lines of 60th Battery in fair sanitary condition when visited by me. Found non-regulation latrines in use. Drew attention of Sergt Major to this fact and gave instructions for the proper latrine to be dug.	
	Resumed hearing of case against LCpl Evans who after requesting a Court Martial was remanded till tomorrow.	
	5665 Sergt Howson of 1st Bn SCOTS GUARDS joined section.	
	4016 Pte Billon of 1st Bn L N LANCS reported for duty also.	
LONG CORNET	Visited with ADMS billets of 1st Bn L.N. LANCS which were now in a fairly good sanitary condition.	G.J.

1247 W 3299 200,000 (E) 8/14 J.B.C. & A. Forms/C. 2118/11.

Instructions regarding War Diaries and Intelligence Summaries are contained in F. S. Regs., Part II. and the Staff Manual respectively. Title pages will be prepared in manuscript.

WAR DIARY
or
INTELLIGENCE SUMMARY
(Erase heading not required.)

Army Form C. 2118.

Hour, Date, Place	Summary of Events and Information	Remarks and references to Appendices
April 29.1915	Party from Section at work assisting in carrying out of middens in lines of 25th BDE RFA AMM COL	
RICHEBOURG	Accompanied A.D.M.S. on special duty. Inspected Transport lines of 7th MOUNTAIN BTTY and discussed with OC certain matters regarding insanitary conditions obtaining. OC promised to attend to these matters. Visited a billet of the 11th BATTERY and found ground after midden had been covered in, in a very bad state. Arranged with Sergeant Major to have this billet put into a satisfactory condition. Saw M.O's in charge of 2nd Bn K.R.R's and 9th LIVERPOOL REGT and arranged to send today Squad from Sanitary Section with lorry to assist fatigue party in clearing up.	
LONG CORNET	Inspected 3rd BDE Hdqrs and surroundings and saw Staff Captain with respect to further treatment of manure middens and other insanitary conditions requiring attention. Condition of this area on the whole satisfactory	
LOCON	Resumed hearing of charge against L Cpl Evans who withdrew his request for a Court Martial and was remanded till tomorrow for consideration of award. At request of 2nd Inter[illegible] inspected a billet and found a foul open drain which required immediate attention. Routine work carried on. Three men have returned from hospital	

1247 W 3299 200,000 (E) 8/14 J.B.C. & A. Forms/C. 2118/11.

Instructions regarding War Diaries and Intelligence Summaries are contained in F. S. Regs., Part II. and the Staff Manual respectively. Title pages will be prepared in manuscript.

WAR DIARY
or
INTELLIGENCE SUMMARY

(Erase heading not required.)

Army Form C. 2118.

Hour, Date, Place	Summary of Events and Information	Remarks and references to Appendices
April 30. 1915 RICHEBOURG HINGES	Sanitary squad from Section at work cleaning up generally in this district.	
PONT D'AVELETTE	Accompanied A.D.M.S. who inspected billets of Gloucester Regt and of 2nd Royal Sussex Regt in this district. Discussed matters concerning manure middens with M.O.s & O.C.s. Area in fair condition with the exception of food being covered & kept free from infection and unsuitable spots for latrines.	
ALLOUAGNE	Accompanied A.D.M.S. & Area of 1st Bn BLACK WATCH and LONDON SCOTTISH finding these lines in good condition	
LACOUTURE	Went with A.D.M.S. to investigate complaint received from O.C. 51st BTTY R.F.A. Inspected lines of 25th Bde A.M. & Col. R.F.A. and found them in good condition with exception of middens which required covering in.	
LOCON	Routine work continued by remainder of Section 7029 Pte BARNES of 2nd WELSH REGT reported for duty with Section 15191 L/Cpl Evans awarded 10 days Field punishment No. 1	G.L.

G. L. [illegible]
Lt R.A.M.C. (T)
O.C. 13 Sanitary Section

1247 W 3299 200,000 (E) 8/14 J.B.C. & A. Forms/C. 2118/11.

Appendix No. 1

SANITATION. A A & Q M G 1st Div

1st Div. No 1414.

CIRCULAR MEMORANDUM -- SANITATION.

In a circular memorandum on Sanitation issued by the 1st Army, dated 31st March, attention is drawn to the fact that flies breed in enormous quantities in horse manure.

The G. O. C. requests that the following instructions be issued to Officers Commanding units which are billetted in farms where middens and manure heaps exist.

1. All middens and manure heaps near billets occupied by troops are to be treated with lime, and covered with a layer of earth.

2. Arrangements are to be made with the owners or occupants that no fresh manure is deposited on the middens, but is removed to a distance of at least 200 yards from the billets and deposited in newly dug pits, or spread out on the ground. In the event of any of the old manure from the middens being required by the owners or occupants, it is to be taken from one corner.

3. Every effort is to be made to clear out wet ditches in the vicinity of billets, and to remove any obstructions to the flow of water, and prevent stagnation as mush as possible.

4. Sufficient Incinerators are to be constructed to enable all rubbish to be burnt.

5. If any difficulty is experienced by the inhabitants in conforming to the instructions regarding the removal of manure, assistance may be given by the loan of horses and drivers, if available.

H. S. L. Ravenshaw.
Lt. Colonel,

15th April 1915. A. A. & Q. M. G, 1st Division.

APPENDIX No 1. DAA & QMG 1st DIV.
CONVICTION QUASHED

A. D. M. S.

First Division.

The Major General has quashed the conviction and ordered the record to be removed.

This N.C.O. should be deprived of his acting rank as he is not fitted to be in charge of men.

Andrew Thorne
Capt.
DAA & QMG 1st Div.

1 May 15

2.

O.C. San. Section.

For your information & necessary action.

[illegible] Lt Col
for ADMS.

2/5/15.

SECRET APPENDIX No 2 ADMS 1st DIV COPY. No 12

R.A.M.C. ORDERS
by
Colonel S. Macdonald, A.M.S. Commanding R.A.M.C.
1st Division 6th April, 1915.

MOVES.

(1) The Bearer Division of No 2 Field Ambulance relieves that of No 1. Field Ambulance at LE TOURET this morning, and will establish when necessary a collecting station at road junction X.16.a.6.0.

(2) The Bearer Division of No 3. Field Ambulance will move on the morning of 7th to billets at road junction at X.5.d.3.4 and will establish a "Collecting station" there.

(3) The Bearer Division of No 1. Field Ambulance will move at a time to be notified later to LOCON and will establish there a "Collecting station".

(4) The Tent Division of No 2 Field Ambulance will move at a time to be notified later to the ECOLE JEUNE FILLES, BETHUNE, and will establish a dressing station there, taking over the North wing of that building for this purpose. This dressing station to be ready to receive casualties by 9 a.m. on the 8th.

O.C. Sanitary Section will detail a fatigue party of 20 men with motor lorry to accompany this unit to assist in preparing the dressing station. This party will remain with and be rationed by No 2 Field Ambulance until no longer required.

TRANSPORT.

Each Bearer Division will be accompanied by not more than 4 motor ambulances, one forage cart, one water cart and one horsed ambulance wagon, which will be parked at the Collecting station clear of the road. The G.S. wagons of the Bearer Divisions will join the 1st line transport of their respective brigades which will be parked at MESPLAUX farm X.14.a.

The remainder of the motor ambulances will remain with the tent divisions ready to be sent up to the collecting stations when required.

The routes for motor ambulances as shown on the traffic map issued to O.C. F.A's on 28th April will be strictly adhered to.

H B Fawcus
Lt Colonel,
for ADMS 1 Div

Copies to:- 1.2 & 3 F.A's 1st, 2nd & 3rd Bdes, ADMS M.G, DMS 1st Army, DDMS 1st Corps, ADMS 2nd London division, San: Section,

May 1915

S 121/5614

No 13 Sanitary Section

~~April~~ 1915

May "

1st Division

121/5614

Summarised but not copied.

No 13. Sanitary Section

Vol I.

Instructions regarding War Diaries and Intelligence Summaries are contained in F. S. Regs., Part II. and the Staff Manual respectively. Title pages will be prepared in manuscript.

WAR DIARY
or
INTELLIGENCE SUMMARY
(Erase heading not required.)

Army Form C. 2118.

Hour, Date, Place	Summary of Events and Information	Remarks and references to Appendices
MAY 14 1915 LACOUTURE	On instructions received from A.D.M.S. 7th DIV I visited with an Interpreter the MAYOR of LACOUTURE and pointed out to him the difficulties experienced in carrying out the orders issued concerning the covering in of manure middens, owing to the opposition of farmers. I especially drew his attention to the difficulties experienced in endeavoring to restrain farmers from throwing fresh manure onto middens which had already been covered in. I inspected with the MAYOR various billets in the place and also pointed out to him the necessity for cleaning out the very offensive ditches which run alongside the main street. The MAYOR promised to give these matters his attention. I reported the result of my interview to the ADMS and D.A.D.M.S.	
RICHEBOURG	Visited billets in this area occupied by 2nd Bn. KINGS ROYAL RIFLE REGT and found them and their surroundings in an extremely unsatisfactory condition. Saw OC and discussed with him steps to be taken to clear up his billeting area. Arranged for fatigue party from this unit to assist Sanitary Section which had proceeded in the morning to work in the village and arranged for a further party of 50 men to assist Section tomorrow.	
	Inspected wagon lines of 116th BATTERY RFA and found them in good condition.	
	Inspected lines of 1st Bn. NORTHAMPTONSHIRE REGT finding lines in good condition with exception of some minor matters. OC promised to have matters attended to.	
LE TOURET	Asked Orderly Officer of ~~26th~~ LOWLAND FIELD Co RE for loan of horses which [illegible] unable to give. Inspected with A.D.M.S. lines of 23RD FIELD Co R.E. and found conditions satisfactory. [illegible] [illegible] to obtain loan of horses from this unit.	
LOCON	Inspected with A.D.M.S. lines of 4th SIEGE BATTERY and found conditions much improved. Routine duties carried out by Section at LOCON.	G.J.

1247 W 3299 200,000 (E) 8/14 J.B.C. & A. Forms/C. 2118/11.

Instructions regarding War Diaries and Intelligence Summaries are contained in F. S. Regs., Part II. and the Staff Manual respectively. Title pages will be prepared in manuscript.

WAR DIARY
or
INTELLIGENCE SUMMARY
(Erase heading not required.)

Army Form C. 2118.

Hour, Date, Place	Summary of Events and Information	Remarks and references to Appendices
May 2nd 1915	Sanitary Section supplied squad for work on lines of 25TH BDE RFA AMM COL. Visited these lines with ADMS and found work proceeding satisfactorily though somewhat hampered by civilians who persisted in throwing refuse and [illegible] on covered in middens	
VENDIN	Visited Headquarters of 1ST BRIGADE. Inspected transport lines of 1ST [illegible] and found them exceedingly satisfactory sanitarily.	
LOCON	Arranged with OC 113TH BATTERY to provide horses for tomorrow for sections which were to go to RICHEBOURG for duty tomorrow. Also arranged with Captain of Gendarmerie for loan of carts. Horses and carts to parade at 8.30 am tomorrow at LACOUTURE where Section would take charge of them.	
	Routine work at LOCON continued by Section. Small party from Section clearing large manure heap at rear of lines of 1st SIGNAL Co RE.	
X	Letter from D.A.A.Q.M.G passed to me through ADMS received quashing conviction of L/Cpl Evans and ordering him to be deprived of his lance stripe. Acted accordingly	X Appendix No. 1
RICHEBOURG	Squad from Sanitary Section at work assisted by 50 men from 2nd BN K.R.R's [initials]	
May 3rd 1915 RICHEBOURG	Squad from Sanitary Section sent to this village, with instructions to take charge of carts and horses which would be at LACOUTURE to meet them. Visited squad and found owing to some misunderstanding the carts and horses had not paraded to time. The carts & horses however came to RICHEBOURG later in the morning. In the meanwhile arranged with [illegible] obtained use of cart and horse from ROYAL ENGINEERS. Party of 50 men from 1st BN BLACK WATCH assisted Section in the work.	

1247 W 3299 200,000 (E) 8/14 J.B.C. & A. Forms/C. 2118/11.

Instructions regarding War Diaries and Intelligence Summaries are contained in F. S. Regs., Part II. and the Staff Manual respectively. Title pages will be prepared in manuscript.

WAR DIARY
or
INTELLIGENCE SUMMARY

(Erase heading not required.)

Army Form C. 2118.

Hour, Date, Place	Summary of Events and Information	Remarks and references to Appendices
May 3rd 1915 HINGES	Visited this village in company with A.D.M.S and D.A.D.M.S. where enquiries were made into case of Scarlet Fever. Made arrangements for immediate disinfection which was duly carried out.	
LOCON	2324 PTE NEVILLE G was this day promoted to the rank of acting Lce Cpl without pay	
	Inspected work being carried out by Section and found same proceeding satisfactorily.	
	Interviewed Capt. of Gendarmerie in respect of complaint re [illegible] cesspit at rear of Generals House.	
	Received complaint from MAYOR of LACOUTURE re shortage of labour for cleaning [illegible] in his village. Letter passed to A.D.M.S.	
	13171 PTE PRYTHERCH was yesterday admitted to Hospital. [signature]	
May 4th 1915 RICHEBOURG	Squad from Sanitary Section continued cleaning of this village and [illegible] by fatigue party of 50 men from LONDON SCOTTISH	
	Visited village with A.D.M.S. Discussed O.C. & M.O.s [illegible] in village steps to be taken to effectually clear village which is in an extremely bad condition.	
	Received instructions from A.D.M.S. re certain details of the work	
LOCON	Visited and inspected work being carried out by Squad from Section at lines of 25th Bde R.F.A. Amm Col near canal	
	Inspected cesspit at rear of Generals House and made arrangements for emptying	
	Arranged for covering in of manure lying spread in lines of 1st Div CYCLISTS	
	Inspected with DMS and A.D.M.S. midden which had been covered in by Section at manoir at LOCON to attend to by urgent matters in company of A.D.M.S. & D.A.D.M.S. [signature]	

1247 W 3299 200,000 (E) 8/14 J.B.C. & A. Forms/C. 2118/11.

Instructions regarding War Diaries and Intelligence Summaries are contained in F. S. Regs., Part II. and the Staff Manual respectively. Title pages will be prepared in manuscript.

WAR DIARY
or
INTELLIGENCE SUMMARY
(Erase heading not required.)

Army Form C. 2118.

Hour, Date, Place	Summary of Events and Information	Remarks and references to Appendices
May 5th 1915 RICHEBOURG	Squad from Sanitary Section at work assisted by fatigue party from 1st Bn SCOTS GUARDS visited and found work making satisfactory progress	
MESPLAUX FARM	Visited this farm, where platoon of 2nd ROYAL MUNSTER FUSILIERS are billeted and found sanitary condition unsatisfactory arranged to have midden pumped out and treated with earth and lime	
LES FACONS	Inspected billets occupied by 115th BATTERY RFA and 24th LONDON REGIMENT found lines in dirty condition. Saw OC of Battery who promised to take steps to have lines cleaned up	
RUE DES CHEVATTES	Saw OC 113TH BATTERY and arranged for horses to assist Section in its work at RICHEBOURG	
MESPLAUX FARM LES FACONS LE TOURET	Inspected billets in these areas, with A.D.M.S., that were reported as being in an insanitary state.	
LOCON	Squad from Section at work re-interring dead horse. Inspected work being carried out by Section at LOCON. [signature]	
May 6 1915 RICHEBOURG	Squad from Sanitary Section assisted by party of 50 men from 1st Bn SCOTS GUARDS completed work of clearing up [illegible] village and directed work. Interviewed M.Os of units, also interviewed Brigadier General and Staff Major in respect of fatigue parties	

Instructions regarding War Diaries and Intelligence Summaries are contained in F. S. Regs., Part II. and the Staff Manual respectively. Title pages will be prepared in manuscript.

WAR DIARY
or
INTELLIGENCE SUMMARY
(Erase heading not required.)

Army Form C. 2118.

Hour, Date, Place	Summary of Events and Information	Remarks and references to Appendices
May 6 1915 CORNET MALO	Inspected lines and billets of 1st DIVISIONAL AMM COL and arranged with OC to send a squad from Sanitary Section to clean up area tomorrow.	
LOCON	Inspected and found work being done by Section proceeding satisfactorily.	
	2208 LCE CPL ALLWRIGHT returned to the Section from 1st BN LOYAL NORTH LANCASHIRE REGT and was reverted to his permanent rank.	
	2209 LCE CPL LAWRENCE was posted to the LOYAL NORTH LANCASHIRE REGT vice PTE ALLWRIGHT	
	* Received instructions from A.D.M.S. that party of 20 men were to be sent on Saturday next to No 2 FIELD AMBULANCE, taking with them 2 days' rations. The Section's lorry was to accompany the party.	* Appendix 2
	15191 PTE EVANS, 13390 PTE KILROY, 6884 PTE JONES, 1353 PTE SMITH, 10267 PTE NOLAN and 12011 PTE STOKES were detailed for duty with 2nd BN R MUNSTER FUSRS as a sanitary squad	PTE EVANS & PTE KILROY attached to Section from 1st BN S. WALES BORDERERS. PTES JONES, SMITH, NOLAN, STOKES from 2ND BN WELCH REGT
May 7 1915 LOCON	Saw O/C No 2 FIELD AMBULANCE and arranged with him for squad detailed for duty to parade at 3.15 am tomorrow, the lorry to ~~accompany them with~~ carry such equipment as may be necessary. The men to carry one day's rations. The men's kit [?] to be packed in lorry, which was to be handed over in the evening. The squad are to march with No 2 FIELD AMBULANCE to BETHUNE. The lorry will follow with transport of AMBULANCE. The squad and lorry will remain at disposal of OC No 2	

1247 W 3299 200,000 (E) 8/14 J.B.C. & A. Forms/C. 2118/11.

Instructions regarding War Diaries and Intelligence Summaries are contained in F. S. Regs., Part II. and the Staff Manual respectively. Title pages will be prepared in manuscript.

WAR DIARY
or
INTELLIGENCE SUMMARY
(Erase heading not required.)

Army Form C. 2118.

Hour, Date, Place	Summary of Events and Information	Remarks and references to Appendices
May 7 1915 LOCON	FIELD AMBULANCE as long as may be required	
	Supplied at request of D A Q M G a quantity of slacked lime (about 28 lbs) and prepared 7 gallons of lime solution	
	Party from Section at work pumping out cesspit at rear of 1st DIVISION HEADQUARTERS.	
CORNET MALO	Squad from Section at work cleaning lines and billets of 1st DIVISION AMMUNITION COLUMN.	
MESPLAUX FARM	Party from Section at work cleaning up billets and surroundings of farm occupied by ROYAL MUNSTER FUSILIERS.	
7.30pm May 7. LOCON	Order re move above cancelled. [initials]	
May 8. 1915 CORNET MALO	Visited lines and billets of 1st DIVISIONAL AMMUNITION COL where Squad from Section were at work continuing cleaning up process. The work had made considerable progress manure heaps covered in surroundings cleaned up and incinerators built. OC complained very strongly of the dirty condition in which billets was left by previous occupants.	
MESPLAUX FARM	Interviewed and arranged with OC & M O i/c 5th R SUSSEX REGT for a fatigue party of 32 men to assist Squad from Section who were working on this billet. Manure middens being pumped out, incinerators erected	

1247 W 3299 200,000 (E) 8/14 J.B.C. & A. Forms/C. 2118/11.

Instructions regarding War Diaries and Intelligence Summaries are contained in F. S. Regs., Part II. and the Staff Manual respectively. Title pages will be prepared in manuscript.

WAR DIARY
or
INTELLIGENCE SUMMARY
(Erase heading not required.)

Army Form C. 2118.

Hour, Date, Place	Summary of Events and Information	Remarks and references to Appendices
May 8. 1915 BETHUNE	Received balance of brassards ordered in accordance with 1st Divisional Routine Order No. paid a/c amounting to 226.30 francs	
HINGES	Inspected insanitary manure midden at billet of Supply Officer ASC and arranged with him to deal with same as soon as possible.	
May. 8. 1915 7pm LOCON	Received verbal instructions from ADMS that a party of 19 men and 3 NCOs from the Section parade at 3am tomorrow at No 2 FIELD AMBULANCE LOCON, in full marching order. To carry 1 day's rations and kit to be packed in lorry which was to accompany the squad and which was to contain any equipment necessary. The party and lorry to report to OC. No 2 FIELD AMBULANCE and to proceed with the Ambulance to BETHUNE	[initials]
3 am May 9 1915 ~~[illegible]~~ LOCON	Squad and lorry paraded as directed. Remainder of Section stays at LOCON under SERGT HATHAWAY and continues routine work.	
	During operations I remained in attendance on the ADMS and DADMS.	
BETHUNE	Reported myself for duty to OC NO 2 FIELD AMBULANCE in evening	
12 midnight LOCON	Returned from BETHUNE	[initials]

1247 W 3299 200,000 (E) 8/14 J.B.C. & A. Forms/C. 2118/11.

Army Form C. 2118.

Instructions regarding War Diaries and Intelligence Summaries are contained in F. S. Regs., Part II. and the Staff Manual respectively. Title pages will be prepared in manuscript.

WAR DIARY
or
INTELLIGENCE SUMMARY

(Erase heading not required.)

Hour, Date, Place	Summary of Events and Information	Remarks and references to Appendices
May 10 1915 LOCON	I remained at disposal of A.D.M.S. during the morning. Squad from Section carrying out routine work.	
HINGES VENDIN	Inspected billets in these areas finding conditions generally satisfactory. G.J.L.	
May 11 1915 LOCON	Inspected ground recently occupied by an Indian Battery R.F.A. finding billets and surrounding in very dirty state. Arranged for party from Section assisted by prisoners from NORTHUMBERLAND HUSSARS to clean up.	
12 noon May 11 1915	Sanitary Squad of 19 men and 3 N.C.O's returned from BETHUNE.	
	Inspected billets provided for No 1 FIELD AMBULANCE. Subsequently detailing a party of 2 N.C.O.s and 15 men from Section to clean up billets.	
2.30pm May 11 1915 BETHUNE	On instructions received from A.D.M.S. lorry proceeded to BETHUNE to assist in removing equipment for No 2 FIELD AMBULANCE. G.J.L.	
May 12 1915 HINGES. LOCON	Squad from Section at work cleaning up billets of 1st BRIGADE. Received orders that Section was to stand by. Rode to HINGES and instructed party at work to return at once. Squad at work on cleaning billets recently occupied by Indians similarly instructed.	

1247 W 3299 200,000 (E) 8/14 J.B.C. & A. Forms/C. 2118/11.

Instructions regarding War Diaries and Intelligence Summaries are contained in F. S. Regs., Part II. and the Staff Manual respectively. Title pages will be prepared in manuscript.

WAR DIARY
or
INTELLIGENCE SUMMARY
(Erase heading not required.)

Army Form C. 2118.

Hour, Date, Place	Summary of Events and Information	Remarks and references to Appendices
12.45 pm May 12 1915 LOCON	Received orders that Section would not move today but that I was to proceed, myself, to BETHUNE	
2.45 pm May 12 1915 BETHUNE	Arrived here from LOCON. Billet and office found for me in RUE LOUIS BLANC. Billets were also found for Section and I sent orders to Staff Sergeant i/c Section to evacuate billets at LOCON and proceed at once here	
6.45 pm do do	Section with lorry arrived from LOCON and were billeted in grounds of College near Place de Lille.	
	Arranged for Squad from Section to clean up tomorrow, commencing at 5am billets of G.O.C., 1st DIVISION HEADQUARTERS and 1st DIVISIONAL ARTILLERY Hdqrs.	
	732 SERGEANT HATHAWAY was this day admitted to Hospital	
5am May 13 1915 BETHUNE	Squads at work on billets of G.O.C. 1st Div Hdqrs and 1st D.A as arranged	
	On instructions of A.D.M.S. interviewed SANITARY OFFICER 47TH (LONDON) DIV. at his office in Boulevard Frederick Desgeorges, and discussed with him steps taken by municipality to deal with cesspools. Inspected dumping ground of for Town refuse. Reported result of interview to A.D.M.S. 1st DIV. on my return. Arranged with CAMP COMMANDANT 1st DIV for horses and drivers to be provided daily and with Captain of Gendarmerie for hire of carts, to be used by SECTION for removal of refuse manure etc from billets.	

1247 W 3299 200,000 (E) 8/14 J.B.C. & A. Forms/C. 2118/11.

Instructions regarding War Diaries and Intelligence Summaries are contained in F. S. Regs., Part II. and the Staff Manual respectively. Title pages will be prepared in manuscript.

WAR DIARY
or
INTELLIGENCE SUMMARY

(Erase heading not required.)

Army Form C. 2118.

Hour, Date, Place	Summary of Events and Information	Remarks and references to Appendices
May 13.1915 BETHUNE	Visited Hotel de Ville and arranged for an interview at 9.30am tomorrow with Town Sanitary authority and for an appointment afterwards with Town Engineer and Surveyor. On instructions of A.D.M.S. visited billets of 9th KINGS LIVERPOOL REGT re difficulty in dealing with pails containing excreta. Saw M.O. i/c and discussed with him the best means of dealing with the difficulty. Reported result of interview to A.D.M.S. on return. [signature]	
9am May 14 1915 BETHUNE	Visited Captain Pigeon with regard to carts for removal of refuse	Capt Pigeon French Military Mission 1st Div
12 noon	Visited billets of Sanitary Section.	
7am		
9.30am	Visited with Sanitary Officer 47th (LONDON) DIV. Town Surveyor and discussed with him arrangements for disposal of refuse excreta etc. A tentative ~~arrangement~~ understanding was reached as to the assistance to be given by the municipal authorities. It was apparent however that from the results of the interview that little if any assistance was to be expected from the Authorities.	
	Lieut MACLENNAN arrived to take up duty and interviewed me with reference to the command of the Section. Referred him to the A.D.M.S.	LIEUT MACLENNAN was originally in charge of Section but had been sent to Hospital and consequently received Sick Leave.
	LIEUT CLAYTON, Sanitary Officer 2ND DIVISION called to make enquiries re carts which were alleged by owners not to have been used. He was informed that none of the carts in question were being used by the Section.	

1247 W 3299 200,000 (E) 8/14 J.B.C. & A. Forms/C. 2118/11.

Army Form C. 2118.

Instructions regarding War Diaries and Intelligence Summaries are contained in F. S. Regs., Part II. and the Staff Manual respectively. Title pages will be prepared in manuscript.

WAR DIARY
or
INTELLIGENCE SUMMARY
(Erase heading not required.)

Hour, Date, Place	Summary of Events and Information	Remarks and references to Appendices
May 14 1915 BETHUNE	Interviewed Madame de Lille and after some difficulty succeeded in obtaining loan of 2 carts for carting manure and refuse. The arrangement of work for Section in the town occupied a considerable portion of the day.	
May 15 1915 BETHUNE	Inspected 1st DIVISION HEADQUARTER billets and directed measures to be taken for cleaning these billets. Squad from Section were detailed to clean up billets and surroundings of 9th Bn KINGS LIVERPOOL and 5th ROYAL SUSSEX REGIMENTS. Visited these billets later and found work making satisfactory progress. Captn Pigeon called at office and stated that he had received letters which he showed me, from owners of 2 carts at LACOUTURE. These carts were sent for work at RICHEBOURG and had not been returned. Promised to give matter my attention. Reported facts to A.D.M.S. Sent for Staff Sergeant and Sergt who stated that carts had been left at RICHEBOURG. SERGT HOWSON was sent in company with a Gendarme in Motor Ambulance to RICHEBOURG. SERGT HOWSON on his return reported that Carts had been found and arrangements made for return of carts forthwith to their respective owners.	

1247 W 3299 200,000 (E) 8/14 J.B.C. & A. Forms/C. 2118/11.

Instructions regarding War Diaries and Intelligence Summaries are contained in F. S. Regs., Part II. and the Staff Manual respectively. Title pages will be prepared in manuscript.

WAR DIARY
or
INTELLIGENCE SUMMARY
(Erase heading not required.)

Army Form C. 2118.

Hour, Date, Place	Summary of Events and Information	Remarks and references to Appendices
May 15 BETHUNE	Sanitary Officer 47th (LONDON) DIV called and stated he had been informed by TOWN COMMANDANT that I was responsible for the sanitation of the whole town. Reported this to A.D.M.S. 1st DIV. who instructed me to see the TOWN COMMANDANT with SANITARY OFFICER 47th DIV. I informed the TOWN COMMANDANT that it was impossible for me to undertake the supervision of the whole town. An interview followed between the TOWN COMMANDANT, The A.D.M.S. The SANITARY OFFICER 47th DIV and myself. Suggestions were made so that the difficulty might be overcome. The A.D.M.S pointed out however that the SANITARY OFFICER 1st DIV had sufficient to do with his section in looking after the billets of his own DIVISION.	
	Visited billets of 9th Bn KINGS LIVERPOOL and 5th ROYAL SUSSEX REGIMENTS where squad from Section was at work cleaning up building incinerators etc. I found work making satisfactory progress.	
	Visited and inspected the ORPHANAGE lately occupied by 1st Bn L.N LANCASHIRE REGT finding billet so bad as to necessitate a report to the A.D.M.S. A fatigue party of 100 men will be required to properly clean this place. Offensive rubbish lying about, latrine pails unemptied, the whole place smelling offensively. Later visited this billet and billets of 5th Bn R Sussex and 9th Bn KINGS LIVERPOOL REGIMENTS with A.D.M.S.	

Army Form C. 2118.

Instructions regarding War Diaries and Intelligence Summaries are contained in F. S. Regs., Part II. and the Staff Manual respectively. Title pages will be prepared in manuscript.

WAR DIARY
or
INTELLIGENCE SUMMARY
(Erase heading not required.)

Hour, Date, Place	Summary of Events and Information	Remarks and references to Appendices
May 15 BETHUNE	At request of TOWN COMMANDANT arranged for removal of refuse from THEATRE and SKATING RINK occupied by SCOTS G.DS 1st BN. Quantity of manure removed from billets of 1st DIVISIONAL ARTILLERY in RUE GAMBETTA. GJL	
May 16. BETHUNE	Visited and inspected ORPHANAGE and found that a fatigue party from 1st BN L N LANCASHIRE REGT had been sent yesterday evening between 6 30pm and 8 30pm to clean up. Work however very imperfectly carried out, floors only superficially swept, stairs thick with dust. Latrine pails emptied but otherwise yard untouched. Sent whole of Section to thoroughly scrub with water and cresol all floors, staircases and passages, to remove refuse and large manurial deposit in yard. Purchased 6 pails and 10 scrubbing brushes necessary for this work. Squad sent to remove manure from billets of G.OC, H.Q 1st DIV and 1st DIV ART. Accompanied A.D.M.S. to various FIELD AMBULANCES and to CONVALESCENT Co in order to obtain men for light duty with the Section. Endeavoured to arrange with French Authorities for cleaning out of cesspools in town. ~~[illegible]~~ GJL	

1247 W 3299 200,000 (E) 8/14 J.B.C. & A. Forms/C. 2118/11.

Instructions regarding War Diaries and Intelligence Summaries are contained in F. S. Regs., Part II. and the Staff Manual respectively. Title pages will be prepared in manuscript.

WAR DIARY
or
INTELLIGENCE SUMMARY
(Erase heading not required.)

Army Form C. 2118

Hour, Date, Place	Summary of Events and Information	Remarks and references to Appendices
May 17 1915 BETHUNE	Visited and inspected Orphanage. Sent fatigue party from Section to complete cleaning up of building and annexe and to remove manure.	
	Received from SANITARY OFFICER 2ND DIV list of pail latrines and wash basins left by him in various billets in town.	
	Squads from Section cleaning up billets at HORLOGERIE and billets recently occupied by 1st BN NORTHAMPTON REGT in CHEMIN DE FER ROAD	
	Visited and inspected billets of 5TH R SUSSEX REGT at TOBACCO FACTORY	
	Obtained 1122 frs 50 cents from Field Cashier to pay out Section and to settle various small bills for articles obtained by local purchase.	
	Paid out SECTION and carried out Routine duties	
	Received letter from a M SARRUT in connection with charges for cleaning out cesspools in town.	
BEUVRY CAMBRIN	Visited these areas and found billets of 1st BN L NORTH LANCASHIRE REGT required attention. Arranged to send Squad to clean these billets tomorrow.	
	Called at Headquarters of 3RD BRIGADE and saw Staff Captain arranging with him to send a Squad under a Sergeant to clean up billets and surroundings in CAMBRIN. Assistance required to be supplied by fatigue party from troops in Brigade area	
	2208 PTE ALLWRIGHT was today admitted to hospital.	

1247 W 3299 200,000 (E) 8/14 J.B.C. & A. Forms/C. 2118/11.

Instructions regarding War Diaries and Intelligence Summaries are contained in F. S. Regs., Part II. and the Staff Manual respectively. Title pages will be prepared in manuscript.

WAR DIARY
or
INTELLIGENCE SUMMARY
(Erase heading not required.)

Army Form C. 2118.

Hour, Date, Place	Summary of Events and Information	Remarks and references to Appendices
May 18 1915 BEUVRY	Squad from Section in charge of NCO cleaning up of billets in this area	
CAMBRIN	Squad from Section in charge of NCO clean up billets and Hqrs 3RD BRIGADE assisted by fatigue party of 30 men from 2nd Bn ROYAL MUNSTER FUSILIERS.	
BETHUNE	Squad sent to clean up Headquarters of 1st DIVISION just evacuated.	
	NCO at SKATING RINK occupied by CONVALESCENT Co supervising the erection of an incinerator.	
	Squad cleaning up horse lines in PLACE LAMARTINE	
	Squad cleaning scrubbing and disinfecting large room at ORPHANAGE	
BEUVRY & CAMBRIN	Inspected work being carried out by section and fatigue party and arranged with Staff Captain 3RD BRIGADE for a fatigue party to assist section here, tomorrow	
BETHUNE	732 SERGT HATHAWAY returned to duty today from hospital.	
CAMBRIN	Arranged with OC 1/10 & 1st Bn L.N. LANCASHIRE REGT for a fatigue party to assist Squad from Section tomorrow in cleaning up billets here	

[illegible initials]

1247 W 3299 200,000 (E) 8/14 J.B.C. & A. Forms/C. 2118/11.

Instructions regarding War Diaries and Intelligence Summaries are contained in F. S. Regs., Part II. and the Staff Manual respectively. Title pages will be prepared in manuscript.

WAR DIARY
or
INTELLIGENCE SUMMARY
(Erase heading not required.)

Army Form C. 2118.

Hour, Date, Place	Summary of Events and Information	Remarks and references to Appendices
May 19. 1915 BEUVRY	Squad under N.C.O. continued cleaning up of billets and surroundings of 1st Bn L. N. LANCASHIRE REGT. Arranged with O.C. for carts and horses for the removal of manure etc from neighbourhood of billets. Fatigue party of 40 men from L.N. LANCASHIRE REGT assisted with the work	
CAMBRIN	Squad under N.C.O. continued work of clearance here and were assisted by a fatigue party from 2nd Bn ROYAL MUNSTER FUSILIERS. Visited and inspected locality and ordered Staff Sergeant to take charge of party.	
SAILLY LABOURSE	Inspected 1st DIVISIONAL HEADQUARTERS here and arranged for squad from section to commence cleaning up in this district, especially at HEADQUARTERS, tomorrow. Asked A.D.C. to arrange for fatigue party to assist in work.	
BETHUNE	Sent party from Section to pump out cellar in ORPHANAGE. Inspected and directed execution of work. Cellar filled with liquid sewage. With interpreter visited the Mairie and interviewed representative of Town Surveyor, with reference to an extensive deposit of offensive refuse in the Bd VOLTAIRE. Was informed that the Town Authorities had made arrangements to have this mass removed and dumped in an old quarry outside the town. I also discussed with the official concerned the question of infectious disease in the town and arranged for a list of all infectious cases to be supplied to A.D.M.S. 1st Div. Called on TOWN COMMANDANT re sanitation, but this official was out. SANITARY OFFICER 47th (Lon) Div called re works proposed to be carried out by his Section (No 19 SANITARY SECTION) in BETHUNE. Inspected billets of 5th R SUSSEX REGT finding same satisfactory. 2545 Pte SUTCLIFFE was today admitted to hospital.	

Army Form C. 2118.

Instructions regarding War Diaries and Intelligence Summaries are contained in F. S. Regs., Part II. and the Staff Manual respectively. Title pages will be prepared in manuscript.

WAR DIARY
or
INTELLIGENCE SUMMARY
(Erase heading not required.)

Hour, Date, Place	Summary of Events and Information	Remarks and references to Appendices
MAY. 20th 1915 BEUVRY	Sent Squad to complete work of cleaning up here	
SAILLY LABOURSE	Squad under 3 NCOs from Section assisted by a fatigue party of 30 men from RAMC. stretcher bearers. Parties at work cleaning up billet of G.O.C. and DIVISIONAL HEADQUARTERS and a party cleaning up in village generally. Later visited district and found work proceeding.	
NOYEAU LES VERMELLES.	Visited 1st BDE HDQRS and saw BRIGADIER arranging with him for a fatigue party of 100 men to parade tomorrow at SAILLY LABOURSE to assist SECTION there. Requested also that a party be detailed daily as work at SAILLY LABOURSE was very considerable. Was informed that a party would be available as long as necessary.	
CAMBRIN	Sent party to clean up HDQRS 25th BDE RFA at CAMBRIN.	
ANNEQUIN	Visited these districts and found conditions improved sanitarily.	
BETHUNE	Visited ORPHANAGE and found that a collection of offensive refuse had been overlooked. Arranged for its removal tomorrow. 11894 PTE EDWARDS and 13319 PTE UPTON were today admitted to hospital. G.J.	
MAY. 21st 1915. SAILLY LABOURSE	Sent Sanitary Squad here to clean up billets and surroundings and to clear manure middens of which there are a large number, mostly offensive, in the village. Fatigue party of 150 men from 1st BN CAMERON HIGHLANDERS assisted section. 5 carts were at work for the purpose of removing manure. Visited the district and directed work, remaining there all day. Several manure middens were dealt with and considerable progress	

1247 W 3299 200,000 (E) 8/14 J.B.C. & A. Forms/C. 2118/11.

Instructions regarding War Diaries and Intelligence Summaries are contained in F. S. Regs., Part II. and the Staff Manual respectively. Title pages will be prepared in manuscript.

WAR DIARY
or
INTELLIGENCE SUMMARY

(Erase heading not required.)

Army Form C. 2118.

Hour, Date, Place	Summary of Events and Information	Remarks and references to Appendices
May 21st 1915 SAILLY LABOURSE	in the work of clearing up was made. Saw BRIGADIER 1st BRIGADE who informed that a party of 50 men only could be supplied tomorrow. Interview with AA & QMG at which steps were discussed as to the clearing of the village and the billets. I was promised assistance for carrying out the work. Inspected latrines and refuse destructors in some of the billets and arranged for incinerators to be erected where necessary.	
BETHUNE	Sent party to ORPHANAGE to clean up offensive refuse discovered yesterday.	
	Routine work, viz removal of refuse from billets of 1st DIV. HDQRS continued.	
	~~Two men [illegible]~~	
	2545 PTE SUTCLIFFE and 13319 PTE UPTON yesterday returned to duty from hospital.	
	[initials]	
May 22 1915 SAILLY LABOURSE	Squad from Section assisted by fatigue party of 50 men from 1st BN SCOTS GUARDS at work continuing clearing of village. Visited locality and personally supervised work. Several more manure middens being dealt with. Saw STAFF CAPTAIN and pointed out that owing to the enormous amount of work to be done it would be advisable if a fatigue party could be obtained for the afternoons as well as for the mornings. STAFF CAPTAIN arranged for this to be done	

1247 W 3299 200,000 (E) 8/14 J.B.C. & A. Forms/C. 2118/11.

Instructions regarding War Diaries and Intelligence Summaries are contained in F. S. Regs., Part II. and the Staff Manual respectively. Title pages will be prepared in manuscript.

WAR DIARY
or
INTELLIGENCE SUMMARY
(Erase heading not required.)

Army Form C. 2118.

Hour, Date, Place	Summary of Events and Information	Remarks and references to Appendices
May 22nd 1915 LABOURSE	Visited lines of 26TH and 1st LOWLAND FIELD COS RE finding Sanitary condition of things very unsatisfactory. Saw M O i/c who consulted me as to the best method of dealing with several large vats containing beer refuse which smelled very offensively. Suggested to him best method, in my opinion, in dealing with this offensive matter and promised after consultation with OC & MO i/c to send party from Section if a fatigue party could be provided to assist them.	
BETHUNE	Complaint re offensive cesspool at FIRE STATION submitted to Town authorities for attention.	
	Routine work at BETHUNE carried out.	
	4983 PTE GEORGE was this day admitted to hospital. GL	
May 23rd 1915 SAILLY LABOURSE	Squad sent to this district to continue cleaning up. Visited locality at 10 am. finding squad at work but that no fatigue was working. Saw ADJUTANT of 1st BN CAMERON HIGHLANDERS who stated that party had been available, as ordered, since 8 am. but no one had come to take it over. Saw SERGT HATHAWAY who stated that men were there but had no shovels and that consequently he could make no use of them. Admonished the SERGT and obtained a party of 50 men forthwith and set them to work at 12.30.	

1247 W 3299 200,000 (E) 8/14 J.B.C. & A. Forms/C. 2118/11.

Instructions regarding War Diaries and Intelligence Summaries are contained in F. S. Regs., Part II. and the Staff Manual respectively. Title pages will be prepared in manuscript.

WAR DIARY
or
INTELLIGENCE SUMMARY
(Erase heading not required.)

Army Form C. 2118.

Hour, Date, Place	Summary of Events and Information	Remarks and references to Appendices
May 23. 1915 SAILLY LABOURSE	Visited Divisional Headquarters and saw AA + QMG asking him for a fatigue party of 60 men to be available in the morning and for another party of 60 men in the afternoon from 2pm to 6pm tomorrow and following 2 days to assist section in completing cleaning up of village.	
12.45pm. 23.5.15 do	Received orders from CAPT THORNE for SECTION to evacuate office and billets occupied by them in BETHUNE and to proceed to [struck out] LABOURSE to occupy billets provided there. Proceeded to	
BETHUNE	BETHUNE where I received written orders from A.D.M.S. to same effect. Arranged accordingly and SECTION with lorry and	
7.30pm. 23.5.15 LABOURSE	equipment arrived at LABOURSE	
BETHUNE	Routine work carried out up to time of evacuation. 1561 STAFF SERGEANT BERWICK was today admitted to hospital. LIEUT GAIR of the 1st LONDON SANITARY Co RAMC T was attached to the SECTION for special duty. G.L.	
May 24. 1915 SAILLY LABOURSE	Sent squad from section to this village to continue work of cleaning up. They were assisted by a fatigue party of 60 men from 1st BN COLDSTREAM GDS in morning and a similar party in the afternoon.	

Instructions regarding War Diaries and Intelligence Summaries are contained in F. S. Regs., Part II. and the Staff Manual respectively. Title pages will be prepared in manuscript.

WAR DIARY
or
INTELLIGENCE SUMMARY
(Erase heading not required.)

Army Form C. 2118.

Hour, Date, Place	Summary of Events and Information	Remarks and references to Appendices
May 24 1915 LABOURSE	Sent CPL PALMER to BETHUNE to see that one of the carts borrowed from a MME DE LILLE for purpose of work there is returned. The other cart was damaged whilst carting soil for covering manure middens, the right hand wheel being broken off owing to its having rotten spokes. The cart is at present lying at SAILLY LABOURSE where the accident happened. A.D.M.S advised and instructions as to its disposal asked for.	
BEUVRY	Visited horse lines of 26TH HEAVY BATTERY which lie to the east of this village on instructions of A.D.M.S. to enquire into and report on drainage plan proposed to be completed at a farm occupied by the BATTERY for the drainage of a manure midden. While there visited and inspected other billets occupied by the BATTERY and found conditions sanitarily unsatisfactory. My report to be handed to A.D. MS tomorrow.	
LABOURSE	On my return here found that SERGT HATHAWAY was absent in BETHUNE without permission.	
	SERGT HOWSON reported Acting LCE CPL NEVILLE for insubordination. The charges against these N.C.O.s adjourned till morning.	
	1622 PTE WRAY was today appointed to the acting rank of Lance Corporal without pay and was instructed to proceed to the 1ST BN NORTHAMPTON	

1247 W 3299 200,000 (E) 8/14 J.B.C. & A. Forms/C. 2118/11.

Instructions regarding War Diaries and Intelligence Summaries are contained in F. S. Regs., Part II. and the Staff Manual respectively. Title pages will be prepared in manuscript.

WAR DIARY
or
INTELLIGENCE SUMMARY.
(Erase heading not required.)

Army Form C. 2118.

Hour, Date, Place	Summary of Events and Information	Remarks and references to Appendices
May. 24. 1915 LABOURSE	REGT and report himself the OC for Sanitary duty vice 2138 Acting LCE CPL SNELLING who yesterday returned from that unit and who is from today reverted to his permanent rank. GW	
May. 25. 1915 LABOURSE	Considered charges against SERGT HATHAWAY and LCE CPL NEVILLE. I severely reprimanded the former for being absent without leave in BETHUNE the previous evening (2 hours absent). I adjourned case against Lce Cpl NEVILLE until tomorrow for further consideration. Forwarded a report of my enquiries and result of inspection of proposed drainage system of a manure midden at BEUVRY in lines of 26TH HEAVY BTTY RFA. Letter received from MO i/c 25TH BRIGADE RFA requesting that a man from the Section be sent to replace a man who was ill, in the Sanitary Squad of this unit. Telephoned to ADMS for an appointment to discuss the discipline of the SECTION. Received wire from 1ST DIV HDQRS requesting that a party be sent to DIVISIONAL HEADQUARTERS at once as billage was in an extremely bad condition.	

(73989) W4141—463. 400,000. 9/14. H.&J.Ltd. Forms/C. 2118/10.

Instructions regarding War Diaries and Intelligence Summaries are contained in F. S. Regs., Part II. and the Staff Manual respectively. Title pages will be prepared in manuscript.

Army Form C. 2118.

WAR DIARY
or
INTELLIGENCE SUMMARY.
(*Erase heading not required.*)

Hour, Date, Place	Summary of Events and Information	Remarks and references to Appendices
May 25. 1915 VEROUIN	In accordance with instructions contained in wire sent party of 8 men and 1 N.C.O. to this village and later visited and inspected the district. Arranged details of work obtaining carts from a French farmer and horses from 1st SIGNAL Co R.E's. Personally supervised the work of squad. Visited various billets and remained in village for some 3 hours.	
SAILLY LABOURSE	Squad at work continuing work of emptying and covering manure middens and attending to various matters requiring immediate attention. The COLDSTREAM GUARDS (1st BN) supplied fatigue parties of 60 men in the morning and afternoon.	
	2207 PTE ALLWRIGHT returned from hospital today. [initials]	
May. 26. 1915 SAILLY LABOURSE	Squad from Section cleaning up assisted in morning and afternoon by fatigue parties of 60 men from 1st BN COLDSTREAM GUARDS. A number of manure middens were again treated either by covering in with earth or by emptying. Liquid required liquid matter being pumped out. Inspected work in progress and obtained loans of further horses and a cart. The latter from an inhabitant and for which I agreed to pay 4 francs per day for its use.	

(73989) W4141—463. 400,000. 9/14. H.&J.Ltd. Forms/C. 2118/10.

Instructions regarding War Diaries and Intelligence Summaries are contained in F. S. Regs., Part II. and the Staff Manual respectively. Title pages will be prepared in manuscript.

WAR DIARY
or
INTELLIGENCE SUMMARY.
(*Erase heading not required.*)

Army Form C. 2118.

Hour, Date, Place	Summary of Events and Information	Remarks and references to Appendices
May 26th 1915 VERQUIN	Squad from Section here continued cleaning up of billets surrounding 1st DIVISION HEADQUARTERS. Visited and inspected work which was proceeding satisfactorily. Saw OC 1st SIGNAL Co and arranged with him for the loan of horses to assist in carting and removing manure.	
LABOURSE	2324 LCE CPL NEVILLE was today reverted to his permanent rank for using insubordinate language to his superior officer. Routine duties carried out. 2187 PTE WHITE was today appointed the acting rank of LCE CPL without pay.	
May 27 1915 SAILLY LABOURSE	Squad from Section continued work in this village assisted by fatigue parties in morning and afternoon of 60 men from 1st BN COLDSTREAM GUARDS. Owing to delay experienced in obtaining carts the morning fatigue party was kept waiting 30 minutes before commencing work.	
VERQUIN	Squad from Section continued work here on HEADQUARTERS billets. Later visited village and found work proceeding satisfactorily.	
BETHUNE	Called on A.D.M.S and D.A.D.M.S but both these officials were out. Obtained money from FIELD CASHIER for the purpose of paying out 2 men of section	

(73989) W4141—463. 400,000. 9/14. H.&J.Ltd. Forms/C. 2118/10.

Instructions regarding War Diaries and Intelligence Summaries are contained in F. S. Regs., Part II. and the Staff Manual respectively. Title pages will be prepared in manuscript.

WAR DIARY
or
INTELLIGENCE SUMMARY.
(Erase heading not required.)

Army Form C. 2118.

Hour, Date, Place	Summary of Events and Information	Remarks and references to Appendices
May 27. 1915. LABOURSE	Visited & inspected billets of 1st Bn GLOUCESTER REGT and found same generally in an insanitary state. Several large middens require to be dealt with as may be required. Routine duties carried out by squad left for the purpose. [illegible]	
May 28. 1915. LABOURSE	Detailed a squad from Section to clean up this village. There are a large number of middens which require to be dealt with and a large number of billets which require attention. Requisitioned a fatigue party from 1st Bn GLOUCESTER REGT and obtained 60 men who assisted squad. Obtained horses and carts from 39TH BRIGADE RFA AMM Col for purpose of removing manure and carting earth for covering manure middens.	
SAILLY LABOURSE	SERGT HOWSON reports that a fatigue party of 50 men from 1st Bn CAMERON HIGHLANDERS has been waiting at SAILLY LABOURSE since 8am. No information has been received by me as to the disposition of this party for use by SANITARY SECTION. At once sent a message to OC of unit to this effect and enquired if party could be available for the afternoon. Reply received to the effect that party would parade at 2 pm. They were also chiefly employed in cleaning up lines of 2[illegible] LOWLAND	

(73989) W4141—463. 400,000. 9/14. H.&J.Ltd. Forms/C. 2118/10.

Instructions regarding War Diaries and Intelligence Summaries are contained in F. S. Regs., Part II. and the Staff Manual respectively. Title pages will be prepared in manuscript.

Army Form C. 2118.

WAR DIARY
or
INTELLIGENCE SUMMARY.
(Erase heading not required.)

Hour, Date, Place	Summary of Events and Information	Remarks and references to Appendices
May 28.1915	FIELD COS RE'S at SAILLY LABOURSE. Received instructions from ADMS to take up my billet at VERQUIN the Section to remain at LABOURSE. Arranged accordingly leaving SERGT HOWSON in charge of section. 2180 PTE KEARNES was this day admitted to hospital, he having, whilst working at VERQUIN, been injured by the prong of a pitchfork passing through one of his fingers.	
May 29 1915 VERQUIN LABOURSE	Received instructions from Headquarters to evacuate Section from LABOURSE today. Visited village and made arrangements for Section to move to VERQUIN A party from Section assisted in morning and afternoon by fatigue parties of 60 men from 1st Bn CAMERON HIGHLANDERS carried on work of cleaning up village. Saw the C.O. 39TH BRIGADE RFA AMM Col and pointed out the necessity for at once dealing with accumulation of manure from the large number of horses under his charge. The C.O. promised to see OC of BRIGADE with reference to this and at the same time I promised to lend assistance from the Section.	

Instructions regarding War Diaries and Intelligence Summaries are contained in F. S. Regs., Part II. and the Staff Manual respectively. Title pages will be prepared in manuscript.

WAR DIARY
or
INTELLIGENCE SUMMARY.
(*Erase heading not required.*)

Army Form C. 2118.

Hour, Date, Place	Summary of Events and Information	Remarks and references to Appendices
May 29 1915 SAILLY LABOURSE	Visited and inspected lines of 23RD and 1st LOWLAND FIELD Co's R.E. in Chateau grounds	
FOUQUIERES	Visited and inspected the lines of 1st DIVISION SUPPLY COLUMN find condition sanitarily very satisfactory	
5.30pm May 29 15 VERQUIN	Section arrived, the lorry having previously brought equipment and men's kit.	
	Reported to A.D.M.S. re complaint as to accumulation of incinerated refuse left by Sanitary Section when evacuating billets at COLLEGE DES GARCONS BETHUNE on May 23 1915. Instructed to proceed and make enquiries there tomorrow	
	Replied to M.O. i/c 25TH BRIGADE re supplying a man to replace a man evacuated through illness from his Sanitary Squad [initials]	
9am May 30 1915 VERQUIN	CPL PALMER reported that PRIVATES NEVILLE and BARWELL were missing. Saw SERGT HOWSON who had not reported ~~[illegible]~~ to me that these men were left behind at LABOURSE although I had seen him the night before on the arrival of the SECTION here, and again this morning at 7am.	
10 am.	Reported matter to A.P.M	

3989) W4141—463. 400,000. 9/14. H.&J.Ltd. Forms/C. 2118/10.

Instructions regarding War Diaries and Intelligence Summaries are contained in F. S. Regs., Part II. and the Staff Manual respectively. Title pages will be prepared in manuscript.

WAR DIARY
or
INTELLIGENCE SUMMARY.
(*Erase heading not required.*)

Army Form C. 2118.

Hour, Date, Place	Summary of Events and Information	Remarks and references to Appendices
May 30 1915 VERQUIN	On instructions of D.A.D.M.S. I visited house in the GRAND RUE to enquire into case of infectious disease. ~~On arrival~~ On arrival at billet which was a farmhouse I found that two Sections of 1st BN SOUTH WALES BORDERERS were in occupation. A room opposite kitchen was used as a bedroom and I found the patient a child of 5. This child is stated to have died of Diphtheria, after an illness of 2 days, on 26th instant. Disinfection had not been carried out. Saw O/C and M/O of unit and made arrangements for the immediate evacuation of billet and suggested to M.O. the desirability of keeping men under observation. Placed an[x] Out of bounds notice on gate. Reported subsequently to D.A.D.M.S.	x Appendix 3
LA BOURSE	Squad sent here to continue work. Squad was assisted by fatigue parties of 60 men from 1st CAMERON HIGHLANDERS in morning and afternoon. Reported that ~~the~~ PTE [illegible] had reported to SERGT HATHAWAY in charge of squad at 7.35am this morning.	
VERQUIN	8571 PTE JONES, A. 11670 PTE WILSON G. 14191 PTE DUGGAN J of 1st BN SOUTH WALES BORDERERS 5018 PTE GEDDES, J of 2nd BN R MUNSTER FUSILIERS and 2635 PTE HOOPER W. H. 1st BN GLOUCESTER REGT reported for [illegible]	

(73989) W4141—463. 400,000. 9/14. H.&J.Ltd. Forms/C. 2118/10.

Instructions regarding War Diaries and Intelligence Summaries are contained in F. S. Regs., Part II. and the Staff Manual respectively. Title pages will be prepared in manuscript.

WAR DIARY
or
INTELLIGENCE SUMMARY.
(*Erase heading not required.*)

Army Form C. 2118.

Hour, Date, Place	Summary of Events and Information	Remarks and references to Appendices
May 30 1915 VERQUIN	for duty today from CONVALESCENT COY 1ST DIV. 11894 PTE EDWARDS returned to duty today from CONVALESCENT Co. [initials]	
6.45am May 31st 1915 VERQUIN	Paraded Section and sent off parties to LABOURSE and VERQUIGNEUL	
LABOURSE	Visited and inspected work being carried by Squad who were assisted morning and afternoon by parties of 60 men from 1st BN CAMERON HIGHLANDERS work proceeding satisfactorily	
VERQUIGNEUL	Visited this village and found work proceeding satisfactorily Squad were being assisted by fatigue party of 50 men from 4th BN ROYAL WELSH FUSILIERS.	
BETHUNE	Visited this town to enquire into complaint re non-removal of incinerated refuse from ECOLE de GARÇONS. Reported to ADMS that matter was not pressing.	
	Called on Madame DE LILLE with reference to cart damaged while in use by Section. MADAME was not at home	
VERQUIN	Received orders from ADMS that Section were to evacuate billets here by 11am tomorrow and were to proceed to billet in RITHEAD near PRIEURE ST PRY arranged accordingly [initials]	

G. L. [signature] Lt. R.A.M.C. T. O/c 13 San Section

(13989) W4141—463. 400,000. 9/14. H.&J.Ltd. Forms/C. 2118/10.

5/

121/6135

1st Division

June 1915.

Summarised but not copied

121/6135.

No 13. Sanitary Section

Vol II

Auto

Instructions regarding War Diaries and Intelligence Summaries are contained in F. S. Regs., Part II. and the Staff Manual respectively. Title pages will be prepared in manuscript.

WAR DIARY
or
INTELLIGENCE SUMMARY.
(*Erase heading not required.*)

Army Form C. [illegible]118.

Hour, Date, Place	Summary of Events and Information	Remarks and references to Appendices
	CONFIDENTIAL WAR DIARY of LIEUT G. Q. LENNANE RAMC OC No 13 SANITARY SECTION from June 1st 1915 to June 30 1915 (Volume 2)	

Instructions regarding War Diaries and Intelligence Summaries are contained in F. S. Regs., Part II. and the Staff Manual respectively. Title pages will be prepared in manuscript.

WAR DIARY
or
INTELLIGENCE SUMMARY.
(Erase heading not required.)

Army Form C. 2118.

Hour, Date, Place	Summary of Events and Information	Remarks and references to Appendices
9am. 1st June 1915. VERQUIN	Paraded section and inspected mens kit. Gave instructions to SERGT HOWSON to evacuate billet and proceed to PITHEAD near PRIEURE ST PRY	
11am.	Section left VERQUIN	
PITHEAD (near) PRIEURE ST PRY	Visited in company with Camp Commandant billet and office of SECTION.	
12noon do	SECTION and lorry arrived	
	Detailed squad to proceed to the CHATEAU at VAUDRICOURT in afternoon for purpose of clearing up stables, middens and surroundings generally and to erect an incinerator at HDQRS 1st DIV.	
2.30pm. VAUDRICOURT	Squad commenced work as directed.	
	I enquired as directed by DADMS into illness of a child of 6 years living with her grandparents Belgian refugees in lodge at Chateau. I examined with permission of grandparents the child. I was accompanied by Liaison Officer, CAPT SOLLET. In my opinion case was not Enteric Fever.	
	Reported to ADMS on my return.	
PITHEAD PRIEURE ST PRY	15200 PTE THOMAS D. 1st BN S WALES BORDERERS and 2064 PTE RIORDAN J. 2nd WELCH REGT reported for duty today from Communication Co 1st Div. 13157 PTE BARNWELL E was awarded 7 days C.C. for "Being absent at 4pm on May 29 1915 [illegible]	

Instructions regarding War Diaries and Intelligence Summaries are contained in F. S. Regs., Part II. and the Staff Manual respectively. Title pages will be prepared in manuscript.

WAR DIARY *or* INTELLIGENCE SUMMARY.

(Erase heading not required.)

Army Form C. 2118.

Hour, Date, Place	Summary of Events and Information	Remarks and references to Appendices
June 1st 1915	fresh billets and remaining absent until 7.35 am. May 30. 1915 GDL	
June 2nd 1915 BETHUNE 11.40 am	Sent squad from SECTION to BETHUNE to clean up billets and surroundings of troops billeted there. Proceeded to BETHUNE arriving there about 11.40 am. Visited ECOLE de JEUNE FILLES occupied by 1st BN SCOTS GUARDS. Saw OC with whom I went round billet finding condition very insanitary - there being a considerable quantity of offensive matter left behind by unit previously occupying billet. The latrine pails had not been emptied and the ground round about was considerably fouled owing to contents of pails having been dumped into pits dug into ground not extensive enough for the purpose. Arranged with C.O. for removal of all the offensive material lying about and for a daily removal of contents of pails to some ground outside Town, the billet to be supervised daily by the Section. Assistance to be rendered when required by a fatigue party from the Regiment.	
	Called upon TOWN COMMANDANT who promised to obtain 3 carts for use of SECTION at BETHUNE daily.	

(73989) W4141—463. 400,000. 9/14. H.&J.Ltd. Forms/C. 2118/10.

Instructions regarding War Diaries and Intelligence Summaries are contained in F. S. Regs., Part II. and the Staff Manual respectively. Title pages will be prepared in manuscript.

WAR DIARY
or
INTELLIGENCE SUMMARY.
(Erase heading not required.)

Army Form C. 2118.

Hour, Date, Place	Summary of Events and Information	Remarks and references to Appendices
June 2nd 1915 PITHEAD (PRIEURE ST PRY)	Correspondence, report and papers re damage to cart at SAILLY LA BOURSE handed to A D M S.	
	2138 L CPL PARKER reported for duty with Section from the LONDON SCOTTISH. 16937 PTE WILKINSON was detailed & reported for duty with 25th BDE R.F.A.	
VAUDRICOURT	Visited and inspected Chateau and found squad clearing up stables and surroundings satisfactorily.	
June 3. 1915 VAUDRICOURT	Sent squad to finish work at Chateau.	
BETHUNE	Sent squad to continue clearing billets and surroundings in town.	
8.30 am	Visited town and proceeded to direct operations for proper sanitation of billets of troops quartered here. With an interpreter visited Marie and obtained list of persons owning carts. Proceeded to 40 Bd FREDERIC DESGEORGES and hired for 4 francs per day each 2 carts from M BILLET. Obtained horses for these from TRANSPORT 1st Bn SCOTS GUARDS, through TOWN COMMANDANT. Asked Town authorities to furnish me with a daily return of notifications of infectious disease which return was promised. Obtained through TOWN COMMANDANT a fatigue party of men from CONVALESCENT Co 47th (LON) DIV who assisted Section in afternoon clearing up MARCHÉ AUX CHEVAUX TOBACCO FACTORY, ORPHANAGE and ECOLES DU PROGRÈS in Rue des [illegible]	

(73989) W4141—463. 400,000. 9/14. H.&J.Ltd. Forms/C. 2118/10.

Instructions regarding War Diaries and Intelligence Summaries are contained in F. S. Regs., Part II. and the Staff Manual respectively. Title pages will be prepared in manuscript.

WAR DIARY
or
INTELLIGENCE SUMMARY.
(Erase heading not required.)

Army Form C. 2118.

Hour, Date, Place	Summary of Events and Information	Remarks and references to Appendices
June 3. 1915 BETHUNE	Town was divided into 4 districts N.S.E.W., to each of which a NCO of the Section, who in civil life was a Sanitary Inspector, was to be appointed, for the purpose of inspecting and reporting daily as to nuisances or other matters requiring attention in the Sanitary interest of troops quartered in the town.	
PITHEAD near Annezin(?)	Routine work here and at Chateau occupied by 2ND ECHELON carried out.	
	2167 L CPL MORELAND from 2ND BN K.R.R. CORPS 2155 " TETLOW from 9TH BN KINGS LIVERPOOL REGT 2107 " CLAYDON from 11th BN GLOUCESTER REGT } reported for duty to day	
	These NCOs together with LCE CPL PARKER are in civil life Sanitary Inspectors and were assigned to various districts of BETHUNE as follows	
	NORTHERN DISTRICT — LCPL MORELAND SOUTHERN do — LCPL CLAYDON EASTERN do — LCPL PARKER WESTERN do — LCPL TETLOW	
	13319 PTE UPTON today was ordered to report to OC LONDON SCOTTISH for Sanitary duty vice L CPL PARKER. 2180 PTE KEARNES returned to duty today from Convalescent Co.	

(73989) W4141—463. 400,000. 9/14. H.&J.Ltd. Forms/C. 2118/10.

Instructions regarding War Diaries and Intelligence Summaries are contained in F. S. Regs., Part II. and the Staff Manual respectively. Title pages will be prepared in manuscript.

WAR DIARY
or
INTELLIGENCE SUMMARY.
(*Erase heading not required.*)

Army Form C. 2118.

Hour, Date, Place	Summary of Events and Information	Remarks and references to Appendices
7am June 4 1915 BETHUNE	Squad at work in BETHUNE cleaning billets and surroundings	
9am	arrived in BETHUNE and saw 4 Sanitary Inspectors and received their reports. Gave necessary orders in relation to them. Inspected billet of SCOTS GUARDS at ECOLE DE JEUNES FILLES and found condition somewhat improved, but found it necessary to draw attention of Sanitary Corporal to some important matters requiring his attention. Interviewed Adjutant 1 RO'C pointing out that it would be necessary for the unit to provide a cart for the purpose of ~~emptying~~ removing excreta in pails to a place arranged for outside the town, twice daily. Gave Adjutant addresses of persons letting out carts on hire and promised to try and arrange for more serviceable pails to be supplied. Ordered LCpl PARKER of Section to inspect daily and supervise removal of offensive matter. Visited D.A.D.O.S. VII Div and endeavoured unsuccessfully to obtain pails which he had in stock, as being more suitable than those already in use at billets.	
6pm. PITHEAD near PRIEURE St PRY	Received an urgent message from O.C. 1st Bn SCOTS GUARDS that latrine pails had not been emptied. Sent SERGT HATHAWAY to BETHUNE immediately to make necessary arrangements. Wrote to O.C.	

(73989) W4141—463. 400,000. 9/14. H.&J.Ltd. Forms/C. 2118/10.

Instructions regarding War Diaries and Intelligence Summaries are contained in F. S. Regs., Part II. and the Staff Manual respectively. Title pages will be prepared in manuscript.

WAR DIARY
or
INTELLIGENCE SUMMARY.
(*Erase heading not required.*)

Army Form C. 2118.

Hour, Date, Place	Summary of Events and Information	Remarks and references to Appendices
June 4 1915 PITHEAD	at same time pointing out the necessity for making his own arrangements to remove these matters.	
	Enquired into charge of absence against ~~Lce Cpl~~ PTE NEVILLE who had reported himself today and adjourned case for evidence.	
	Indents for equipment signed and forwarded to D.A.D.O.S. 1st Div	
	Routine work carried out at Pithead and Chateau.	
	1607 L. CPL MARTIN reported today to O.C. 1st BN GLOUCESTER REGT for Sanitary duty vice Lce Cpl CLAYDON.	
	2187 L. CPL WHITE reported today to O.C. 2ND BN KING'S ROYAL RIFLES vice LCE CPL MORELAND	
	1613 PTE READING reported today to O.C. 9TH KINGS LIVERPOOL REGIMENT vice LCE CPL TETLOW.	
	[initials]	
7am. June 5th 1915 BETHUNE	Sent squad to ~~complete~~ continue cleaning up of billets and surroundings	
9 am	arrived at BETHUNE and received Sanitary Inspectors' reports gave necessary orders in connection therewith. Obtained a list of persons, owners of carts, from M SARRUT but I was unable to obtain vehicles. Visited Maire and drew attention to previous complaints as to dumping refuse in BDE VOLTAIRE. The town authorities had promised to remove a considerable accumulation of rubbish refuse etc but this had not been done. M Sarrut stated	

Instructions regarding War Diaries and Intelligence Summaries are contained in F. S. Regs., Part II. and the Staff Manual respectively. Title pages will be prepared in manuscript.

WAR DIARY
or
INTELLIGENCE SUMMARY.
(*Erase heading not required.*)

Army Form C. 2118.

Hour, Date, Place	Summary of Events and Information	Remarks and references to Appendices
June 5. 1915 BETHUNE	that he could not find sufficient vehicles for its removal, but that he was willing now to arrange for its being burned if Sanitary Section would assist. I promised to consider his proposal as this rubbish is sure to attract and breed countless flies during the hot weather besides being an intolerable nuisance in consequence of effluvia being given off. Asked for a ground outside town for dumping excreta. I was referred to a contractor who was prepared to undertake the removal and disposal of excreta, manure, refuse etc. I received no notification of any infectious disease during the day	
	Called on O.C. 1st Bn SCOTS GUARDS with reference to the removal of contents of pail latrines. Inspected billets of unit which were not as satisfactorily kept as might be. Saw Quartermaster and drew his attention to these defects, which he promised to have remedied.	
	Called at Headquarters 1st BRIGADE and asked for fatigue party of 30 men for duty with Section and for as many as horses as may be required. Request granted	
PITHEAD	Routine duties carried out at billets and chateau	[initials]
June 6. 1915 BETHUNE	Squad in town clearing up billets and surroundings	

74

(73989) W4141—463. 400,000. 9/14. H.&J.Ltd. Forms/C. 2118/10.

Instructions regarding War Diaries and Intelligence Summaries are contained in F. S. Regs., Part II. and the Staff Manual respectively. Title pages will be prepared in manuscript.

WAR DIARY
or
INTELLIGENCE SUMMARY.
(*Erase heading not required.*)

Army Form C. 2118.

Hour, Date, Place	Summary of Events and Information	Remarks and references to Appendices
8.30am June 6. 1915 BETHUNE	Arrived in town saw Sanitary Inspectors and received reports afterwards giving necessary instructions Visited and inspected billets of COLDSTREAM GUARDS 1st Bn and found same satisfactory. Gave directions as to disposal of contents of pail latrines to Quartermaster of Regiment. Received note from OC. 2ND Bn R SUSSEX REGT asking where carts could be obtained. This note passed to me by Town Commandant. Obtained cart for use by unit and handed address of owner to OC. Called on several entrepreneurs and succeeded in obtaining by requisition at 1 franc per cart per day, 4 carts additional carts. One cart for use by SCOTS GUARDS, one for use by 2ND Bn ROYAL SUSSEX REGT the remainder to be used by SANITARY SECTION. Horses and fatigue parties requisitioned from 1st BRIGADE Hdqrs for duty with SECTION tomorrow. 4 extra horses requisitioned for carts. Visited and inspected billets of 2ND Bn R SUSSEX REGT and found same in good condition. Saw M.O. i/c and handed him requisition for cart mentioned above and asked him to hand same to OC. Visited and inspected ECOLE DE JEUNES FILLES (1st SCOTS GUARDS) finding conditions improved but leaving room for improvement yet. Saw OC & M.O. i/c of unit and handed the former requisition for cart ~~to~~ mentioned above. Informed OC ~~that~~ a Sanitary Inspector	

(73989) W4141—463. 400,000. 9/14. H.&J.Ltd. Forms/C. 2118/10.

Army Form C. 2118.

WAR DIARY
or
INTELLIGENCE SUMMARY.
(*Erase heading not required.*)

Instructions regarding War Diaries and Intelligence Summaries are contained in F. S. Regs., Part II. and the Staff Manual respectively. Title pages will be prepared in manuscript.

Hour, Date, Place	Summary of Events and Information	Remarks and references to Appendices
June 6. 1915 BETHUNE	would call each morning to supervise removal of contents of latrine pails. There should be therefore no further excuse for the sanitation of this billet not being maintained	
FOUQUERIEUL	Accompanied A.D.M.S. and inspected billets of Shoemakers' Shop 1st Div. Found same requiring to be cleansed. Inspected lines and billets of 23RD Co R.E. at Fontinelle Farm and with exception of a very offensive manure midden found conditions sanitarily satisfactory.	
ANNEZIN	Visited and inspected lines of 1st DIVISION AMM. COL finding conditions unsatisfactory. No proper arrangements for disposal of refuse. Insanitary water supply etc.	
	Visited and inspected billets of CYCLIST COY finding same in an unsatisfactory sanitary state	
VAUDRICOURT	Visited Headquarters and found that at Stable Yard in Chateau the sanitary conditions were not being maintained. Reported this matter to CAMP COMMANDANT	
PITHEAD (PRICURE ST. PRY)	Routine duties carried out here and at Chateau. Men bathed in afternoon	
	[initials]	
June 7. 1915 BETHUNE	Squad from Section clearing up various billets and surroundings. Cpl Tetlow reported result of his morning inspection. Visited and inspected the Caserne Montmorency	

(73989) W4141—463. 400,000. 9/14. H.&J.Ltd. Forms/C. 2118/10.

Instructions regarding War Diaries and Intelligence Summaries are contained in F. S. Regs., Part II. and the Staff Manual respectively. Title pages will be prepared in manuscript.

WAR DIARY
or
INTELLIGENCE SUMMARY.
(Erase heading not required.)

Army Form C. 2118.

Hour, Date, Place	Summary of Events and Information	Remarks and references to Appendices
June 7 1915 BETHUNE	occupied by 2ND BN K.R.R CORPS. Found plague of flies caused by large heap of manure and dirty state of stables within the precincts of the Barracks used by the French Gendarmes. Steps were being taken, and had been taken by the KRRs, assisted by Squad from the SECTION to clear up billet and surroundings and the work was proceeding very satisfactorily. Saw M.O. i/c unit, who had discarded pail latrines in use by his unit and was using shallow trenches in ground at rear of Barracks easily accessible and not too distant. I approved of this step and inspected the trench latrines which were in good order. I suggested that paraffin should be sprinkled round margins to prevent flies. A spray was lent for use in sprinkling ground of Barrack Square with cresol also rooms in billet to mitigate nuisance from flies. Reported action to A.D.M.S. on return and sent special report as to cause of fly nuisance.	
	Visited Headquarters of the 1st Bn L.N. LANCASHIRE REGT and later M.O i/c. Found at Hqrs billet a large heap of manure left by unit previously occupying billet. Arranged for its removal by Sanitary Section today. Saw with M.O. a N.C.O. with suspicious symptoms of Enteric, advised immediate evacuation of patient. Discussed recent cases of suspected Paratyphoid in this unit and advised precautionary measures in all suspected cases. Especially diarrhoeal cases.	
	Left written instructions for SERGT HOWSON as to removal of manure heap found in lines of L.N. LANCS, for L CPL TETLOW to report at once to OCs of 2ND BN K.R.R CORPS and L.N.LANCS and for a spray to be sent on loan to M.O. i/c 2ND K.R.R.C.	

(73989) W4141—463. 400,000. 9/14. H.&J.Ltd. Forms/C. 2118/10.

Instructions regarding War Diaries and Intelligence Summaries are contained in F. S. Regs., Part II. and the Staff Manual respectively. Title pages will be prepared in manuscript.

WAR DIARY
or
INTELLIGENCE SUMMARY.
(*Erase heading not required.*)

Army Form C. 2118.

Hour, Date, Place	Summary of Events and Information	Remarks and references to Appendices
June 7. 1915 BETHUNE	A fatigue party of 30 men from 1st Bn SCOTS GUARDS and 4 horses from SCOTS GUARDS transport assisted SECTION in its work today	
11 am June 7. 1915 ANNEZIN	Inspected lines of 1st DIVISIONAL AMMUNITION COLUMN. Saw MO i/c Company Officers and finally OC. 4 sections billeted in this area Nos 2 & 3 being well kept sanitarily. No 1 SECTION not satisfactory, lines not well kept and measures for disposal of rubbish unsatisfactory. Found that water from pump was being used by men without previous sterilization, pointed this fact out to MO i/c and later to OC. Discussed with MO state of No 4 SECTION visited previous day and arranged to send a party from SANITARY SECTION tomorrow to assist his fatigue party in putting Nos 1 & 4 SECTIONS in better sanitary order. Ascertained that men of No 1 Section were drinking unsterilised water, which was unnecessary as unit has two water carts. Reported facts to ADMS.	
FONTINELLE FARM	Accompanied ADMS on his inspection of new Convalescent Camp at FONTINELLE FARM.	
PITHEAD PRIEURE ST PRY	Routine work carried out at billet of SECTION and Chateau occupied by 2nd Echelon mess. [initials]	

(73989) W4141—463. 400,000. 9/14. H.&J.Ltd. Forms/C. 2118/10.

Instructions regarding War Diaries and Intelligence Summaries are contained in F. S. Regs., Part II. and the Staff Manual respectively. Title pages will be prepared in manuscript.

WAR DIARY
or
INTELLIGENCE SUMMARY.
(*Erase heading not required.*)

Army Form C. [illegible]118.

Hour, Date, Place	Summary of Events and Information	Remarks and references to Appendices
June 8. 1915. BETHUNE	Squad from Section assisted by a fatigue party of 30 men from 1st Bn Black Watch at work at billets. Visited Bethune and saw Sergeant in charge of squad. Cpl Tetlow reported no matter requiring my attention in his district. Watering can lent M.O. i/c 2nd Bn K.R.R.s for use in Caserne Montmorency (French Barracks). Visited and inspected Headquarters and billets of 1st Bn Black Watch and 2nd Bn R Sussex Regt. Saw M.O.'s i/c of these units and arranged for sanitary matters to be adjusted in their respective billets.	
FONTNELLE FARM	Squad from Section at work on billets and lines of the 23rd Field Co R.E.s.	
ANNEZIN	Squad from Section at work on lines of 1st Divisional Ammunition Column.	
PITHEAD PRIEURE ST PRY	Heard case against 2324 Pte Neville and awarded him 7 days C.C. Forwarded application of L Cpl Howes for leave to A.D.M.S. Received 100 latrine pails for use in Bethune. Routine work continued at billet and at Chateau	

[illegible]

Instructions regarding War Diaries and Intelligence Summaries are contained in F. S. Regs., Part II. and the Staff Manual respectively. Title pages will be prepared in manuscript.

WAR DIARY
or
INTELLIGENCE SUMMARY.
(Erase heading not required.)

Army Form C. [illegible]118.

Hour, Date, Place	Summary of Events and Information	Remarks and references to Appendices
June 9 1915 BETHUNE	Squad from Section at work Visited town and saw Sergt in charge of squad. Received reports of SERGT PARKER and L CPL TETLOW. Saw Town Surveyor and discussed with him steps to be taken with regard to refuse tipping place at RUE VOLTAIRE. Also obtained site off BEUVRY ROAD for dumping excreta and refuse. Inspected billets of SCOTS GUARDS 1st BN at COLLEGE de JEUNE FILLES finding sanitary conditions improved. Inspected billets of COLDSTREAM GUARDS at TOBACCO FACTORY, saw M O i/c and arranged for fitting of newpail latrines and other sanitary measures. Visited billets of 1st BN L N LANCASHIRE REGT saw MO i/c and arranged for various sanitary measures for the better sanitation of billets, such as additional incinerators, removal of refuse & cleaning of floors of billets. Visited billets of 2ND BN KINGS ROYAL RIFLES at CASERNE MONT-MORENCY saw MO i/c and discussed further measures to be taken for sanitation of billets. Inspected dumping ground near ORPHANAGE. Inspected billets of LONDON SCOTTISH at ORPHANAGE saw O.C. and discussed with him steps to be taken to improve sanitation of billets. Conditions on the whole satisfactory	

Instructions regarding War Diaries and Intelligence Summaries are contained in F. S. Regs., Part II. and the Staff Manual respectively. Title pages will be prepared in manuscript.

WAR DIARY
or
INTELLIGENCE SUMMARY.
(*Erase heading not required.*)

Army Form C. 2118.

Hour, Date, Place	Summary of Events and Information	Remarks and references to Appendices
June 9.1915 FONTNELLE FARM	Squad from Section completed covering of manure midden in lines of 23RD FIELD Co. R.E.	
ANNEZIN	Squad from SECTION at work on billets of Miners of 1ST DIVISION AMM COL. Visited locality and saw M.O. i/c. Found work satisfactory, completed SECTION & removed to more suitable billets.	
PITHEAD PRIEURE ST PRY	2137. Acting L. CPL PARKER appointed to rank of ACTING L. SERGT without pay. 2523 CORP. BISHOP of 2ND LONDON SANITARY Co. RAMC reinforced Section today. Routine work carried out at billets and at Chateau occupied by 2ND ECHELON MESS.	[signature]
June 10.1915 BETHUNE	Squad from SECTION at work. Visited town and inspected billets of 1ST BN SCOTS GUARDS at ECOLE de JEUNES FILLES. Inspected urine pit being dug constructed there. Visited billets of 2ND BN. K.R.R. CORPS at CASERNE MONTMORENCY and saw M.O. in charge. Manure not removed from Gendarmerie stables. Arranged for its removal. Saw O.C. 1ST BN L.N. LANCASHIRE REGT and discussed with him sanitary measures for the protection of his unit	

(73989) W4141—463. 400,000. 9/14. H.&J.Ltd. Forms/C. 2118/10.

Instructions regarding War Diaries and Intelligence Summaries are contained in F. S. Regs., Part II. and the Staff Manual respectively. Title pages will be prepared in manuscript.

WAR DIARY
or
INTELLIGENCE SUMMARY.
(Erase heading not required.)

Army Form C. 2118.

Hour, Date, Place	Summary of Events and Information	Remarks and references to Appendices
June 10 1915 VAUDRICOURT	Visited with A.D.M.S. 1st DIVISION HEADQUARTERS. Saw OC 1st SIGNAL Co. and inspected his transport lines. After discussing with him steps for dealing with manure arranged for party from Section to clear up his billets and surroundings tomorrow and for a fatigue party from his unit to assist Sappers Kerosene for dealing with manure & refuse.	
LABEUVRIERE LAPUGNOY	Visited these districts to enquire into cases of Typhoid amongst the civil population reported by MO i/c 13th Bn R SUSSEX REGT. Reported result of investigation to A.D.M.S.	
PITHEAD PRIEURE St PRY	Sent report re SERGT HOWSON to A.D.M.S.	
	Received voucher re leave for L.CPL HEWES.	
	Routine work carried out at billets and Chateau.	
	G.J.	
June 11 1915 BETHUNE	Squad from Section at work. Visited town and inspected billets of 2ND BN KINGS ROYAL RIFLES at CASERNE MONTMORENCY. Visited INSTITUTION St VAAST and saw OC No 2 FIELD AMBULANCE. Discussed with him drainage system of premises which was stopped and gave rise to an effluvia nuisance. Also inspected a large manure heap in garden adjoining which requires to be dealt with immediately	

Instructions regarding War Diaries and Intelligence Summaries are contained in F. S. Regs., Part II. and the Staff Manual respectively. Title pages will be prepared in manuscript.

WAR DIARY
or
INTELLIGENCE SUMMARY.
(*Erase heading not required.*)

Army Form C. [illegible]118.

Hour, Date, Place	Summary of Events and Information	Remarks and references to Appendices
June 11.1915 BETHUNE	Arranged to send Sanitary Inspection Squad from Section to deal with these matters as suggested. Also discussed with OC state of billets of this unit at ANNEZIN and permission to inspect same.	
	Visited and inspected COLLEGE de GARCONS, PLACE de LILLE	
	Took interpreter and purchased pitch forks at a cost of 30 francs for use of San Section.	
	Paid LCpl HAWES who left BETHUNE STATION at 1.30 pm today for leave for England	
	Obtained by requisition 2 extra carts. 6 carts are now in use by Section	
	Opened new office at 7. GRAND PLACE	
ANNEZIN	Visited village and inspected work being carried out on billets and lines of CYCLIST Co. Saw OC and discussed with him steps to be taken to secure improved Sanitary Conditions.	
	Visited No 2 FIELD AMBULANCE TENT SUB DIVISION at Boys' School. Saw O.C. and discussed with him steps to be taken to deal with the sanitation of the billets and surroundings - especially with regard to difficult manure middens and foul ditch near AMBULANCE STATION. Arranged to let him have necessary equipment for dealing with these matters. Also arranged to send small party from Sanitary Section tomorrow to assist his fatigue party.	
PITHEAD PRIEURE St PRY	Received reports from Sanitary Inspectors and gave orders necessary in connection therewith. Reported several matters to A.D.M.S. - especially as to the provision of suitable harness for horses drawing carts, and nuisance re manure at CASERNE MONTMORENCY. Gave orders for disinfection of room at Orphanage BETHUNE. Routine work carried out.	

Instructions regarding War Diaries and Intelligence Summaries are contained in F. S. Regs., Part II. and the Staff Manual respectively. Title pages will be prepared in manuscript.

WAR DIARY
or
INTELLIGENCE SUMMARY.
(Erase heading not required.)

Army Form C. 2118.

Hour, Date, Place	Summary of Events and Information	Remarks and references to Appendices
June 11 1915 VAUDRICOURT	Party from Section in charge of NCO cleaning up surroundings of 1ST DIVISION HEADQUARTERS and lines of 1ST SIGNAL Co RE	
June 12 1915 BETHUNE	Squad from Section at work. Inspected billets of 2ND BN K.R.R.Corps and L.N. LANCASHIRE REGT. Saw OC's of both units and discussed with them steps to be taken to deal with the sanitation of their units. At request of MO i/c L.N.LANCASHIRES examined man suffering from an acute febrile attack [illegible] but here a influenza. Advised immediate evacuation. Advised O/C K.R.Rs to provide screen for latrines used by his unit and raised question of using pail system. Visited Institution St Vaast and saw Captain FORSYTH RAMC as to matters of sanitation. Saw MO i/c GLOUCESTERSHIRE REGT (1st BN) and discussed matters of sanitation with [illegible] as his billets	
ANNEZIN	Squad at work assisting fatigue party from No 2 FIELD AMBULANCE TENT SUB DIV. to clean up billets and surroundings	
VAUDRICOURT	Squad at work continuing cleaning up of billets of 1ST SIGNAL Co RE.	
LABEUVRIERE	Inspected lines of 5TH BN R SUSSEX REGT and arranged to send party from Section tomorrow	
LABUISSIERE	Obtained 1475 fcs for purpose of paying our men of Section	

(73989) W4141—463. 400,000. 9/14. H.&J.Ltd. Forms/C. 2118/10.

Instructions regarding War Diaries and Intelligence Summaries are contained in F. S. Regs., Part II. and the Staff Manual respectively. Title pages will be prepared in manuscript.

WAR DIARY
or
INTELLIGENCE SUMMARY.
(*Erase heading not required.*)

Army Form C. 2118.

Hour, Date, Place	Summary of Events and Information	Remarks and references to Appendices
June 12 1915 PITHEAD PRIEURE St PRY	Arranged for SERGT HOWSON attached to SECTION to return to his unit the 1st Bn SCOTS GUARDS tomorrow.	
	Received notification of infectious disease (Enteric) in 1st Bn S. WALES BORDERERS, which appeared to have been sent in error. Reported to ADMS for enquiries.	
	Routine work continued at billets and at Chateau.	
	Men paid out.	
June 13 1915 LABEUVRIERE	Squad from Section cleaning up lines and billets of 5th Bn. ROYAL SUSSEX REGT, assisted by fatigue party of 20 men from that unit. 2 carts at work. Saw M.O. i/c and arranged with him for fatigue party of 50 men tomorrow and 6 carts to assist Section in work of covering the numerous manure middens and remedying insanitary conditions.	
ANNEZIN.	Two men from Section assisting fatigue party of TENT SUB DIV No 2 FIELD AMBULANCE till 11 am. when party was dismissed by N.C.O. in charge.	
VAUDRICOURT	Party at work continuing clearance of lines of 1st SIGNAL Co. Visited and found work proceeding satisfactorily.	
FONTENELLE FARM.	Sent L/CPL MORELAND to assist fatigue party by his advice & supervision in improving as far as possible sanitary conditions at CONVALESCENT Co. Subsequently approved report of his work.	
9.15 am BETHUNE	SERGT PARKER reported that no fatigue party had paraded. Saw Staff Captain 3RD BRIGADE and found that party had been requisitioned as usual but that matter had been apparently overlooked. Was promised	

(73989) W4141—463. 400,000. 9/14. H.&J.Ltd. Forms/C. 2118/10.

Instructions regarding War Diaries and Intelligence Summaries are contained in F. S. Regs., Part II. and the Staff Manual respectively. Title pages will be prepared in manuscript.

WAR DIARY
or
INTELLIGENCE SUMMARY.
(Erase heading not required.)

Army Form C. 2118.

Hour, Date, Place	Summary of Events and Information	Remarks and references to Appendices
June 13. 1915. BETHUNE	fatigue party of 50 men for 2pm which however did not turn up till 3pm. leaving but [illegible] during which their services could be utilised. Reported to ADMS	
11 am	Obtained fatigue party of 24 men from CONVALESCENT Co through the Town Commandant.	
	Visited and inspected CASERNE MONTMORENCY saw MO's 2ND BN KINGS ROYAL RIFLES. Found steps being taken to deal with all sanitary requirements. Found also that in spite of all efforts to the contrary French Gendarmes were still dumping manure in barrack yard. Reported this to ADMS.	
PITHEAD PRIEURE ST PRY	Pte WILSON reported absent without leave since [illegible] 10.30 am	
	Routine work continued at billet and chateau.	
	SERGT HOWSON rejoined his unit today. (1ST BN SCOTS GUARDS	G.W.
June 14. 1915. LABEUVRIERE	Squad from section at work assisted by fatigue party, 50 men from R SUSSEX REGT 5TH BN. 2 carts and one two horsed limber. 6 manure middens covered. SERGT HATHAWAY reported bicycle stolen whilst he was inspecting billets. MP MILITARY POLICE and subsequently ADMS advised.	
BETHUNE	Fatigue party of 50 men from 4TH BN R WELSH FUSILIERS at work under supervision of Sanitary Inspectors dealing with nuisances. Saw SERGT PARKER and gave necessary orders in connection with horse pool. Interviewed Mayor of Town with Town Commandant with reference to complaint made by the Mayor as to Sanitary state of billets in the town. There seemed no ground for his complaints. Inspected in company with ADMS billets of 4th BN R WELSH FUSILIERS in the RUE FAUBOURG D'ARRAS. Billets scattered over a	

(73989) W4141—463. 400,000. 9/14. H.&J.Ltd. Forms/C. 2118/10.

Instructions regarding War Diaries and Intelligence Summaries are contained in F. S. Regs., Part II. and the Staff Manual respectively. Title pages will be prepared in manuscript.

WAR DIARY
or
INTELLIGENCE SUMMARY.
(*Erase heading not required.*)

Army Form C. 2118.

Hour, Date, Place	Summary of Events and Information	Remarks and references to Appendices
June 14. 1915 BETHUNE	[illegible] area and generally speaking in an insanitary condition. Some billets having no sanitary conveniences whatever, the men having to walk a considerable distance to a latrine. Attention of CO & MO's drawn to these matters and to urgent need of keeping billets and surroundings in a good sanitary state.	
	Visited CASERNE MONTMORENCY, found manure heap had been removed. Saw Adjutant and MO's and arranged for a system of pail latrines to be installed. Attention of these officers drawn to the fact that pails would have to be emptied daily into ground outside town, which would be pointed out to them. Arranged also that a Corporal from the Section should supervise the work daily.	
	Saw BRIGADIER 3RD BRIGADE and arranged to have cesspools at schools in Rue Michelet cleared. Made necessary arrangements with contractor M. Sauvage BETHUNE for this and other billets.	
	Asked for fatigue party of 50 men from 8 am to 12 noon and from 2 pm to 4 pm, for tomorrow from 3RD BRIGADE	
PITHEAD. PRIEURE St PRY	PTE WILSON reported at 10.30 this morning.	
	Routine work continued at billets and Chateau.	
	217 PTE HARPER and 57 PTE RIVERS reported today as reinforcements from ROUEN. [initials]	
June 15 1915 LABEUVRIERE	Squad from Section continued work of clearance assisted by fatigue party and horses and carts. Visited area in afternoon and found work proceeding satisfactorily.	

(73989) W4141—463. 400,000. 9/14. H.&J.Ltd. Forms/C. 2118/10.

Instructions regarding War Diaries and Intelligence Summaries are contained in F. S. Regs., Part II. and the Staff Manual respectively. Title pages will be prepared in manuscript.

WAR DIARY
or
INTELLIGENCE SUMMARY.
(Erase heading not required.)

Army Form C. 2118.

Hour, Date, Place	Summary of Events and Information	Remarks and references to Appendices
June 15. 1915 BETHUNE	Sanitary inspectors at work inspecting billets and supervising work of fatigue parties. Gave necessary orders in connection with inspectors' reports. Visited Mayor of Town and asked for assistance in obtaining man for cleaning cesspools. Promised to arrange for a man to clean out cesspits at ECOLE MICHELET this evening as work was urgent.	
	Visited Tobacco factory occupied by 1st BN GLOUCESTER REGT and found same in satisfactory condition. Transport lines inspected, found men bivouacing there, as this ground had been fouled for months past and unfit for bivouacing purposes, suggested to OC & MO i/c that the men should be prevented from using this ground in this manner.	
	At Headquarters of GLOUCESTER REGT found filthy collection of rubbish and remains of used dressing in a disused room and basement. Place in foul condition. Gave orders for SANITARY SECTION to put the place in order.	
	Inspected lines of 2nd HEAVY BATTERY R.G.A AMM COL & saw OC with regard to a large heaps of manure which required removing at once. Directed his attention to the necessity of disposing of manure from his lines in a suitable area.	
	Found that work of covering and burning 2 large heaps of offensive refuse which had accumulated during a considerable time past, had been carried out in a very satisfactory manner by Section.	

(73989) W4141—463. 400,000. 9/14. H.&J.Ltd. Forms/C. 2118/10.

Instructions regarding War Diaries and Intelligence Summaries are contained in F. S. Regs., Part II. and the Staff Manual respectively. Title pages will be prepared in manuscript.

WAR DIARY
or
INTELLIGENCE SUMMARY.
(*Erase heading not required.*)

Army Form C. 2118.

Hour, Date, Place	Summary of Events and Information	Remarks and references to Appendices
June 15. 1915 BETHUNE	Requisitioned for party of 50 men from 3RD BRIGADE for tomorrow. Saw a large heap of manure in BRIGADE TRANSPORT lines, which I inspected at request of Staff Captain. Gave orders for this to be covered with earth and lime immediately by Sanitary Section.	
	Accompanied A.D.M.S. in his inspection of transport lines of 1ST BN GLOUCESTER REGT, Billets of 2ND BN ROYAL MUNSTER FUSILIERS at ORPHANAGE and 2ND H.B. R.G.A. Ammn Col.	
PITHEAD. PRIEURE ST PRY	Investigated case against PTE NILSON and adjourned it till tomorrow for evidence.	
	Routine work continued at billets and chateau	
	Paid Pte RIVERS and PTE HARPER 25/00 each	
	PTE HOOPER reported absent from 12 noon today from party at work at LABEUVRIERE	
June 16 1915 BETHUNE	Sent party with 4 N.C.O.S to BETHUNE to continue work there. Visited BETHUNE and saw with Interpreter Town Surveyor in reference to cleaning out of Cesspools in Billets at BETHUNE. Although promised on 2 days running to have a contractor provided, work had not yet been carried out. Reported to A.D.M.S. and later saw Capt STUBBS M.O. i/c Bth. Worth who arranged for his Interpreter to see to the matter and report later the result of his efforts	

(73989) W4141—463. 400,000. 9/14. H.&J.Ltd. Forms/C. 2118/10.

Army Form C. 2118.

WAR DIARY
or
INTELLIGENCE SUMMARY.
(Erase heading not required.)

Instructions regarding War Diaries and Intelligence Summaries are contained in F. S. Regs., Part II. and the Staff Manual respectively. Title pages will be prepared in manuscript.

Hour, Date, Place	Summary of Events and Information	Remarks and references to Appendices
June 16.1915 BETHUNE	I have had again to report to the A.D.M.S. that great difficulty is experienced in getting any assistance from the Town Authorities who themselves appear to take no satisfactory steps to promote Sanitation in their town. Visited Ecole des Michelets, Rue du Michelet finding work of cleaning this large billet well in hand except for cesspools. Read reports of Sanitary Inspectors on Special Duty in the Town and gave necessary orders in relation thereto. Fatigue party of 50 men, provided by Brigade, at work with Sanitary Section. All billets, refuse removal, latrine pails etc being carried out.	
LABEUVRIERE	Sent squad of 13 men and 2 N.C.O.s to continue work of cleaning up billets and surroundings at LABEUVRIERE. No fatigue party available for the assistance of the Squad from Section owing to changing over of BRIGADES.	
PITHEAD PRIEURE ST PRY	Routine work continued at billet and chateau. G.J.L.	
June 17.1915. LABEUVRIERE	Sent squad from SANITARY SECTION to LABEUVRIERE to continue work of cleaning up billets and surroundings.	
BETHUNE	Sent party from SANITARY SECTION, to BETHUNE, with 4 N.C.O.s (Sanitary Inspectors) to continue work of cleaning up billets and surroundings	

(73989) W4141—463. 400,000. 9/14. H.&J.Ltd. Forms/C. 2118/10.

Instructions regarding War Diaries and Intelligence Summaries are contained in F. S. Regs., Part II. and the Staff Manual respectively. Title pages will be prepared in manuscript.

WAR DIARY
or
INTELLIGENCE SUMMARY.
(*Erase heading not required.*)

Army Form C. 2118.

Hour, Date, Place	Summary of Events and Information	Remarks and references to Appendices
9.30am June 17 1915 BETHUNE	Visited town and inspected CASERNE MONTMORENCY occupied by 1st Bn COLDSTREAM GUARDS. Saw Quartermaster. Inspected billets with him and arranged for latrines temporarily to be dug in adjoining ground pending arrival of additional pails ordered from D.A.D.O.S. Found conditions fairly satisfactory and that French Gendarmerie were taking steps to clean out their stables within the Barrack precincts.	
	Visited Ecole des Mickelew, Rue des Mickelew and found squad at work cleansing and scrubbing floors etc of this billet which is required for the use of troops, work proceeding satisfactorily and cesspools partly emptied by contractor, employed by SANITARY SECTION. Work of SECTION completed with exception of cesspools which are to be finished by tomorrow morning.	
	Visited Orphanage occupied by 2ND BN ROYAL MUNSTER FUSRS, and saw C.O. who accompanied me in my inspection of billets and surroundings. Found that the work of fixing new pail latrines seats was nearly completed as well as the arrangements for removal of contents to ground appointed by SANITARY SECTION for the purpose. Arranged to send some men from the SECTION to supervise erection of incinerator on transport lines of unit and other matters which appeared to me to require attention. On the whole the condition of this billet was found to be satisfactory.	
	Visited ECOLE de JEUNE FILLES occupied by 2ND BN WELCH REGT finding that latrine pails had not been emptied of contents by	

(73989) W4141—463. 400,000. 9/14. H.&J.Ltd. Forms/C. 2118/10.

Instructions regarding War Diaries and Intelligence Summaries are contained in F. S. Regs., Part II. and the Staff Manual respectively. Title pages will be prepared in manuscript.

WAR DIARY
or
INTELLIGENCE SUMMARY.
(*Erase heading not required.*)

Army Form C. 2118.

Hour, Date, Place	Summary of Events and Information	Remarks and references to Appendices
June 17 1915 BETHUNE	previous unit before leaving (11th Bn S WALES BORDERERS). Saw the O.C. and arranged to provide a cart from the SANITARY SECTION to temporarily assist the unit until their own arrangements are completed. Reported to A.D.M.S.	
FOUQUIERES	Sent party under NCO to clean up a collection of manure and refuse near lines of DIVISIONAL CAVALRY	
PITHEAD PRIEURE ST PRY	Routine work continued on fosse and chateau	
	Heard charge against PTE RIORDAN, 2nd Bn WELCH REGT, attached to the SANITARY SECTION for duty, placed under arrest by order of Capt AITKEN A.D.V.S., a witness, of using insubordinate language to his NCO. Adjourned consideration of award until tomorrow morning 9 am.	
	Awarded PTE WILSON 7 days confinement to camp, for while on duty with the SANITARY SECTION at LABEUVRIERE absenting himself without leave from 10.30 am on June 13. 1915 and remaining absent until 10.30 am on June 16. 1915. Pte Wilson forfeits 3 days pay.	
	[signature]	

(73989) W4141—463. 400,000. 9/14. H.&J.Ltd. Forms/C. 2118/10.

Instructions regarding War Diaries and Intelligence Summaries are contained in F. S. Regs., Part II. and the Staff Manual respectively. Title pages will be prepared in manuscript.

WAR DIARY
or
INTELLIGENCE SUMMARY.
(*Erase heading not required.*)

Army Form C. 2118.

Hour, Date, Place	Summary of Events and Information	Remarks and references to Appendices
June 18 1915 LABEUVRIERE	Sent Squad from SANITARY SECTION to LABEUVRIERE to continue work of cleaning up billets and surroundings there — Assisted by fatigue party of 50 men in the morning and 30 men in the afternoon from units billetted there.	
FOUQUIERES.	Sent squad from SANITARY SECTION to clean up lines and billets of DIVISIONAL SUPPLY COLUMN at FOUQUIERES and ditches lining roadway which were in a very foul state. The squad were assisted by a fatigue party of 12 men from DIVISIONAL CAVALRY. Visited and inspected lines of this unit and found work proceeding satisfactorily.	
BETHUNE	Sent party under 4 N.C.Os (Sanitary Inspectors) from SANITARY SECTION to BETHUNE to continue work of supervision of sanitation of the Town. Squad assisted by 100 men morning and afternoon supplied by the 1st BRIGADE HQRS, from units billetted in the Town.	
10.30am	Visited Town and inspected billets of 2ND BN WELCH REGT at Ecole de Jeunes Filles. Saw Co. and went round with him and discussed steps to be taken to maintain satisfactory condition in which this billet had been placed. Arranged to lend equipment from SECTION to assist in keeping up high standard of cleanliness.	
	Visited Ecole des Michelets, Rue du Michelet and found that contractor had not completed work of emptying foul cesspools there. Visited Mairie and received an assurance that work would be proceeded with, without further delay. Called at BRIGADE HQRS and informed Brigade Major billets there would not be ready for occupation until this work was completed.	

Army Form C. 2118.

Instructions regarding War Diaries and Intelligence Summaries are contained in F. S. Regs., Part II. and the Staff Manual respectively. Title pages will be prepared in manuscript.

WAR DIARY
or
INTELLIGENCE SUMMARY.
(Erase heading not required.)

Hour, Date, Place	Summary of Events and Information	Remarks and references to Appendices
June 19 1915 BETHUNE	Visited Clock factory and inspected billets of 25th BRIGADE RFA AMM COL finding conditions fairly satisfactory. Saw MO i/c and pointed out certain matters which required to be attended to, to improve sanitation of this billet. Arranged to send fatigue party to complete covering in of large manure heap and arranged that the manure from these horse lines should be removed to the appointed place outside the town. Visited and inspected with MO i/c the horse lines of 25th BRIGADE RFA AMM COL opposite Clock factory. Found a large manure heap of several hundred tons lying there and which ~~[illegible]~~ had accumulated for months past and was still being added to. There was abundant evidence that large quantities of flies were breeding there and as it would take too much time and labour to remove arranged to treat the mass in situ with earth and lime. All further dumping of manure to cease there and fresh manure to be removed daily to ground appointed outside town. Visited and inspected wagon lines of 4th Bn R WELSH FUSRS. finding a great improvement since my last inspection 3 or 4 days ago. Received reports of 4 Sanitary Inspectors from SECTION and gave necessary orders in relation thereto. Sent party from SECTION in the evening to BETHUNE to arrange for the disinfection of cesspools at Ecole and Michelets after these had been emptied by contractor. Sent load of lime to Timber Yard occupied by 25th BRIGADE AMM. COL in readiness for fatigue party tomorrow. Visited billet of LONDON SCOTTISH finding fixed closets at Ecole Libre being used by men. These are in a foul state and unfit for use and	

(73989) W4141—463. 400,000. 9/14. H.&J.Ltd. Forms/C. 2118/10.

Instructions regarding War Diaries and Intelligence Summaries are contained in F. S. Regs., Part II. and the Staff Manual respectively. Title pages will be prepared in manuscript.

WAR DIARY
or
INTELLIGENCE SUMMARY.
(*Erase heading not required.*)

Army Form C. 2118.

Hour, Date, Place	Summary of Events and Information	Remarks and references to Appendices
June 18 1915 BETHUNE	I arranged for their discontinuance. Trench latrines to be dug in the yard pending pails being provided.	
PITHEAD. PRIEURE St PRY	Awarded Pte RIORDAN, ~~[illegible]~~ 2ND WELCH REGT attached to Sanitary Section for duty 28 days Field Punishment No 1 and returned him to his Regiment to undergo punishment.	
	Routine work at billets and chateau continued.	
	L CPL HOWES returned today off leave from England. [initials]	
June 19 1915. BETHUNE	Sent Squad from SANITARY SECTION to BETHUNE to continue work of cleaning up billets and surroundings. Later visited town and inspected work of cleansing up Ecole des Michelets finding billets in good sanitary state except that the cleaning out of cesspools had not been completed. Saw Contractor who informed me he proposed completing this work tonight.	
	Visited billets of 20TH BRIGADE. RFA AMM COL at Clock Factory and Timber Yard finding work being carried out by SANITARY SECTION there, including treatment of a ~~mass~~ mass of some hundred tons of manure progressing satisfactorily. Inspected Ecole de Jeunes Filles finding billets there of 2ND BN WELCH REGT satisfactory. Inspected transport lines of LONDON SCOTTISH finding small heap of manure not removed, the Regiment being under orders for LAPUGNOY. Arranged for this to be removed.	

(73989) W4141—463. 400,000. 9/14. H.&J.Ltd. Forms/C. 2118/10.

Army Form C. 2118.

Instructions regarding War Diaries and Intelligence Summaries are contained in F. S. Regs., Part II. and the Staff Manual respectively. Title pages will be prepared in manuscript.

WAR DIARY
or
INTELLIGENCE SUMMARY.
(*Erase heading not required.*)

Hour, Date, Place	Summary of Events and Information	Remarks and references to Appendices
June 19. 1915 BEUVRY	Sent squad to BEUVRY to clean up billets and surroundings of [illegible] there.	
PITHEAD PRIEURE ST PRY	Received reports of SERGT PARKER and 3 other Sanitary Inspectors on special duty in BETHUNE and gave necessary orders in reference thereto. Received orders to stand by in readiness to move from PITHEAD. Routine work continued at billets and chateau. 4147 PTE J.H. PLANE of 2ND Bn R SUSSEX REGT, 1496 PTE REDDING S.J. and 7311 PTE ARCHER D.J. of the 1st Bn GLOUCESTER REGT today joined the Section from the CONVALESCENT Co. [illegible]	
June 20. 1915 PITHEAD	SECTION under orders to stand by. Small squad sent from SECTION under 4 Sanitary Inspectors to BETHUNE to continue work of inspection and cleaning of billets there. Remainder of men at PITHEAD awaiting orders. Parade and kit inspection at 7.30am and 3pm. Inspected equipment of SECTION and arranged for articles damaged or missing to be replaced. Routine work carried out at billets and chateau.	
BETHUNE	Squad assisted by fatigue party of 100 men of 1st Bn GLOUCESTERS	

 20 latrine [illegible] sent to the CASERNE MONTMORENCY

Army Form C. 2118.

WAR DIARY
or
INTELLIGENCE SUMMARY.
(Erase heading not required.)

Instructions regarding War Diaries and Intelligence Summaries are contained in F. S. Regs., Part II. and the Staff Manual respectively. Title pages will be prepared in manuscript.

Hour, Date, Place	Summary of Events and Information	Remarks and references to Appendices
June 20 1915 VERQUIN	Visited and inspected billets of 9TH KINGS LIVERPOOL REGT at VERQUIN. Saw O/C and M/O i/c and inspected with M.O. in detail billets of the men. The men partly billeted in the mine and partly in single farm house billets in the village. The latter were for the most part unsatisfactory being generally dirty. In one case advised M.O to immediately evacuate billet. Difficulty experienced in finding ground for latrines, owing to opposition of owners. Advised M.O to take his interpreter and try to persuade civilians to permit ground in their gardens to be utilised for this purpose. Found evidence that the Sanitary Squad of unit was not carrying out its duties satisfactorily, the latrines etc already constructed being in some cases badly looked after. M.O's attention drawn to this matter and to the fact that at one billet it was reported that men were drinking unsterilised water. Calling to order.	
VAUDRICOURT	Visited HQrs at VAUDRICOURT and found that lines of LOWLAND FIELD Co. R.E. were not at VAUDRICOURT PARK as I had been advised. [initials]	
June 21 1915 VERQUIN	Sent squad from ~~A~~ SANITARY SECTION to VERQUIN to clean up billets and surroundings of 9TH Bn KINGS LIVERPOOL REGT assisted by squad of 30 men and 2 limbers with horses	

(73989) W4141—463. 400,000. 9/14. H.&J.Ltd. Forms/C. 2118/10.

Instructions regarding War Diaries and Intelligence Summaries are contained in F. S. Regs., Part II. and the Staff Manual respectively. Title pages will be prepared in manuscript.

WAR DIARY
or
INTELLIGENCE SUMMARY.
(*Erase heading not required.*)

Army Form C. 2118.

Hour, Date, Place	Summary of Events and Information	Remarks and references to Appendices
June 21 1915 BETHUNE	Sent party to BETHUNE to continue work of cleaning up billets and surroundings there. Visited town and received reports of Sanitary Inspectors. Visited and inspected Ecole de Garcons, Ecole de Michelet, Tobacco factory and Orphanage. Inspected transport lines of 2ND BN ROYAL MUNSTER FUSILIERS, GLOUCESTER REGT. Visited HEADQUARTERS 3RD BRIGADE and saw BRIGADIER in reference to use of Ecole de Michelet for troops. Saw A.D.M.S. at office in BETHUNE and M.O. ic 1st BN L. N. LANCASHIRE. Visited and inspected billets and lines of 25TH BRIGADE R.F.A. and found work proceeding satisfactorily.	
BOIS DE MONTAGNES	Visited and inspected lines of 1st LOWLAND FIELD Co R.E. and found conditions fairly satisfactory. Called attention to matters requiring to be dealt with to improve sanitary state of the camp.	
PITHEAD PRIEURE St PRY	Read reports of N.C.O.s from Section specially detailed for duty as Sanitary Inspectors in BETHUNE and gave necessary orders in connection therewith.	
	Routine work carried out at billets and chateau.	
	11670 PTE WILSON reported absent without leave. Later reported to have been taken prisoner by M.M.P. and handed over to 1ST BN L. N. LANCASHIRE REGT.	

GW

Instructions regarding War Diaries and Intelligence Summaries are contained in F. S. Regs., Part II. and the Staff Manual respectively. Title pages will be prepared in manuscript.

WAR DIARY
or
INTELLIGENCE SUMMARY.
(Erase heading not required.)

Army Form C. 2118.

Hour, Date, Place	Summary of Events and Information	Remarks and references to Appendices
22nd June 1915 VERQUIN	Sent squad from SECTION to VERQUIN to continue cleaning up of billets and surroundings of 9TH KINGS LIVERPOOL REGT assisted by fatigue party of 30 men 2 waggons and 4 horses	
BETHUNE	Sent party under N.C.O. to BETHUNE to continue work there. Visited BETHUNE at 9 a.m. and saw Sanitary Inspectors and read their reports giving necessary orders in connection therewith. Visited billets in Rue des Marais of 1st Bn LOYAL NORTH LANCASHIRE REGT saw C.O. & M.O.'s and discussed with latter cases of measles recently occurring in the unit and suggested steps for the prevention of the spread of the disease. Visited and inspected Transport Lines of the unit and found them generally in better condition than when occupied by previous unit. Gave some directions for improving and maintaining sanitary state of these lines. Visited lines lately occupied by French Troops, adjoining, which had been left in a very insanitary state finding that a considerable improvement had been effected by the SANITARY SECTION, the work still proceeding. Visited ECOLE DE JEUNES FILLES finding conditions satisfactory. Visited ECOLE DE JEANNE D'ARC occupied by a Company of 1st Bn L. N. LANCASHIRE REGT and arranged for a pail system to be installed at this billet in place of the foul latrines which had been in use - temporary earth trenches being used - the ground unsuitable and insufficient for this purpose. Visited ECOLE MICHELET finding billets there now occupied by 4TH Bn ROYAL WELSH FUSILIERS conditions fairly satisfactory. Visited TOBACCO FACTORY and inspected billets and surroundings there of 1st Bn GLOUCESTER REGT, finding conditions satisfactory.	

Army Form C. 2118.

Instructions regarding War Diaries and Intelligence Summaries are contained in F. S. Regs., Part II. and the Staff Manual respectively. Title pages will be prepared in manuscript.

WAR DIARY
or
INTELLIGENCE SUMMARY.

(Erase heading not required.)

Hour, Date, Place	Summary of Events and Information	Remarks and references to Appendices
June 22 1915 BETHUNE	Visited CASERNE MONTMORENCY occupied by 1st Bn COLDSTREAM GUARDS finding sanitary conditions there greatly improved, the new pail system nearly completed and in working order. Saw Staff Captain 2ND BRIGADE with reference to 1st Bn S WALES BORDERERS and ECOLE de JEUNES FILLES billets. Also with reference to fatigue parties and their hours of working.	
	On order of A.D.M.S. visited Mairie and saw Town Surveyor in reference to Water Supply submitted report to A.D.M.S. on my return. Saw Town Surveyor re employment of Contractor for cleaning out cesspools. Promised to send a man from ESSARS to see me.	
Bois des Montagnes	Saw O.C. R.E's re water supply of LOWLAND FIELD Co R.E at BOIS DES MONTAGNES. Arranged to test water tomorrow at 2.30 pm	
PITHEAD PRIEURE ST PRY	Received into custody Pte WILSON attached to SANITARY SECTION handed over by M. Pond enquiries with charge of drunkenness against him. Adjourned case till morning for Summary of Evidence for Court-martial.	
	Routine work carried out at billets and Chateau.	G.J.
June 23 1915 BEUVRY	Sent squad from SANITARY SECTION to BEUVRY to continue work of cleaning up billets and surroundings there temporarily discontinued. The squad was assisted by a fatigue party of 40 men from 1st Bn S.WALES BORDERERS 3 horses and carts in the morning and 30 men of same unit and 3 horses and carts in the afternoon.	

(73989) W4141—463. 400,000. 9/14. H.&J.Ltd. Forms/C. 2118/10.

Instructions regarding War Diaries and Intelligence Summaries are contained in F. S. Regs., Part II. and the Staff Manual respectively. Title pages will be prepared in manuscript.

WAR DIARY
or
INTELLIGENCE SUMMARY.
(*Erase heading not required.*)

Army Form C. 2118.

Hour, Date, Place	Summary of Events and Information	Remarks and references to Appendices
June 23 1915 BETHUNE	Sent party from SANITARY SECTION to BETHUNE to continue work there - here to BETHUNE at 11am and received reports of Sanitary Inspectors there giving necessary orders in relation thereto. Visited CASERNE MONTMORENCY and inspected billets there of COLDSTREAM GUARDS (1st BN) finding conditions satisfactory. Visited ECOLES JULES FERRY and inspected billets occupied there by A Company of 1st BN NORTHAMPTONSHIRE REGT. Saw M.O. i/c and arranged with him for the substitution of a pail system in place of the present insanitary closets. Pails sent in from SANITARY SECTION and seats to be fitted by unit. Removal of pail contents to be carried out daily under supervision of the Sanitary Inspector from the SECTION to ground appointed for the purpose. Visited Mairie and saw Town Surveyor re water supply of Town in continuation and confirmation of my report of interview to A.D.M.S. yesterday. Also with reference to names of Contractors willing to undertake cleaning out of cesspools at billets occupied by Troops. Paid % amounting to 138 fcs to Contractor for cleaning out of cesspools at ECOLE MICHELET	
PITHEAD PRIEURE & PRY	SECTION assisted by fatigue party of 150 men and 6 horses & carts. Arranged for taking of summary of evidence by Capt IRVINE RAMC of charge of drunkenness against Pte WILSON. Prepared necessary documents for request for F.G.C.M.	
	Received & considered reports of Sanitary Inspectors detailed for special duty in BETHUNE and gave necessary orders in connection therewith.	
	1496 PTE REDDING S.J. today admitted to hospital	

(73989) W4141—463. 400,000. 9/14. H.&J.Ltd. Forms/C. 2118/10.

WAR DIARY
or
INTELLIGENCE SUMMARY.
(Erase heading not required.)

Army Form C. 2118.

Instructions regarding War Diaries and Intelligence Summaries are contained in F. S. Regs., Part II. and the Staff Manual respectively. Title pages will be prepared in manuscript.

Hour, Date, Place	Summary of Events and Information	Remarks and references to Appendices
June 24.1915 BETHUNE	Sent party with 4 NCOs (Sanitary Inspectors) to BETHUNE to continue work of inspecting and cleaning up billets. Visited BETHUNE and read reports of Sanitary Inspectors as to state of billets being vacated by 1st DIVISION TROOPS.	
PITHEAD PRIEURE St PRY	Remainder of SECTION standing by. Sent list of latrine pails provided by 1st DIVISION and left behind in charge of Town Commandant at various large billets in BETHUNE to TOWN COMMANDANT. Section evacuated PITHEAD at 3.30pm and marched to MARLES	
MARLES LES MINES	LES MINES to take over new billets there arriving at 6.30pm. Arranged for fatigue party to be provided by 2ND BN R. MUNSTER FUSRS for duty with SANITARY SECTION at MARLES LES MINES tomorrow and horses from same unit's transport.	
June 25.1915 MARLES LES MINES	SECTION at work at MARLES LES MINES cleaning up village and surroundings which were in a very dirty state. The SECTION was assisted by fatigue party of 75 men and 8 horses from 2ND BN R. MUNSTER FUSRS. Carts were obtained from local farmers by requisition. Work had to be discontinued in the afternoon owing to very heavy storm of rain which occurred.	
BETHUNE	Visited BETHUNE and called on TOWN COMMANDANT in reference to the return of 6 carts requisitioned for use of SANITARY SECTION while working in BETHUNE. Sent list of owners to TOWN COMMANDANT and subsequently requested him that in the event of them not being wanted by the Sanitary Section of Division replacing 1st Division they should be forthwith returned to their respective owners.	

Instructions regarding War Diaries and Intelligence Summaries are contained in F. S. Regs., Part II. and the Staff Manual respectively. Title pages will be prepared in manuscript.

WAR DIARY
or
INTELLIGENCE SUMMARY.
(*Erase heading not required.*)

Army Form C. 2118.

Hour, Date, Place	Summary of Events and Information	Remarks and references to Appendices
June 26. 1915 LAPUGNOY	Sent Squad from SANITARY SECTION to LAPUGNOY to clean up billets and surroundings of 1st Bn L. N. LANCASHIRE REGT. Assisted by fatigue party of 50 men from this unit. Visited and inspected district and found work progressing satisfactorily.	
MARLES LES MINES	Squad from SANITARY SECTION engaged in cleaning up village of MARLES LES MINES assisted by fatigue party from CYCLIST SECTION and 4 carts and horses obtained from SIGNAL Co RE. Party from SECTION cleaning up billets of Headquarters 1st DIV. in village. Application, by letter, of PTE BARWELL for extension of leave. 3 days extra granted by order of G. O. C.	
June 27. 1915 MARLES-LES-MINES	SECTION standing by for orders. Party from SANITARY SECTION at work cleaning up Headquarters billets and surroundings.	
9.30 pm	Received orders from Headquarters to evacuate billets of SANITARY SECTION at MARLES-LES-MINES and to proceed tomorrow to MINEHEAD at PRIEURE ST PRY.	
LOZINGHEM	Visited lines of DIVISIONAL SUPPLY COLUMN at LOZINGHEM.	

(73989) W4141—463. 400,000. 9/14. H.&J.Ltd. Forms/C. 2118/10.

Instructions regarding War Diaries and Intelligence Summaries are contained in F. S. Regs., Part II. and the Staff Manual respectively. Title pages will be prepared in manuscript.

WAR DIARY
or
INTELLIGENCE SUMMARY.
(*Erase heading not required.*)

Army Form C. 2118.

Hour, Date, Place	Summary of Events and Information	Remarks and references to Appendices
27 June 1915 BURBURE	Visited and inspected billets of 1st BN COLDSTREAM GUARDS at BURBURE also billets of 1st BN CAMERON HIGHLANDERS Saw M.O. i/c of both Units - which were under orders to move - Condition of billets fairly satisfactory but manure middens not touched as units were moving tomorrow. Discussed with M.O. i/c 1st BN COLDSTREAM GUARDS, case of measles in one of the billets and steps to be taken to prevent risk of spread of infection. GJ	
28 June 1915 MARLES LES MINES	SANITARY SECTION under orders to evacuate billet at MARLES-LES-MINES, and to proceed to PITHEAD near PRIEURE ST PRY to take over billet there. Evacuation completed by 2.30pm. SECTION arriving at PITHEAD at 5pm. Party from SECTION at work cleaning up Headquarters billets at MARLES-LES-MINES prior to evacuation. GJ	
[illegible] June 1915. VERQUIN	Sent squad from SANITARY SECTION to VERQUIN to clean up billets and surroundings there.	

(73989) W4141—463. 400,000. 9/14. H.&J.Ltd. Forms/C. 2118/10.

Instructions regarding War Diaries and Intelligence Summaries are contained in F. S. Regs., Part II. and the Staff Manual respectively. Title pages will be prepared in manuscript.

WAR DIARY
or
INTELLIGENCE SUMMARY.
(*Erase heading not required.*)

Army Form C. 2118.

Hour, Date, Place	Summary of Events and Information	Remarks and references to Appendices
29 June 1915. VERMELLES.	Visited VERMELLES and inspected billets of 2ND BN ROYAL MUNSTER FUSILIERS. The conditions generally were unsatisfactory, the billets in most cases being more or less in an insanitary state. Tried to see MO i/c with a view to taking steps to mitigate the unsatisfactory conditions prevailing in this village which lies close to the trenches, and has been practically devastated by shell fire, during the previous heavy fighting here when it was occupied alternately by the French troops and by the enemy. It is practically a large cemetery and owing to the amount of fallen bricks and debris lying round billets and to the proximity to the firing line a very difficult matter to deal with the ~~...~~ insanitary conditions which undoubtedly exist. I saw Adjutant of unit suggested steps which might be taken to improve to some extent at least the billets and surroundings. There are several other units or parts of units billeted here. Reported specially to A.D.M.S. on my return.	
BETHUNE	Visited BETHUNE to see that 6 carts which had been by SANITARY SECTION there had been taken over or returned to their respective owners. Saw O.C. SANITARY SECTION 2ND DIV. who informed me he had taken over carts and proposed taking over pails provided by SANITARY SECTION 1ST DIV. at large billets in the town. Called on TOWN COMMANDANT in whose custody the pails and carts above mentioned were left, when 1ST DIV. evacuated BETHUNE as a billeting area.	

Army Form C. 2118.

Instructions regarding War Diaries and Intelligence Summaries are contained in F. S. Regs., Part II. and the Staff Manual respectively. Title pages will be prepared in manuscript.

WAR DIARY
or
INTELLIGENCE SUMMARY.
(Erase heading not required.)

Hour, Date, Place	Summary of Events and Information	Remarks and references to Appendices
29 June 1915 PITHEAD PRIEURE ST PRY	Sent Squad from SANITARY SECTION to clear out offensive sullage pit at 2ND ECHELON MESS. PRIEURE ST PRY.	
	Received orders to arrange for attendance of PTE WILSON, 1ST BN S. WALES BORDERERS, attached for duty to SANITARY SECTION at C.M. at LABOURSE 3pm. Arranged accordingly. PTE WILSON sent back under escort to await promulgation of decision of C.M.	
	4149 PTE J.H. PLANE, attached to SECTION from 2ND Bn R SUSSEX RAGT was today admitted to Hospital.	
	[initials]	
30 June 1915 VERQUIN	Sent Squad from SANITARY SECTION to VERQUIN to clean up billets and surroundings of 1ST Bn SCOTS GUARDS. Visited VERQUIN and saw M.O i/c SCOTS GUARDS who promised to assist party in the morning with 24 men of his unit and 2 horses. No men available and only one horse supplied. In the afternoon 100 men 1ST BN CAMERON HIGHLANDERS were supplied by 1ST BDE H.Q. to assist squad from SECTION	
LABOURSE	Sent Squad from SANITARY SECTION to LABOURSE to clean up village and surroundings. Visited LABOURSE and saw BRIGADE MAJOR 1ST DIV ART. and inspected HQrs of BRIGADE and surroundings	

(73989) W4141—463. 400,000. 9/14. H.&J.Ltd. Forms/C. 2118/10.

Instructions regarding War Diaries and Intelligence Summaries are contained in F. S. Regs., Part II. and the Staff Manual respectively. Title pages will be prepared in manuscript.

WAR DIARY
or
INTELLIGENCE SUMMARY.
(*Erase heading not required.*)

Army Form C. 2118.

Hour, Date, Place	Summary of Events and Information	Remarks and references to Appendices
30. June 1915 LABOURSE	which were in a very insanitary state. Arranged for fatigue party from 1st Bn SOUTH WALES BORDERERS to assist Squad.	
NOYELLES LES VERMELLES	Visited NOYELLES-LEZ-VERMELLES occupied as Brigade Headquarters 3RD BRIGADE and by 4th Bn ROYAL WELSH FUSILIERS. Saw M.O. and Adjutant and inspected billets of his unit which I found very dirty and insanitary. This village being close to the firing line has suffered considerably from shell fire and has up till lately been occupied by French troops. There are numerous very offensive manure middens in front of the billets in addition to other objectionable features. The surroundings were found to be in a very dirty state. No latrines appearing to have been used by previous occupants. The ground in the immediate vicinity of village being fouled by human excreta. Arranged for fatigue party with horses and carts to be provided tomorrow to assist Squad from SANITARY SECTION. Visited Chateau where 3rd BDE HQRS situated. Saw Staff Officer and inspected Sanitary State of Chateau & surroundings which were insanitary. Arranged for N.C.O. from SANITARY SECTION to assist fatigue party provided by BRIGADE.	
VERQUIGNEUL	Visited VERQUIGNEUL and inspected billets of 5th Bn R. SUSSEX REGT. This village very dirty and will require a lot of attention from SANITARY SECTION.	
PITHEAD PRIEURE ST PRY	Sent party from SANITARY SECTION to clean out offensive sewage soakage pit at 2ND ECHELON MESS.	

(73989) W4141—463. 400,000. 9/14. H.&J.Ltd. Forms/C. 2118/10.

Army Form C. 2118.

Instructions regarding War Diaries and Intelligence Summaries are contained in F. S. Regs., Part II. and the Staff Manual respectively. Title pages will be prepared in manuscript.

WAR DIARY
or
INTELLIGENCE SUMMARY.

(*Erase heading not required.*)

Hour, Date, Place	Summary of Events and Information	Remarks and references to Appendices
30 June 1915	Saw G.O.C. who drew my attention to foul state of cellar in a house at LE ROUTOIRE close to trenches which required to be remedied. Promised to give matter immediate attention.	
10pm.	C.M. Papers re PTE WILSON forwarded at 10pm promulgating sentence.	
	2324 PTE NEVILLE of the SANITARY SECTION was today admitted to Hospital.	
	G.J.	

(73989) W4141—463. 400,000. 9/14. H.&J.Ltd. Forms/C. 2118/10.

S

July '15

121/6401

1st Division

Summarised but not copied

121/6401

No 13 Sanitary Section

Vol III

Instructions regarding War Diaries and Intelligence Summaries are contained in F. S. Regs., Part II. and the Staff Manual respectively. Title pages will be prepared in manuscript.

WAR DIARY

or

INTELLIGENCE SUMMARY.

(*Erase heading not required.*)

Army Form C. 2118.

Hour, Date, Place	Summary of Events and Information	Remarks and references to Appendices
	CONFIDENTIAL WAR DIARY of LIEUT G. O LENNANE RAMCT O.C. No 13 SANITARY SECTION 1st DIV FROM 1st July 1915 TO 31st July 15 (Volume 4)	

(73989) W4141—463. 400,000. 9/14. H.&J.Ltd. Forms/C. 2118/10.

Instructions regarding War Diaries and Intelligence Summaries are contained in F. S. Regs., Part II. and the Staff Manual respectively. Title pages will be prepared in manuscript.

WAR DIARY
or
INTELLIGENCE SUMMARY.
(Erase heading not required.)

Army Form C. 2118.

Hour, Date, Place	Summary of Events and Information	Remarks and references to Appendices
July 1st 1915 VERQUIN	Sent squad from SANITARY SECTION to VERQUIN to clean up billets and surroundings there assisted by 100 men fatigue party from 1st Bn CAMERON HIGHLANDERS in the morning. Owing to a misunderstanding by Sergeant in charge of SANITARY SECTION services of fatigue party 100 men 1st Bn SCOTS GUARDS not availed of in the afternoon. 4 horses and carts at work with SECTION here. Visited village and found work proceeding satisfactorily	
LABOURSE	Sent squad from SANITARY SECTION to LABOURSE to continue work of cleaning up billets and surroundings there, assisted by fatigue party of 50 men 1st Bn SOUTH WALES BORDERERS. 2 horses and carts at work with Sanitary Squad. Visited village finding work proceeding satisfactorily	
NOYELLES LEZ VERMELLES	Sent party under 2 N.C.Os to NOYELLES-LEZ-VERMELLES to clean up billets and surroundings there. Assisted by a fatigue party of 100 men 4th Bn ROYAL WELSH FUSILIERS and 4 horses and carts. Also the H.Qrs. of 3RD BRIGADE which was in a very dirty state there being a formidable manure midden in the Chateau Farm requiring to be treated. Visited village finding work proceeding satisfactorily	
VERMELLES	~~Visited~~ Sent small party to VERMELLES to search for evidence of nuisance	
LE ROUTOIRE	Visited VERMELLES and LE ROUTOIRE, the Headquarters of 1st Bn GLOSTER REGT in response to a complaint as to foul cesspool and other offensive conditions there. The Headquarters are reached from VERMELLES through the communication trench and consist of 2 ruined farm houses. I inspected the surroundings generally with M.O. i/c of unit. There was a cesspool in the courtyard of one of the farm houses quite full and smelling offensively. There were said to be a number of Germans buried in ground immediately adjoining this cesspool and that these had been ~~imperfectly~~ imperfectly buried and there was some evidence of effluvium nuisance from this heap. The latrines and urine pit were dug in an adjoining garden and there was also provision made for burying refuse.	

(73989) W4141—463. 400,000. 9/14. H.&J.Ltd. Forms/C. 2118/10.

Instructions regarding War Diaries and Intelligence Summaries are contained in F. S. Regs., Part II. and the Staff Manual respectively. Title pages will be prepared in manuscript.

WAR DIARY
or
INTELLIGENCE SUMMARY.
(Erase heading not required.)

Army Form C. 2118.

Hour, Date, Place	Summary of Events and Information	Remarks and references to Appendices
July 1st 1915 LE ROUTOIRE	The conditions were especially owing to foul cesspool and the number of dead bodies buried in the precincts of the Headquarters, insanitary; and I made suggestions to the M.O. as to the best method of mitigating the nuisance, which he promised to put into action. Reported to A.D.M.S. on return.	
SAILLY LABOURSE	Visited SAILLY LABOURSE and saw O.C. and M.O.'s with reference to the complaint received as to the insanitary state of the billets of the 9th Bn KINGS LIVERPOOL REGT.	
PITHEAD PRIEURE ST PRY	Sent party to Chateau to continue cleaning out offensive sewage pit in rear of 2ND ECHELON MESS.	
	~~Saw F.G.C.M.~~ Sentence of F.G.C.M. on PTE WILSON promulgated on parade 10 days F.P. No 2. [signature]	
July 2ND 1915 VERQUIN	Sent party to VERQUIN to continue cleaning up of billets and surroundings there. Assisted by fatigue party of 100 men 1st Bn CAMERON HIGHLANDERS in the morning and 100 men 1st Bn SCOTS GUARDS in the afternoon. Visited district and accompanied ADMS in his inspection of billets of CAMERON HIGHLANDERS and SCOTS GUARDS. Work proceeding satisfactorily.	
LABOURSE	Sent Squad from SECTION to LABOURSE to continue cleaning up billets and surroundings. Assisted by fatigue party of 50 men 1st Bn SOUTH WALES BORDERERS. Party delayed owing to difficulty of obtaining carts. Visited district and saw C.O. & Adjutant 1st S. WALES BORDERERS in reference to complaint as to fatigue being kept waiting and tried to arrange to obtain carts. Saw fatigue party put on useful work	

(73989) W4141—463. 400,000. 9/14. H.&J.Ltd. Forms/C. 2118/10.

Army Form C. 2118.

Instructions regarding War Diaries and Intelligence Summaries are contained in F. S. Regs., Part II. and the Staff Manual respectively. Title pages will be prepared in manuscript.

WAR DIARY
or
INTELLIGENCE SUMMARY.
(*Erase heading not required.*)

Hour, Date, Place	Summary of Events and Information	Remarks and references to Appendices
July 2 1915 LABOURSE	Visited LABOURSE again in afternoon and found work proceeding satisfactorily though no carts were obtainable. Saw M.O. i/c in reference to steps to be taken to continue sanitation of billets of his unit.	
NOYELLES LEZ VERMELLES	Sent squad from SANITARY SECTION to NOYELLES LEZ VERMELLES to continue cleaning up of billets and surroundings and 3RD BRIGADE HQRS at the Chateau. Visited the district and found work proceeding satisfactorily. Saw BRIGADIER with reference to supply of fatigue party and horses and discussed complaint received re SOUTH WALES BORDERERS at LABOURSE	
SAILLY LABOURSE	Visited SAILLY LABOURSE where small party from SANITARY SECTION were at work. Conditions of this village very unsatisfactory. Found work proceeding slowly owing to no fatigue party having been obtained. Arranged for fatigue party with horses from 2ND BRIGADE to be available for work with SANITARY SECTION tomorrow.	
PITHEAD PRIEURE ST PRY	G.O.C. 1st DIV. called at my office with the A.D.M.S. in reference to my visit of inspection to Headquarters of 1st BN GLOSTER REGT at LE ROUTOIRE and the trenches near VERMELLES Sector. [signature]	
3rd July 1915 VERQUIN	Sent squad to VERQUIN to continue work of cleaning billets and surroundings. Squad assisted by 100 men and 4 horses morning and afternoon. Morning party supplied by 1st BN CAMERON HIGHLANDERS and that in the afternoon by 1st BN SCOTS GUARDS. Visited locality finding work proceeding satisfactorily.	

(73989) W4141—463. 400,000. 9/14. H.&J.Ltd. Forms/C. 2118/10.

Instructions regarding War Diaries and Intelligence Summaries are contained in F. S. Regs., Part II. and the Staff Manual respectively. Title pages will be prepared in manuscript.

WAR DIARY
or
INTELLIGENCE SUMMARY.
(*Erase heading not required.*)

Army Form C. 2118.

Hour, Date, Place	Summary of Events and Information	Remarks and references to Appendices
3rd July 1915 LABOURSE	Sent squad from SANITARY SECTION to LABOURSE to continue work of clearing up billets and surroundings there. Assisted by fatigue party of 50 men from 1st BN GLOUCESTER REGT and horses. Visited LABOURSE and called at MAIRIE to requisition carts for use with the SANITARY SECTION	
SAILLY LABOURSE	Sent squad from SANITARY SECTION to SAILLY LABOURSE to clean up billets and surroundings of 1st BN L NORTH LANCASHIRE REGT. Conditions very unsatisfactory the billets in many cases being far from ~~satisfactory~~ sanitary. Saw M.O. i/c unit and arranged to supply latrine pails at 2 of the billets, no suitable ground being available. Visited Mairie and requisitioned carts for use of SECTION. 2ND BRIGADE unable to supply fatigue party to assist.	
NOYELLES LEZ VERMELLES	Sent squad from SANITARY SECTION to continue clearing up of billets and surroundings of 2ND BN R MUNSTER FUSILIERS at NOYELLES-LEZ-VERMELLES and 3RD BRIGADE H.Qs. Squad assisted by 100 men 2ND BN R MUNSTER FUSILIERS with horses and carts. Visited locality and found work proceeding satisfactorily, a great improvement being already perceptible in the village and surroundings which had been in a filthy state previously.	
PITHEAD PRIEURE ST PRY	Investigated charge against 2545 Pte SUTCLIFFE attached from 1st BN L.N. LANCASHIRE REGT and admonished him. 021672 DR PRATT ASC M.T was today sent to hospital.	

[signature]

(73989) W4141—463. 400,000. 9/14. H.&J.Ltd. Forms/C. 2118/10.

Instructions regarding War Diaries and Intelligence Summaries are contained in F. S. Regs., Part II. and the Staff Manual respectively. Title pages will be prepared in manuscript.

WAR DIARY
or
INTELLIGENCE SUMMARY.
(*Erase heading not required.*)

Army Form C. 2118.

Hour, Date, Place	Summary of Events and Information	Remarks and references to Appendices
4 July 1915 NOYELLES LEZ VERMELLES	Sent squad from Section to continue work at NOYELLES LEZ VERMELLES assisted by fatigue party of 100 men (2ND BN R MUNSTER FUSILIERS). Visited locality finding work proceeding satisfactorily (Village heavily shelled in the afternoon - with several casualties amongst troops) Accompanied A.D.M.S. in his inspection of billets etc at NOYELLES LEZ VERMELLES	
SAILLY LABOURSE	Sent squad from SECTION to continue work at SAILLY LABOURSE no fatigue party available to assist	
LABOURSE	Sent squad from SECTION to LABOURSE to continue work of cleaning up billets and surroundings there assisted by fatigue party of ~~40~~ 50 men of 1st BN GLOUCESTER REGT	
PITHEAD PRIEURE ST PRY	2023 CPL BISHOP 1632 L.CPL PALMER and 57 PTE HARPER were this day admitted to hospital	
	Obtained leave of absence to proceed to England (8 days)	
	Obtained 150 fcs from Field Cashier to pay cartage and cleaning of cesspool at BETHUNE	
	Paid 176 fcs to ~~Capt [illegible]~~ CAPT IRVINE to pay these bills	
	GL	

(73989) W4141—463. 400,000. 9/14. H.&J.Ltd. Forms/C. 2118/10.

Army Form C. 2118.

WAR DIARY
or
INTELLIGENCE SUMMARY.
(Erase heading not required.)

Instructions regarding War Diaries and Intelligence Summaries are contained in F. S. Regs., Part II. and the Staff Manual respectively. Title pages will be prepared in manuscript.

Hour, Date, Place	Summary of Events and Information	Remarks and references to Appendices
5 July 1915. PITHEAD PRIEURE ST PRY	LIEUT LENNANE left for ENGLAND today having been granted 8 days leave. CAPT IRVINE RAMC took over command of the SECTION temporarily.	
SAILLY LABOURSE LABOURSE VERQUIN	Visited SAILLY LABOURSE, LABOURSE, and VERQUIN with A.D.M.S. inspected several farms etc and found that there was still a considerable amount of work to be done. Parties working at SAILLY LABOURSE, LABOURSE and NOYELLES.	
LABOURSE	SERGT HATHAWAY and party at LABOURSE working in Chateau farm. A fatigue party of 50 men were supplied from 8 – 12 noon and work was continued - pumping out middens etc. 4 horses & 2 carts were in use. No fatigue party was available in afternoon and the work was continued by the Sanitary Squad. It was noticed that the middens previously covered over with etc at a former date have once again been allowed to get into an unsatisfactory condition owing to neglect and carelessness of the new occupants of the billets. Orders issued for this party to continue work and a fatigue party etc applied for from 2ND BRIGADE.	
SAILLY LABOURSE	Fatigue party of 1st Bn L N LANCASHIRE REGT, middens covered in manure removed from large heap near the church. Fatigue party employed cleaning up roads etc. Only two carts were available which hampered the work one cart was damaged (wheel) owing to the horse taking fright.	

Instructions regarding War Diaries and Intelligence Summaries are contained in F. S. Regs., Part II. and the Staff Manual respectively. Title pages will be prepared in manuscript.

WAR DIARY
or
INTELLIGENCE SUMMARY.
(Erase heading not required.)

Army Form C. 2118.

Hour, Date, Place	Summary of Events and Information	Remarks and references to Appendices
5 July 1915. NOYELLES.	Removed manure from a large midden (14 loads) small midden covered up. Several small yards cleaned up and sprayed. BRIGADE HQRS Chateau removing of liquid manure & covering up midden. The removal of the liquid manure was hampered by want of a pump and suitable appliances a fatigue party of 50 men & 4 carts. Work to continue when pump is available & when fatigue party can be obtained from 1st BRIGADE.	
PITHEAD PRIEURE ST PRY	7646 PTE LOVE attached to SECTION from 4th R WELSH FUSILIERS was this day admitted to hospital. [initials]	
6. July 1915 PITHEAD	L CPL TETLOW and 3 men worked in Chateau Grounds (2nd Echelon) built incinerator dug refuse pit, constructed grease trap and latrines burnt horse manure etc.	
SAILLY LABOURSE	Visited working party here under SERGT PARKER gave detailed instructions and personally pointed out the work to be done. Saw the O.C. 2nd Bn K.R.R.C. re working party which had been arranged for by the 2nd BDE. Owing to no shovels being available at 8am. the party did not parade. The C.O. promised to get spades as soon as possible and to increase the fatigue party to 100 men. The roads in this area were very thickly littered with horse droppings a party was detailed to clear the roads. Fatigue party of 50 men paraded at 11am. Manure heaps covered up as follows 1. Maxim Section and officers billet 1st Bn L. N. LANCS. 2. Cottage beside do do. 3. Cottage near Hdqrs L. N. LANCS.	

Instructions regarding War Diaries and Intelligence Summaries are contained in F. S. Regs., Part II. and the Staff Manual respectively. Title pages will be prepared in manuscript.

WAR DIARY
or
INTELLIGENCE SUMMARY.
(*Erase heading not required.*)

Army Form C. 2118.

Hour, Date, Place	Summary of Events and Information	Remarks and references to Appendices
July 6. 1915 SAILLY LABOURSE	4. Corner of main road opposite Church. Portion of manure heap near Church removed, ditches & roadside near church cleaned. Work done at transport Section of R.E's. Tins buried and refuse cleared up etc. Roads cleaned. 2 horses and large civilian cart employed. Limber cart of 9th KINGS LIVERPOOL REGT employed. A Farmer's cart was also in use for a short time. Manure being removed from 9th KINGS LIVERPOOL transport yard.	
LABOURSE	Chateau Farm (RFA Hdqrs) incinerator built several loads of manure removed from large manure midden. Saw OC 1st Bn COLDSTREAM GUARDS and obtained fatigue party of 30 men & 2 horses. All the roads thoroughly cleaned up and the large accumulations of horse droppings removed. 23RD Co's R.E. billets - a certain amount of work was also done here. These lines are now satisfactory. Arrangements made to continue work here tomorrow.	
PITHEAD PRIEURE ST PRY	Aeroplane Ground near railway crossing Rue St Pry. Ground cleaned up, incinerator constructed, collections of rubbish from roads and ditches burnt. This area is used by the 2nd DIVISION as a dumping ground. ~~Arrangements made to send a~~ report sent to A.D.M.S. 1st DIV Arrangements made to continue work at SAILLY LABOURSE and NOYELLES tomorrow. [initials]	

(73989) W4141—463. 400,000. 9/14. H.&J.Ltd. Forms/C. 2118/10.

Instructions regarding War Diaries and Intelligence Summaries are contained in F. S. Regs., Part II. and the Staff Manual respectively. Title pages will be prepared in manuscript.

WAR DIARY
or
INTELLIGENCE SUMMARY.
(*Erase heading not required.*)

Army Form C. 2118.

Hour, Date, Place	Summary of Events and Information	Remarks and references to Appendices
July 7. 1915 LABOURSE	Work continued. Fatigue party not available until the afternoon. The manure midden at Chateau Farm almost cleared out. Roads cleaned up. In the afternoon a fatigue party of SCOTS GUARDS available. Arrangements made to continue work tomorrow.	
SAILLY LABOURSE	Fatigue party only available in the morning. SANITARY SECTION 2 NCOs and 6 men continued work, middens covered in, also manure heaps covered up at top of road near barrier. Some more manure removed from transport lines behind church, the remainder was covered over with earth. Roads and several billets surroundings cleaned, one large farm cart and 1 limber cart employed. Arrangements made to continue work.	
NOYELLES	Large midden cleaned out 14 load removed and turned over etc. Small middens covered with earth etc. Large collection of tins buried & tannery yard cleaned etc. CHATEAU. Work continued cleaning out liquid manure from under tower turning over and covering with earth. Pumping water from another large midden. The farmers are throwing rubbish and manure in middens already cleaned out; informed that this was prohibited. Fatigue party of 30 men and 4 horses employed. Arrangements made to continue work. Work at Headquarters continued.	
July 1915	Squads working at NOYELLES, SAILLY LABOURSE and LABOURSE visited these places with D.A.D.M.S. and gave the necessary instructions for carrying on the work	

(73989) W4141—463. 400,000. 9/14. H.&J.Ltd. Forms/C. 2118/10.

Army Form C. 2118.

Instructions regarding War Diaries and Intelligence Summaries are contained in F. S. Regs., Part II. and the Staff Manual respectively. Title pages will be prepared in manuscript.

WAR DIARY
or
INTELLIGENCE SUMMARY.

(Erase heading not required.)

Hour, Date, Place	Summary of Events and Information	Remarks and references to Appendices
July 8.1915. NOYELLES	Liquid manure pumped out from 5 middens, covered over, sprayed etc. This area is now in a satisfactory Sanitary Condition. Saw the M.O. 1/6 BLACK WATCH and gave the necessary instructions re billets etc	
SAILLY LABOURSE	Sergt PARKER and squad from SANITARY SECTION also fatigue party of 50 men and 4 horses continued the work in this area, middens cleared out etc. roads and surroundings of billets cleared. This area is now in a satisfactory Sanitary Condition	
LABOURSE	SERGT HATHAWAY and party from SANITARY SECTION 50 men and 4 horses in the afternoon. CHATEAU FARM The midden has now been emptied of manure etc thoroughly cleaned and disinfected, also the chateau yard and surroundings. Covered in midden in 1st Bn GOLDSTREAM GUARDS billet. Roads & surroundings of billets cleaned. This area is now in a satisfactory Sanitary Condition	
FOUQUEREUIL	Inspected lines of 4th Bn R WELSH FUSILIERS at FOUQUEREUIL. The billets generally required more attention, several manure middens have not been dealt with in accordance with routine orders. Incinerators are not being sufficiently used. Collections of tins in billets and surroundings. In A Co billet PLATOONS 1 & 2 the men were sleeping beside a stinking pig stye. Recommended that these men be taken from this billet. Horse lines satisfactory - more care is required re storage of food. The number of flies in the billet was exceptional. Found that the men use water direct from the pump for drinking. Saw the OC and personally pointed out the matters that required attention. It was arranged that two of the middens were to be covered up etc. The Sanitary Corporal reported that the Sanitary Squad were taken for a parade today from 10 a.m. to 2 p.m. and consequently were not able to attend to their duties. They have previously been taken off their duty for a route march when stationed at Annezin(?). I pointed this out to OC	

(73989) W4141—463. 400,000. 9/14. H.&J.Ltd. Forms/C. 2118/10.

Instructions regarding War Diaries and Intelligence Summaries are contained in F. S. Regs., Part II. and the Staff Manual respectively. Title pages will be prepared in manuscript.

WAR DIARY
or
INTELLIGENCE SUMMARY.
(Erase heading not required.)

Army Form C. 2118.

Hour, Date, Place	Summary of Events and Information	Remarks and references to Appendices
July 9. 1915 VERQUIN	SERGT HATHAWAY and party working at VERQUIN Incinerator built emptying our midden, covering midden etc. The fatigue of 30 men were only obtained for one hour during the morning and from 2 to 4 in the afternoon. Arrangements made to continue work tomorrow. Inspected lines and billets of 1st Bn SOUTH WALES BORDERERS at VERQUIN and found them generally in a satisfactory condition.	
PITHEAD PRIEURE St PRY	SERGT PARKER and 6 men covered etc a large heap of manure in a field close to road almost beside Chateau St Pry. The road ditches etc cleared out. In the afternoon this party brought a large pump from the Bomb Factory for use of the SANITARY SECTION. The motor lorry was inspected by an Officer from HEADQUARTERS and found to be in urgent want of repairs. Arrangement made to send it to the DIVISIONAL SUPPLY COLUMN WORKSHOP tomorrow.	
	a.e.s.	
July 10. 1915.	The motor pump which we received yesterday from the Bomb Factory is out of order and the lorry driver could not get the engine to work. Reported to Motor Ambulance Repair workshop	
VERQUIN	Work continued at VERQUIN. Sgts HATHAWAY, PARKER & SANITARY SECTION also a fatigue party of 50 men and 4 horses and carts. Large midden emptied of water, turned and covered over with earth. 3 other middens treated in the usual manner, cleaned up several rubbish heaps adjoining roads, burned tins etc. This area is now in a very satisfactory sanitary condition	
NOYELLES	Visited NOYELLES with CORPL MORELAND visited billet from which a suspected case of Small Pox was sent to C.C.S. billet 176? 8. Side of road	

(73989) W4141—463. 400,000. 9/14. H.&J.Ltd. Forms/C. 2118/10.

Instructions regarding War Diaries and Intelligence Summaries are contained in F. S. Regs., Part II. and the Staff Manual respectively. Title pages will be prepared in manuscript.

WAR DIARY
or
INTELLIGENCE SUMMARY.
(*Erase heading not required.*)

Army Form C. 2118.

Hour, Date, Place	Summary of Events and Information	Remarks and references to Appendices
July 10 1915 NOYELLES	The contacts (1st Bn Black Watch) were isolated in this billet which had been thoroughly disinfected. NOYELLES is in a satisfactory sanitary condition. The M.O. i/c the regiment there was informed re the keeping of the middens free from manure rubbish etc.	
SAILLY LABOURSE	Billet in SAILLY LABOURSE lately occupied by 2nd Bn K.R.R. Corps disinfected - case of scarlet fever - location of billet Estaminet L 2 & 77. All rooms sprayed with formalin (2 rooms & a passage). Inspected the Chateau grounds and kitchens of Officers mess and gave instructions for necessary work to be done etc. SAILLY LABOURSE is in a satisfactory sanitary condition.	
LABOURSE	Saw M.O. i/c 1st Bn Scots Guards and explained to him the necessary steps to be taken re middens. Cleaning up roads etc. This village is in a very satisfactory sanitary condition.	
HESDIGNEUL	Visited HESDIGNEUL and inspected lines etc of 30th Battery R.F.A. Several matters require more attention. These were pointed out to sanitary man - all the officers were away.	
PITHEAD PRICURE ST PRY	Motor lorry of the Section sent to Divisional Supply Column Motor Repair Shop by orders of the Inspecting Officer Mechanical Transport from G.H.Q. 176 fly traps received from D.A.D.O.S. Under instructions from A.D.M.S. these fly traps are to be distributed to Field Ambulances Convalescent to H.Q.RS. Infantry Brigades. 1 D.A and 1 D.R.E. etc. It was decided not to issue these traps for use in the trenches. 7644 Pte Love returned from hospital.	[illegible]
July 11 1915	Sanitary Section had a holiday	
HESDIGNEUL	Inspected 30th Bty lines etc at HESDIGNEUL, they were not in a satisfactory condition. Many matters required more attention. Arranged to send out party from Sanitary Section to clean up this area.	[illegible]

Army Form C. 2118.

Instructions regarding War Diaries and Intelligence Summaries are contained in F. S. Regs., Part II. and the Staff Manual respectively. Title pages will be prepared in manuscript.

WAR DIARY
or
INTELLIGENCE SUMMARY.
(*Erase heading not required.*)

Hour, Date, Place	Summary of Events and Information	Remarks and references to Appendices
July. 12. 1915 HESDIGNEUL	SERGTS HATHAWAY, PARKER and party worked at HESDIGNEUL 2 incinerators built. Grease traps dug. latrines covered in. Surroundings of billets cleaned, manure cleared up. Incinerator also built for 113th BTTY RFA, collected tins and other rubbish which was satisfactorily disposed of. The area occupied by troops of the 1st DIVISION is now in a satisfactory state.	
BETHUNE	CORPL CLAYDON and party went to No 2 FIELD AMBULANCE, ECOLE JULES FERRY and cleaned out closet midden.	
VAUDRICOURT	Inspected 2ND BN R MUNSTER FUSILIER lines, a lot of work is necessary in this area, covering in middens etc. Arrangements made for SANITARY SECTION to work here tomorrow.	
FOUQUIERES	Inspected billets of NORTHUMBERLAND HUSSARS arrangements made to have a large midden full of water emptied. 2523 CPL BISHOP and 1632 L CPL PALMER of the SECTION today returned from hospital. A.E.H.	
July. 13. 1915 PITHEAD PRIEURE ST PRY FOUQUIERES	Took over command of SECTION today from CAPT IRVINE RAMC. Visited with CAPT IRVINE, HDQRS. NORTHUMBERLAND HUSSARS. Party from SANITARY SECTION at work under CPL BISHOP, emptying large and offensive sump in yard.	
VAUDRICOURT	Visited and inspected billets of 2ND BN R MUNSTER FUSILIERS, finding squad from SANITARY SECTION, assisted by 30 men of R MUNSTER FUSRS at work. Saw M.O. i/c who stated his unit was moving today. Work found to be proceeding satisfactorily.	

(73989) W4141—463. 400,000. 9/14. H.&J.Ltd. Forms/C. 2118/10.

Army Form C. 2118.

Instructions regarding War Diaries and Intelligence Summaries are contained in F. S. Regs., Part II. and the Staff Manual respectively. Title pages will be prepared in manuscript.

WAR DIARY
or
INTELLIGENCE SUMMARY.
(Erase heading not required.)

Hour, Date, Place	Summary of Events and Information	Remarks and references to Appendices
July. 13. 1915 PIT HEAD PRIEURE ST PRY	PTES. 3167 HOOLIGAN, 4416 O'KEEFE 5393 BARRY, 5290 COLLINS 6742 KENNY and 4957 DONOVAN, of the 2ND BN R. MUNSTER FUSILIERS reported for duty with the SECTION today. GW	
July 14. 1915 FOUQUIERES.	Visited Headquarters NORTHUMBERLAND HUSSARS where party from SANITARY SECTION was at work. Found work of pumping sump pit proceeding satisfactorily.	
VAUDRICOURT	Visited VAUDRICOURT where squad from SANITARY SECTION at work, dealing with manure middens. Found work proceeding satisfactorily. 3 carts being employed. ~~[illegible]~~ Examined R SERGT LACEY DIV. HDQRS STAFF suffering from an acute attack of diarrhoea and had him evacuated to No 3 FIELD AMBULANCE. Later visited village with LIEUT ~~[illegible]~~ Strain RAMC to take samples of water for analysis. Two samples taken from wells in village where water carts are filled.	
BETHUNE	Visited BETHUNE and inspected billet of 2ND BN K.R.R.CORPS. at the Orphanage. The rooms at this billet were being cleansed and were in fair condition sanitarily. Latrine pails in use and in order but insufficient in number. 10 additional pails being required. Saw O.C. and M.O. i/c and discussed with him points requiring attention e.g. supply of pails, removal and disposal of contents etc. Ablutionary arrangements were being attended to. Part of the cellar of this building was again flooded with somewhat offensive liquid but as billets are occupied at this side of the building there is no immediate hurry for its removal. Visited and inspected billets of 2ND BN R. SUSSEX REGT in RUE DE LA GARE. Those inspected were generally in a fair condition. Saw Company	

(73989) W4141—463. 400,000. 9/14. H.&J.Ltd. Forms/C. 2118/10.

Instructions regarding War Diaries and Intelligence Summaries are contained in F. S. Regs., Part II. and the Staff Manual respectively. Title pages will be prepared in manuscript.

WAR DIARY
or
INTELLIGENCE SUMMARY.
(Erase heading not required.)

Army Form C. 2118.

Hour, Date, Place	Summary of Events and Information	Remarks and references to Appendices
July 14 1915 BETHUNE	Officers in reference to minor matters. Called on Town Commandant in reference to his telegram re payment for cart hired for use of SANITARY SECTION and pointed out to his clerk that steps had already been taken to settle cartage % of SECTION but owner refused payment until his cart was returned. The cart is at present being used by S.O. 2ND DIVISION. 13158 PTE BARWELL, 13478 PTE ROBERTS of 1st BN S. WALES BORDERS and 7644 PTE LOCKE, 4th R WELSH FUSRS were today detailed to report for Sanitary duty with 1st DIV. HQRS.	
July 15 1915 FOUQUIERES	Sent squad from SECTION to continue work of pumping out large sump at Headquarters NORTHUMBERLAND HUSSARS. Visited Hdqrs and found work proceeding satisfactorily but somewhat impeded by heavy rain. Inspected horse lines of 1st DIVISIONAL TRAIN finding conditions on the whole fairly good.	
BETHUNE	Sent party from SECTION to BETHUNE to do any necessary work at billets of 9th KINGS LIVERPOOL REGT. Visited BETHUNE and inspected in detail billets of this unit finding them for the most part unsatisfactory and in several cases insanitary. Unable to see M.O. Reported to A.D.M.S. on my return generally and specially in respect of billet occupied by No 2 PLATOON, which was in my opinion unfit for occupation, a foul stable and closet ventilating into billet. Accompanied A.D.M.S. in his inspection of this billet later and to Co. of unit re evacuation of billet. Visited Orphanage occupied as billet by 2ND BN K.R.R.C. finding food and other refuse being dumped into pits used for contents of pails instead of being burned in incinerator. 2180 ACTING L/CPL WHITE today rejoined SECTION from duty with 2ND BN K.R.R.C. (and reverts to his permanent rank). 1566 PTE ROBINSON (R.A.M.C.) today joined section from 1st D.S.C.	

(73989) W4141—463. 400,000. 9/14. H.&J.Ltd. Forms/C. 2118/10.

Instructions regarding War Diaries and Intelligence Summaries are contained in F. S. Regs., Part II. and the Staff Manual respectively. Title pages will be prepared in manuscript.

WAR DIARY
or
INTELLIGENCE SUMMARY.
(*Erase heading not required.*)

Army Form C. 2118.

Hour, Date, Place	Summary of Events and Information	Remarks and references to Appendices
July 16. 1915 VERQUIGNEUL	Sent Squad from SECTION to VERQUIGNEUL to clean up billets and surroundings of 26TH BDE RFA Amm Col and HDQRS. 26th BDE RFA. Visited locality and found work proceeding satisfactorily, latrines, incinerators, middens covered and roads cleansed.	
FOUQUIERES	Sent Squad from SECTION to continue work at HDQRS NORTHUMBERLAND HUSSARS of removing contents of large sump. Visited locality and obtained Cart for use of SECTION from OC DIV. TRAIN.	
BETHUNE	Sent Squad from SECTION to BETHUNE to continue work of cleaning up billets & surroundings of 9th BN KINGS LIVERPOOL REGT (Rue Faubourg d'Arras). Visited locality and saw O.C. and M.O. i/c unit and with latter visited billet occupied by A.Co. No 2 PLATOON part of which should if possible be evacuated. Reported to ADMS on return. Obtained fatigue party of 50 men from Co. to assist Sanitary Squad.	
	Visited Orphanage occupied by 2ND BN K.R.R. CORPS where Section were also at work and had erected an incinerator and dug refuse pit to prevent refuse being deposited as was found yesterday in improper places. Saw M.O. to request him to assist in preventing further objectionable practices of this nature which he promised to do	
PITHEAD PRIEURE ST-PRY	Received 25 latrine pails from DADOS 1st DIV. Sent 15 pails to 1st BN L.N. LANCASHIRE REGT and 10 pails to 2ND BN K.R.R. CORPS at ORPHANAGE BETHUNE	
	Consulted by ADMS as to number of pails required for use by Battalions in proposed new scheme for latrine system.	Ptes 13402 INNES 10575 STAPLETON 10591 DAVIES 15146 MURPHY and 13447 BRADY of the 1st Bn SOUTH WALES BORDERERS today joined the Section
	Obtained 845 francs from Field Cashier to pay SECTION	GL

(73989) W4141—463. 400,000. 9/14. H.&J.Ltd. Forms/C. 2118/10.

WAR DIARY
or
INTELLIGENCE SUMMARY.
(*Erase heading not required.*)

Instructions regarding War Diaries and Intelligence Summaries are contained in F. S. Regs., Part II. and the Staff Manual respectively. Title pages will be prepared in manuscript.

Army Form C. 2118.

Hour, Date, Place	Summary of Events and Information	Remarks and references to Appendices
17 July 1915 VERQUIGNEUL SAILLY LABOURSE	Sent Squad from SANITARY SQUAD to VERQUIGNEUL and SAILLY LABOURSE to continue work of ~~cleaning~~ dealing with flooded manure middens. Visited locality and found work progressing satisfactorily. Saw M.O. i/c 1st Bn SOUTH WALES BORDERERS and discussed steps to be taken to deal with ~~the~~ Sanitary state of the village which has been much improved.	
LABOURSE	Visited LABOURSE and inspected billets of 1st NORTHAMPTON REGT finding two of the billets, those occupied by D Co PLATOON 15 and A Co PLATOON 4 unfit for habitation. Saw M.O. i/c and Company Officer and advised immediate evacuation. There were other unsatisfactory features of the sanitary state of these billets and surroundings to which the attention of the M.O. i/c was drawn e.g. absence of incinerators, state of manure middens, cleanliness of roadway and approach etc. to all of which matters he promised to give his attention.	
	Visited and inspected Chateau, Hdqrs and surroundings of 1st DIV. ART. and saw BRIGADE MAJOR with whom I inspected the buildings and surroundings. The place was swarming with flies largely due to neglect on part of those responsible for maintaining cleanliness. Arranged to send an experienced man from the SECTION to spray out kitchen and other parts of buildings, and to supervise and instruct men responsible for maintaining cleanliness there.	
FOUQUIERES.	Sent Squad to continue work of emptying out sump at Hdqrs of NORTHUMBERLAND HUSSARS. Visited Hdqrs & saw C.O. and found work was [illegible] through lack of sufficient carts. Obtained 2 carts through French Mission and one from O.C. Unit. Arranged for 4 carts and horses to be at work tomorrow to complete job if possible.	
PITHEAD PRIEURE St PRY	Fly traps issued to 25th BRIGADE R.F.A. Hdqrs and to NORTHUMBERLAND HUSSARS.	
	Reported to A.D.M.S. condition of billets of 1st NORTHAMPTON REGT.	

Instructions regarding War Diaries and Intelligence Summaries are contained in F. S. Regs., Part II. and the Staff Manual respectively. Title pages will be prepared in manuscript.

WAR DIARY
or
INTELLIGENCE SUMMARY.
(Erase heading not required.)

Army Form C. 2118.

Hour, Date, Place	Summary of Events and Information	Remarks and references to Appendices
17 July. 1915 PITHEAD	5018 PTE GEDDES 4416 PTE O'KEEFE 4857 PTE DONOVAN, 6742 PTE KENNY 5290 PTE COLLINS 3167 PTE HOOLIGAN of the 2ND BN R MUNSTER FUSRS and 13402 PTE INNES of the 1ST BN S. WALES BORDERERS were today detailed to report to the O.C. 2ND BN R MUNSTER FUSILIERS for Sanitary duty.	
18 July 1915 SAILLY LABOURSE	Sent Squad to SAILLY LABOURSE to continue work of emptying flooded manure middens. Visited locality finding work proceeding somewhat slowly. Visited Mayor's House to pay claim for cart damaged while being used by SECTION. Mayor absent.	
LABOURSE	Visited Hdqrs of 1ST DIV ART and saw BRIGADE MAJOR with reference to work being performed by Sanitary Squad of his unit under the supervision of a competent N.C.O. from the SANITARY SECTION	
FOUQUIERES	Visited and inspected FOUQUIERES and the Hdqrs NORTHUMBERLAND HUSSARS finding work on this units Hdqrs proceeding satisfactorily.	
VERQUIN LABEUVRIERE VERQUIGNEUL LABOURSE	Visited VERQUIN, LABEUVRIERE, VERQUIGNEUL finding conditions sanatorily fairly satisfactory. Visited Hdqrs 1ST NORTHAMPTON REGT at LABOURSE and saw M.O. i/c who informed me that the two insanitary billets had been evacuated and the other matters to which his attention had been [illegible] were dealt with as suggested.	
PITHEAD	SANITARY SECTION had half day off duty 2155 L.CPL TETLOW rejoined the Section from leave to England	

(73989) W4141—463. 400,000. 9/14. H.&J.Ltd. Forms/C. 2118/10.

Instructions regarding War Diaries and Intelligence Summaries are contained in F. S. Regs., Part II. and the Staff Manual respectively. Title pages will be prepared in manuscript.

WAR DIARY
or
INTELLIGENCE SUMMARY.
(Erase heading not required.)

Army Form C. 2118.

Hour, Date, Place	Summary of Events and Information	Remarks and references to Appendices
19 July 1915 · SAILLY LABOURSE	Sent Squad from SANITARY SECTION to SAILLY LABOURSE to continue pumping out middens there. Visited locality, finding work proceeding somewhat slowly. Sent on [illegible] cart to [illegible]. Inspected Chateau and [illegible], Hdqrs 2ND BRIGADE finding conditions unsatisfactory, refuse manure etc lying about. Inspected Transport lines of ROYAL MUNSTER FUSILIERS – Satisfactory.	
	Saw O.C. Transport ROYAL MUNSTER FUSILIERS as to supplying [illegible] for use of SECTION at SAILLY LABOURSE	
FOUQUIERES	Sent Squad from SECTION to FOUQUIERES to continue work of cleaning out midden at Hdqrs NORTHUMBERLAND HUSSARS. Visited locality finding work proceeding fairly satisfactorily.	
BETHUNE	Sent Squad from SECTION to BETHUNE to continue work in the billeting area. Visited district and arranged for the carrying out by SECTION of paving work & latrines. Work proceeding satisfactorily but cement not procurable at BETHUNE.	
	Called on M. SARIUT at Mairie as to where cement can be obtained. Gave several addresses but stated that it was doubtful if it could be obtained here.	
PITHEAD PRIEURE ST. PRY	SERGT. PARKER reported PTES KEARNES, SNELLING and RIVERS of the SANITARY SECTION for failing to obey orders given them. Investigated case at 9 am tomorrow morning.	[initials]
20. July 1915. SAILLY LABOURSE	Sent Squad from SANITARY SECTION to SAILLY LABOURSE to continue work of pumping out middens there. Visited locality finding work proceeding satisfactorily. Visited CHATEAU Hdqrs 2ND WELSH REGT. The place swarms with flies and there is abundant evidence of neglect on part of previous occupants of the Chateau and grounds of [illegible]	

Instructions regarding War Diaries and Intelligence Summaries are contained in F. S. Regs., Part II. and the Staff Manual respectively. Title pages will be prepared in manuscript.

WAR DIARY
or
INTELLIGENCE SUMMARY.
(*Erase heading not required.*)

Army Form C. 2118.

Hour, Date, Place	Summary of Events and Information	Remarks and references to Appendices
20 July. 1915 SAILLY LABOURSE	region in respect of elementary Sanitary precautions. Inspected Transport Lines of 2nd Bn R MUNSTER FUSRS – Satisfactory	
LA BOURSE	Visited LABOURSE finding Sanitary state of village fairly good. Called on O/c 23RD FIELD Co R E and left supply of fly traps.	
BETHUNE	Sent Squad from SANITARY SECTION to BETHUNE to continue work there at Billets occupied by 1ST DIVISION TROOPS. Visited BETHUNE and paid off a/c's due for hire of carts and for cleaning out cesspool when DIVISION previously occupied town as billeting area. Called on OC SANITARY SECTION 2ND DIVISION re carts now in his possession.	
FOUQUIERES	Sent Squad from SECTION to continue cleaning out of sump at Hdqrs NORTHUMBERLAND HUSSARS. Visited Hdqrs finding work practically completed a very heavy and disagreeable task requiring the assistance of Vidange cart, pump and several carts and horses. Visited and inspected lines of DIVISIONAL CYCLISTS at FOUQUIERES finding conditions sanitary satisfactory except that the pump water in yard of billet was being used for drinking purposes without Sterilisation (Reported to ADMS.) No water cart being available for their use.	
VAUDRICOURT	Called at Hdqrs DIV. RE at VAUDRICOURT to ask for supply of cement and timber for the carrying out of Sanitary work in BETHUNE by Sanitary Section. Informed no cement at present available but that 3 barrels will be supplied when consignment expected arrives. Timber a part of it will be supplied at once.	
PITHEAD PRIEURE ST PRY	Obtained 75 fcs. from Field Cashier to pay an a/c for Sanitary Work at BETHUNE in cleaning out cesspool by Contractor named Sauvage. Investigated charge against PTES KEARNES SNELLING & RIVERS and adjourned consideration till tomorrow.	

Instructions regarding War Diaries and Intelligence Summaries are contained in F. S. Regs., Part II. and the Staff Manual respectively. Title pages will be prepared in manuscript.

WAR DIARY
or
INTELLIGENCE SUMMARY.
(*Erase heading not required.*)

Army Form C. 2118.

Hour, Date, Place	Summary of Events and Information	Remarks and references to Appendices
21ST July 1915 NOYELLES	Sent Squad from Sanitary Section to NOYELLES to clean up billets and surroundings of 1st BN L. NORTH LANCASHIRE REGT and 2ND BDE HDQRS, especially to clean and cover up middens flooded by recent rains. Visited locality finding conditions unsatisfactory. Saw BRIGADE MAJOR and asked for large fatigue party to assist SANITARY SECTION tomorrow. Inspected in detail billets of 1st BN L NORTH LANCASHIRE REGT with MO i/c	
SAILLY LABOURSE	Sent Squad from SANITARY SECTION to SAILLY LABOURSE to continue cleaning up middens etc. assisted by fatigue party of 30 men from 2ND WELCH REGT. Visited locality finding work proceeding satisfactorily. Obtained extra horses and limber from Transport Officer 2ND ROYAL MUNSTER FUSILIERS to assist SECTION	
BETHUNE	Sent party from SANITARY SECTION to BETHUNE to continue work of looking after 1st DIVISION billeting area. Work continued at Orphanage of preparing suitable Sanitary Conveniences for use of troops. Also cleaning up surroundings of COLDSTREAM GUARDS in Rue Faubourg d'Arras and making new drain for removal of waste waters, making new soakage pit etc. Visited BETHUNE and paid 38 francs to Mr Augustin Bugc for carts used by Sanitary Section	
PTHEAD.	Sent Cpl CLAYDON for wood to Hdqrs RE and Cpl MORELAND to BETHUNE to repair piston of drainage cart pump	
22ND July 1915 NOYELLES-LEZ-VERNELLES	Sent Squad from SANITARY SECTION to NOYELLES-LEZ-VERNELLES to continue work of cleaning up billets and surroundings of 1st BN LOYAL NORTH LANCASHIRE REGT and the Hdqrs 2ND INF BRIGADE at Chateau	

Army Form C. 2118.

Instructions regarding War Diaries and Intelligence Summaries are contained in F. S. Regs., Part II. and the Staff Manual respectively. Title pages will be prepared in manuscript.

WAR DIARY
or
INTELLIGENCE SUMMARY.
(*Erase heading not required.*)

Hour, Date, Place	Summary of Events and Information	Remarks and references to Appendices
22 July 1915 NOYELLES-LEZ-VERMELLES	The cellars of the Chateau were filled with filthy water smelling like sewage which had to be pumped out and cellars cleansed and disinfected. Visited NOYELLES finding work proceeding satisfactorily. Saw MO 1/C L. NORTH LANCASHIRE REGT and inspected work already done by the Sanitary Squad at work. Village was heavily shelled and work could only be carried on at intervals	
SAILLY LABOURSE	Sent small party to clean up Chateau du Pres at SAILLY LABOURSE. Horses of 39th BDE RFA stalled there and manure being allowed to accumulate. The Chateau itself and surroundings have been allowed to get into a dirty state. Visited locality finding work proceeding satisfactorily.	
ANNEZIN	Sent Squad from SECTION to ANNEZIN to clean up billets and surroundings of 1ST BLACK WATCH assisted by 50 men of the unit. Visited locality and saw CO. and MO i/c - who promised to give every assistance. Advised MO i/c to evacuate one insanitary billet, where men were sleeping in a cowhouse in which animals (cattle) also were stalled - which he promised to do at once. Found work proceeding satisfactorily	
BETHUNE	Sent party to BETHUNE to continue work of cleaning up billets and surroundings of 1ST BN COLDSTREAM GUARDS and of The LONDON SCOTTISH	
FOUQUIERES	Inspected Hdqrs of NORTHUMBERLAND HUSSARS with ADMS finding work there completed satisfactorily by Squad from SANITARY SECTION	
FOUQUEREUIL	Accompanied ADMS. in his inspection of Brit River Camp near FOUQUEREUIL with reference to suitable site for latrine pails etc	

(73989) W4141—463. 400,000. 9/14. H.&J.Ltd. Forms/C. 2118/10.

Army Form C. 2118.

WAR DIARY
or
INTELLIGENCE SUMMARY.
(*Erase heading not required.*)

Instructions regarding War Diaries and Intelligence Summaries are contained in F. S. Regs., Part II. and the Staff Manual respectively. Title pages will be prepared in manuscript.

Hour, Date, Place	Summary of Events and Information	Remarks and references to Appendices
July 22 1915 PITHEAD	Returning from NOYELLES in small light ambulance car, driver of car ran over a large dog. Car swerved and ran into a house. Car being completely wrecked. S.O. was the only occupant of three injured sustaining slight injuries to hand and knee. Report furnished to A.D.M.S.	
23. July 1915 NOYELLES	Sewr Squad to continue work at NOYELLES assisted by a fatigue party from 1st BN L NORTH LANCASHIRE REGT. Work of pumping cellars at Chateau continued. Also manure middens at billets of 1st BN L N. LANCASHIRE REGT covered etc	
ANNEZIN	Sewr Squad from SANITARY SECTION to continue work of cleaning up billets and surroundings of 1st BN BLACK WATCH at ANNEZIN. Sewage manure middens covered over & drained, incinerators built, roadways and ditches cleaned up. Squad assisted by 50 men of BLACK WATCH	
BETHUNE	Sewr party to BETHUNE to continue work of supervising sanitary state of billeting area there and providing impervious paving for latrines at Orphanage	
PITHEAD	Routine work carried out at Minehead A.D.M.S. arrived back from leave Returned Vidange car and pump with accessories to CORPS H.D.QRS at LA BUISSIERE 2412 PTE DOWNHAM and 2405 PTE DUTTON joined the Section today as reinforcements from the 2ND LONDON SANITARY CO. RAMC T.	

Instructions regarding War Diaries and Intelligence Summaries are contained in F. S. Regs., Part II. and the Staff Manual respectively. Title pages will be prepared in manuscript.

WAR DIARY
or
INTELLIGENCE SUMMARY.
(*Erase heading not required.*)

Army Form C. 2118.

Hour, Date, Place	Summary of Events and Information	Remarks and references to Appendices
24 July 1915 NOYELLES	Sent Squad from SANITARY SECTION to NOYELLES to continue work of clearing up Hdqrs and billets and surroundings of 1st BN L NORTH LANCASHIRE assisted by fatigue party of 30 men from this unit.	
ANNEZIN	Sent Squad from SANITARY SECTION to continue work of clearing up billets and surroundings of 1st BLACK WATCH at ANNEZIN assisted by a fatigue party of 10 men of this unit.	
LABOURSE	Sent Squad from SANITARY SECTION to clean up roadway and surroundings North end of village of LABOURSE	
BETHUNE	Disinfected room at Orphanage BETHUNE after case of Scarlet Fever amongst LONDON SCOTTISH	
PITHEAD	Routine work continued at Minehead and PRIEURE St PRY	
2.30pm PRIEURE St PRY	732 SERGT HATHAWAY proceeded on 7 days leave to England	
	34 fcs 10c paid by CPL MORELAND for various articles purchased in BETHUNE required for use of SECTION. [initials]	
25 July 1915 PITHEAD	Squad from SECTION to clean up 2ND ECHELON HDQRS and surroundings at PRIEURE St PRY	
9.30 am	Kit inspection	
10. am	Section inspected by ADMS	
	1940 CPL WORKMAN and 27456 PTE FOUNTAIN of the 2ND WELCH REGT reported for duty today with Section. 19575 PTE STAPLETON 1st S.WALES BORDERERS today admitted to hospital with injuries to head (how sustained not known)	

(73989) W4141—463. 400,000. 9/14. H.&J.Ltd. Forms/C. 2118/10.

Instructions regarding War Diaries and Intelligence Summaries are contained in F. S. Regs., Part II. and the Staff Manual respectively. Title pages will be prepared in manuscript.

WAR DIARY
or
INTELLIGENCE SUMMARY.
(*Erase heading not required.*)

Army Form C. 2118.

Hour, Date, Place	Summary of Events and Information	Remarks and references to Appendices
25th July 1915 PITHEAD.	Rest of SANITARY SECTION had a holiday	
FONTINELLE FARM FOUQUIERES	Accompanied ADMS on his inspection of CONVALESCENT Co. at FONTENELLE FARM and No 3 FIELD AMBULANCE at FOUQUIERES	
	[initials]	
26. July, 1915. ANNEZIN.	Sent Squad from SANITARY SECTION under SERGT PARKER to continue work of cleaning up billets and surroundings of 2ND BN ROYAL MUNSTER FUSRS. Squad assisted by fatigue party of 20 men from R. MUNSTERS. Visited locality and found work proceeding satisfactorily. The ADMS visited district later and I drew his attention to some matters of an urgent character eg insanitary billets, manure middens blocked culvert in roadway and an offensive slaughterhouse	
LABOURSE	Sent squad from SANITARY SECTION under L CPL HOWES to LABOURSE to clean up roadway at north end of village, which had to be discontinued on Saturday owing to heavy shelling. Visited locality in the evening finding some progress had been made. Called at Hdqrs 5th Bn R. SUSSEX REGT and San Co. and MO i/c. The former stated he could not let me have a fatigue party as his men were being utilised for trench digging, but promised with the MO i/c to assist SECTION all he can. Arranged to send a squad from SECTION tomorrow to clean up billets and surroundings and build incinerators etc. Difficulty is being experienced with some of the inhabitants	

Instructions regarding War Diaries and Intelligence Summaries are contained in F. S. Regs., Part II. and the Staff Manual respectively. Title pages will be prepared in manuscript.

WAR DIARY
or
INTELLIGENCE SUMMARY.
(Erase heading not required.)

Army Form C. 2118.

Hour, Date, Place	Summary of Events and Information	Remarks and references to Appendices
26 July 1915 LABOURSE	of this village as regards Sanitation and I advised M.O. i/c 5th Bn R SUSSEX REGT to see the work which he promised to do at once	
BETHUNE	Visited BETHUNE with A.D.M.S. and inspected work being carried out by SANITARY SECTION at BETHUNE at ORPHANAGE	
PITHEAD	Sent party from SECTION to clean billets and surroundings of 2ND ECHELON. Inspected the work which was being carried out under CORPL WORKMAN and party very satisfactorily.	
	Saw G.O.C. who drew my attention to some nuisances at VERMELLES	
	2523 CPL BISHOP of the SANITARY SECTION was today admitted to hospital.	
27 July 1915 LABOURSE	Sent Squad from Sanitary Section to LABOURSE to continue work of cleaning up roads ditches and surroundings generally of village. Squad under CPL WORKMAN was assisted by fatigue party of 30 men of 5th R SUSSEX REGT and 4 horses and 2 limbers were employed in removing refuse.	
ANNEQUIN	Sent squad from SANITARY SECTION to ANNEQUIN to continue work of cleaning up billets and surroundings of 2ND BN ROYAL MUNSTER FUSILIERS. The squad under SERGT PARKER was assisted by	

Instructions regarding War Diaries and Intelligence Summaries are contained in F. S. Regs., Part II. and the Staff Manual respectively. Title pages will be prepared in manuscript.

WAR DIARY
or
INTELLIGENCE SUMMARY.
(Erase heading not required.)

Army Form C. 2118.

Hour, Date, Place	Summary of Events and Information	Remarks and references to Appendices
27 July 1915 ~~[illegible]~~ ANNEZIN	a fatigue party of 40 men of the ROYAL MUNSTER FUSILIERS Visited district with A.D.M.S. and CAPT STULLET of the MISSION FRANÇAISE and saw Maire Official with reference to a blocked culvert in front of No 2 FIELD AMBULANCE, which is causing a foul accumulation of water in the ditch at side of road. Assistance promised to the SANITARY SECTION in locating source of obstruction who have undertaken to clear obstruction. Also drew officials' attention to the foul state of slaughter house in village. Offal being allowed to accumulate and then when putrid thrown into an adjoining field close to men's billets. Also to the objectionable practice of civilian inhabitants throwing manure and other refuse into places already cleansed by the SANITARY SECTION. To all these matters Maire officials promised attention.	
BETHUNE	Sent party to BETHUNE under CPL TETLOW which cleaned up offensive dumping ground in front of Officers Hospital. Also round billets in Rue Faubourg d'Arras.	
LABUISSIERE	Attended Conference on Sanitation at D.D.M.S. Office at LABUISSIERE presided over by DMS at which representatives 1st 47th and 15th DIVISIONS were present. The sanitation of the billeting areas of the Divisions represented was discussed especially with regard to the disposal of human excreta manure etc and the adoption of a coordinated system for dealing with these matters.	
PITHEAD PRIEURE ST PRY	CORPL CRAYDON and party cleaning up ditches in front of FRENCH MISSION at FOSSE	

Army Form C. 2118.

Instructions regarding War Diaries and Intelligence Summaries are contained in F. S. Regs., Part II. and the Staff Manual respectively. Title pages will be prepared in manuscript.

WAR DIARY
or
INTELLIGENCE SUMMARY.
(Erase heading not required.)

Hour, Date, Place	Summary of Events and Information	Remarks and references to Appendices
28 July 1915 LABOURSE	Sent squad from SANITARY SECTION under Cpl WORKMAN to LABOURSE to continue work there assisted by a fatigue party of 20 men from 5th R SUSSEX REGT. Cleaned up billets and covered in manure middens - No 2 PLATOON A.Co. 16 PLATOON D.Co. and 74th Co RE Hdqrs. Sprayed out Hdqrs and surroundings 1st D.A. Cleaned up roadway and ditches leading to SAILLY LABOURSE and removed all tins and refuse	
ANNEZIN	Sent squad from SECTION under SERGT PARKER to ANNEZIN to continue work there, assisted by fatigue party of 50 men ROYAL MUNSTER FUSRS. Visited area and accompanied BRIGADIER 3RD BRIGADE on his inspection of billets of 2ND BN R. MUNSTER FUSRS. Billets were with the exception of those receiving attention from the SANITARY SECTION generally in fair condition. Section at work cleaning blocked culvert opposite No 2 FIELD AMBULANCE a large quantity of filth being removed and the ditches and roadways cleansed; 4 carts being used for the purpose. Cleaned up field adjoining slaughter house in which offal had been thrown. Cleared out large manure midden at one of A.Co's R MUNSTER FUSRS billets. Inspected lines of No 1 SECTION 1st D.A.C. and saw SERGT MAJOR, no officer being present with reference to the state of his lines which were not as satisfactory as they might be. Advised new incinerator to be built at more suitable site and directed ditch bounding his bivouacs to be cleared	
BETHUNE	Sent party under Cpl MORELAND to clean out ditches and clean up roadway Rue Faubourg St Pry BETHUNE and ditches running alongside	

(73989) W4141—463. 400,000. 9/14. H.&J.Ltd. Forms/C. 2118/10.

Instructions regarding War Diaries and Intelligence Summaries are contained in F. S. Regs., Part II. and the Staff Manual respectively. Title pages will be prepared in manuscript.

WAR DIARY
or
INTELLIGENCE SUMMARY.
(*Erase heading not required*.)

Army Form C. 2118.

Hour, Date, Place	Summary of Events and Information	Remarks and references to Appendices
July [illegible]. 1915 BETHUNE	railway lines. Cpl CLAVDON engaged in making [illegible] seats for [illegible] closets at Orphanage BETHUNE	
PITHEAD	2860 PTE YOUNG, 2459 PTE DAY, 2635 PTE MACK 3127 PTE RATCLIFFE 2709 PTE WILLIAMS and 2424 PTE THOMAS of the 1st BN GLOUCESTER REGT today reported for duty with SECTION	
	2405 PTE DOTTEN of the SECTION was today admitted to hospital.	
July. 29 1915 LABOURSE	Sent squad from SECTION under CPL WORKMAN to continue work at LABOURSE assisted by fatigue party of 30 men from 5th R SUSSEX REGT 4 horses and 2 limbers and horse and cart from R.F.A. Covered in manure middens billets of C COY & D. COY 5th R. SUSSEX. Removed 6 loads manure from 117 BTTY R.F.A waggon lines and covered well lime and earth. Pumped out manure midden 7th Co R.E	
ANNEZIN.	Sent squad from SECTION under SERGT PARKER to ANNEZIN to continue work of cleaning out ditches and culverts [illegible] locality and later accompanied A.D.M.S. and C.R.E. to Mairie to secure cooperation of French Authorities in repairing damaged culvert. Squad carrying out work satisfactorily assisted by fatigue party of 50 men from 2nd BN R MUNSTER FUSRS.	
BETHUNE	Sent party to BETHUNE under CPL MORELAND to continue work of cleaning up ditches and other places requiring attention	
	Sent CPL CLAVDON to BETHUNE to Ecole [illegible] Caserne No 2 Field Ambce in some Carpentry work	

(73989) W4141—463. 400,000. 9/14. H.&J.Ltd. Forms/C. 2118/10.

Instructions regarding War Diaries and Intelligence Summaries are contained in F. S. Regs., Part II. and the Staff Manual respectively. Title pages will be prepared in manuscript.

WAR DIARY
or
INTELLIGENCE SUMMARY.
(Erase heading not required.)

Army Form C. 2118.

Hour, Date, Place	Summary of Events and Information	Remarks and references to Appendices
29 July 1915 PITHEAD.	Sent for Vidange cart to LABUISSIERE and had it sent on to No 2 FIELD AMBULANCE at ANNEZIN to clean out cesspool there. Sent for cement for use of SECTION at BETHUNE. Two barrels obtained and removed to Orphanage. 8871 Pte JONES 15900 Pte THOMAS 1010 Pte HUNT, 15166 Pte MURPHY of the 1st Bn S. WALES BORDERERS, 27456 Pte FOUNTAIN of 2nd WELCH REGT. 3127 Pte RATCLIFFE, 2860 Pte YOUNG 2459 Pte DAY of the 1st GLOUCESTER REGT were detailed to report to OC 1st DIV. AMM-COL for Sanitary Duty. 14576 Pte DAVIES 1st Bn S. WALES BORDERERS was detailed to report to OC 1st DIVISIONAL TRAIN for Sanitary duty. 19575 Pte STAPLETON, 1st S. WALES BORDERERS reported for duty from hospital.	
30 July, 1915 LABOURSE	Sent squad from SANITARY SECTION to LABOURSE to continue work there under CPL WORKMAN assisted by fatigue party 25 men from 5th Bn R SUSSEX REGT. Pumped out and covered in midden Officers billet 23 Field Co RE. Cleaned up archway in front of Transport 2nd Bn K.R.R.C. and covered in manure heap. Removed 4 loads manure – 4 horses and 2 limbers used by squad	
ANNEZIN.	Sent squad from SECTION to ANNEZIN to continue work there assisted by fatigue party of 50 men from 2nd Bn R MUNSTER FUSILIERS. Cleaned up roads at	

(73989) W4141—463. 400,000. 9/14. H.&J.Ltd. Forms/C. 2118/10.

Instructions regarding War Diaries and Intelligence Summaries are contained in F. S. Regs., Part II. and the Staff Manual respectively. Title pages will be prepared in manuscript.

WAR DIARY
or
INTELLIGENCE SUMMARY.
(Erase heading not required.)

Army Form C. 2118.

Hour, Date, Place	Summary of Events and Information	Remarks and references to Appendices
30 July 1915 ANNEZIN	various places in village – removed sludge from ditch. Also cleansed ditch for a considerable length also main thoroughfare – 2 carts used by SECTION	
	Visited district and saw M.O. to R MUNSTER FUSRS. Also accompanied A.D.M.S. in his inspection of billets etc of R MUNSTER FUSRS. Drew attention to neglect at one of billets of R MUNSTER FUSRS in not using incinerator for burning refuse tins etc	
	Vicarage Cart sent to ANNEZIN and used by Squad from SECTION in cleaning out cesspools at Schools there occupied by No 2 FIELD AMBULANCE.	
FOUQUEREUIL	Visited Butte River Camp and arranged for latrines etc to accommodate a Battalion to be encamped there tomorrow. SANITARY SECTION to undertake all necessary Sanitary work.	
BETHUNE	Sent party under Cpl MORELAND to BETHUNE to complete cement work at latrines in Orphanage.	
	Sent Cpl CLAYDON to Sec to some carpentering work for No 2 FIELD AMBULANCE at ECOLES JULES FERRY.	
PITHEAD	11813 Pte GRAHAM 1st Bn SCOTS GUARDS 15359 Pte SMITH 1st Bn SOUTH WALES BORDERERS, 3368 Pte GRAIG and 2969 Pte LIDDLE 1st Bn BLACK WATCH and 1294 Pte COLEMAN of 2ND Bn R. MUNSTER Fus. today reported for duty with the SECTION	[initials]

(73989) W4141—463. 400,000. 9/14. H.&J.Ltd. Forms/C. 2118/10.

Instructions regarding War Diaries and Intelligence Summaries are contained in F. S. Regs., Part II. and the Staff Manual respectively. Title pages will be prepared in manuscript.

WAR DIARY
or
INTELLIGENCE SUMMARY.
(*Erase heading not required.*)

Army Form C. 2118.

Hour, Date, Place	Summary of Events and Information	Remarks and references to Appendices
July 31st 1915 ANNEZIN	Sent Squad from SANITARY SECTION under SERGT PARKER to ANNEZIN to continue work there. Cleansed cesspools at Schools occupied by No 2 FIELD AMBULANCE. Cleaned up roadways ditches etc.	
BRETTE RIVER CAMP (FOUQUEREUIL)	Sent Squad to Brette River Camp under CPL WORKMAN and L/Cpl CLAYDON to prepare camp for reception of troops. Pail latrines erected and seats made by SANITARY SECTION fixed, incinerator for burning excreta and refuse, making grease trap, selecting suitable sites for ablutionary and bathing facilities etc etc. Visited camp and found work progressing satisfactorily.	
BETHUNE	Went to BETHUNE to obtain articles required by SANITARY SECTION in connection with the work at Brette River Camp. Visited BETHUNE and saw M. Sarrut at Mairie with reference to unsanitary state of BOR VOLTAIRE reported to me by A.D.M.S. – Pointed out to M. Sarrut that the continued use of this area as a public tipping place for refuse and filth was a menace to health and asked that steps might be taken by Municipality to put a stop to this nuisance. M. Sarrut promised to arrange for a Gendarme to be placed on Guard and that a cart would be supplied and I promised to arrange for a party from the SANITARY SECTION to clear up this foul mass. Reported to A.D.M.S. result of interview on return. Sent party from SECTION to BETHUNE under CPL ~~WORKMAN~~ MORELAND to complete work of concreting ground at ORPHANAGE for latrine pails. Visited Orphanage finding work proceeding satisfactorily.	
PITHEAD PRIEURE ST PRY	Paid 8 frs for cart hire at ANNEZIN. Also 10 frs for sawdust for use at Brette River Camp. 1294 Pte COLEMAN of 2ND R MUNSTER FUSRS was detailed Enpois for Sanitary duty to O.C. of his unit.	

S

August 1915

1st Division

Summarised but not copied

121/6801

No 13 Sanitary Section

Vol IV

August 15

ams

Army Form C. 2118

Instructions regarding War Diaries and Intelligence Summaries are contained in F. S. Regs., Part II. and the Staff Manual respectively. Title Pages will be prepared in manuscript.

WAR DIARY
or
INTELLIGENCE SUMMARY
(Erase heading not required.)

Place	Date	Hour	Summary of Events and Information	Remarks and references to Appendices
			CONFIDENTIAL. WAR DIARY of LIEUT G Q LENNANE RAMCT OC No 13 SANITARY SECTION FROM 1 AUGUST 1915 TO 31 AUGUST 1915 (VOLUME 5)	

Army Form C. 2118.

Instructions regarding War Diaries and Intelligence Summaries are contained in F. S. Regs., Part II. and the Staff Manual respectively. Title pages will be prepared in manuscript.

WAR DIARY
or
INTELLIGENCE SUMMARY.
(*Erase heading not required.*)

Hour, Date, Place	Summary of Events and Information	Remarks and references to Appendices
AUGUST 1ST 1915 BRETTE RIVER CAMP	Sent squad to BRETTE RIVER CAMP under CPL NORKMAN and LCE CPL TETLOW to build suitable type of incinerators for burning contents of latrine pails. Visited camp and supervised work. Saw C.O. and later BRIGADIER, 2ND BRIGADE and went round camp with them pointing out steps that were being or to be taken to secure sanitation of camp. Later accompanied A.D.M.S and OC. 5TH BN ROYAL SUSSEX REGT in the inspection by A.D.M.S. of work already ~~being~~ carried out.	
VERQUIN.	Accompanied A.D.M.S. in his inspection of sites etc for latrine pails and Excreta Destructors at VERQUIN. Saw Co. and M.O. i/c 2ND BN KINGS ROYAL RIFLE CORPS in reference to details of Sanitation.	
2nd August 1915 (BRETTE RIVER CAMP) GARDEN CITY CAMP	Sent squad from SECTION to GARDEN CITY CAMP and started incinerator for the burning of contents of latrine pails. Saw M.O. i/c who stated that incinerator was not capable of disposing of sufficient quantity of excreta and was giving rise to an	

Instructions regarding War Diaries and Intelligence Summaries are contained in F. S. Regs., Part II. and the Staff Manual respectively. Title pages will be prepared in manuscript.

WAR DIARY
or
INTELLIGENCE SUMMARY.
(*Erase heading not required.*)

Army Form C. 2118.

Hour, Date, Place	Summary of Events and Information	Remarks and references to Appendices
August 2 1915 GARDEN CITY CAMP	effluvium nuisance - the incinerator in question was only built for experimental purposes and appeared to be working quite satisfactorily and no appreciable nuisance was evident although I remained close to the incinerator which had then received the contents of 9 pails for about an hour - reasonable time had not been given for testing incinerator built by Section, before being interfered with. Later in the day the N.C.O. up in charge reported to me that this M.O. had partially demolished the incinerator with the intention, I was informed, of insuring its efficiency and told him that his regimental Sanitary Squad would be able to deal with the matter themselves. Sent a further load of bricks for the making of incinerators and reported matter to A.D.M.S. for instructions. Received orders to take no further action.	
ANNEZIN	Sent Squad from SECTION to ANNEZIN under SERGT PARKER to continue work of cleaning up ditches etc there. Not much progress could be made in cleaning out ditch facing No 2 FIELD AMBULANCE owing to the fact that until stoppage lower downstream is cleared it is impossible, owing to the depth of water.	

Instructions regarding War Diaries and Intelligence Summaries are contained in F. S. Regs., Part II. and the Staff Manual respectively. Title pages will be prepared in manuscript.

WAR DIARY
or
INTELLIGENCE SUMMARY.
(Erase heading not required.)

Army Form C. 2118.

Hour, Date, Place	Summary of Events and Information	Remarks and references to Appendices
August 2. 1915 ANNEZIN	to clear out our portion of this ditch - Referred to A.D.M.S. for instruction	
BETHUNE	Sent Squad from SANITARY SECTION to BETHUNE to empty with vidange cart cesspools at ECOLE JULES FERRY - occupied by No 2 FIELD AMBULANCE. Also lent services of carpenter from SECTION to assist No 2 FIELD AMBULANCE in carrying out some carpentry work.	
VERMELLES	Accompanied Capt THORNE, Hqrs 1st DIV - to VERMELLES and inspected billets there of 1st BN GLOUCESTER REGT, some details of 4TH BN R. WELSH FUSRS, 2ND BN R MUNSTER FUSRS and R.F.A. The Sanitary state of these billets were for the most part very unsatisfactory - there being evidence almost everywhere of neglect of cleanliness and of care in the proper disposal of refuse. In one place close to Medical Inspection room of ROYAL MUNSTER FUSRS in an empty house the floor was being used as a midden. The condition of some of the yards at the rear of some of the Gunners' billets was especially bad. Saw M.O's i/c 1st GLOUCESTER REGT and 2ND R MUNSTER FUSRS and with the former	

(73989) W4141—463. 400,000. 9/14. H.&J.Ltd. Forms/C. 2118/10.

Instructions regarding War Diaries and Intelligence Summaries are contained in F. S. Regs., Part II. and the Staff Manual respectively. Title pages will be prepared in manuscript.

WAR DIARY
or
INTELLIGENCE SUMMARY.
(*Erase heading not required.*)

Army Form C. 2118.

Hour, Date, Place	Summary of Events and Information	Remarks and references to Appendices
August 2. 1915. VERMELLES	inspected in detail this units billets. He agreed generally as to the unsatisfactory state but stated that, which is doubtless correct, his unit had taken over the billets in the unsatisfactory state described above. I suggested to both M.O.s the desirability of at once providing a large fatigue party to remedy the objectionable and insanitary condition of these billets and surroundings. Special report made to A.D.M.S.	
PITHEAD (PRIEURE ST PRY)	Obtained a supply of iron for making incinerators and paid for same	
	4729 Pte POET admitted to hospital	
	732 SERGT HATHAWAY returned to duty from leave from England.	
August 3. 1915 ANNEZIN	Sent Squad under SERGT PARKER to ANNEZIN to erect suitable types of incinerators for burning contents of latrine pails. Two incinerators erected in lines of D A COLUMN.	
BETHUNE	Sent squad under CPL WORKMAN to BETHUNE to clean up refuse tipping place, Boulevard Voltaire, Part of the Squad were engaged	

(73989) W4141—463. 400,000. 9/14. H.&J.Ltd. Forms/C. 2118/10.

Instructions regarding War Diaries and Intelligence Summaries are contained in F. S. Regs., Part II. and the Staff Manual respectively. Title pages will be prepared in manuscript.

WAR DIARY
or
INTELLIGENCE SUMMARY.
(*Erase heading not required.*)

Army Form C. 2118.

Hour, Date, Place	Summary of Events and Information	Remarks and references to Appendices
August 3. 1915 BETHUNE	with Vidange Cart in emptying our cesspool at ECOLE JULES FERRY occupied by No 2 FIELD AMBULANCE. Visited BETHUNE and inspected area occupied by 1ST DIVISION as a billeting area finding condition fairly good. Sent 2 barrels of cement to ORPHANAGE for use of SANITARY SECTION of the 2ND DIVISION and advised by telegram.	
PITHEAD (PRIEURE ST PRY)	Erected special type of incinerator and pail system at rear of SECTION's billet for disposal of contents of latrines by incineration.	
	Routine party at work cleaning up SECTION's billet and surroundings and 2ND ECHELON MESS.	
	Sent food safe made by SECTION to Hdqrs 5TH BN R SUSSEX REGT at GARDEN CITY. Also supply of iron for incinerators.	
	2167 L Cpl MORELAND admitted to Hospital.	
	[signature]	

(73989) W4141—463. 400,000. 9/14. H.&J.Ltd. Forms/C. 2118/10.

Army Form C. 2118.

Instructions regarding War Diaries and Intelligence Summaries are contained in F. S. Regs., Part II. and the Staff Manual respectively. Title pages will be prepared in manuscript.

WAR DIARY
or
INTELLIGENCE SUMMARY.

(*Erase heading not required.*)

Hour, Date, Place	Summary of Events and Information	Remarks and references to Appendices
August 4. 1915 BETHUNE	Sent Squad to BETHUNE to continue work there under Cpl WORKMAN. Visited district finding work of cleaning up tipping place at Boulevard Voltaire proceeding satisfactorily. Part of squad with Vidange cart completed emptying out of cesspools at ECOLE JULES FERRY occupied by No 2 FIELD AMBULANCE.	
	Visited ORPHANAGE and inspected concrete work which had been completed by SECTION at the latrines. Also found work at washing place which had been delayed for lack of cement had been finished. Brick drain requires to be provided to carry away sullage water. Otherwise condition of this billet improved. Saw M.O. i/c 1st BN L. N. LANCASHIRE REGT, the Unit occupying the ORPHANAGE, and discussed with steps to be taken to deal with the disposal of contents of latrine pails.	
ANNEZIN	Accompanied A.D.M.S. to ANNEZIN inspected lines of No 1 SECTION D.A.COLUMN. Conditions were fairly satisfactory except that a better type of incinerator is required. Adjoining ground close to slaughterhouse still very foul.	
	Inspected billets of 1st BN NORTHAMPTON REGT and at one of	

(73989) W4141—463. 400,000. 9/14. H.&J.Ltd. Forms/C. 2118/10.

Army Form C. 2118.

Instructions regarding War Diaries and Intelligence Summaries are contained in F. S. Regs., Part II. and the Staff Manual respectively. Title pages will be prepared in manuscript.

WAR DIARY
or
INTELLIGENCE SUMMARY.

(Erase heading not required.)

Hour, Date, Place	Summary of Events and Information	Remarks and references to Appendices
August 4. 1915 ANNEZIN	these billets found that incinerator was broken down and refuse was lying about and food refuse, tins etc, was being placed in pit without being first incinerated. Attention of CO and M.O. i/c called to this insanitary billet by A.D.M.S.	
	Sent Squad to ANNEZIN under Cpl HOWES to build on lines of 1st D.Amm Col. suitable type of incinerator for burning contents of latrine pails.	
PITHEAD. (PRIEORE ST PRY)	Attended conference of M.O's at A.D.M.S.' office in connection with Sanitation.	
	4729 Pte POET returned from Hospital	
August. 5. 1915 ANNEZIN.	Sent Squad from SECTION to continue work at ANNEZIN under SERGT PARKER and CPL TETLOW to build suitable ~~type~~ types of incinerators on lines of DIV AMM. COLUMN. One beehive type built on lines of No 2 SECTION D.A.C.	
BETHUNE	Sent party to BETHUNE under CPL WORKMAN to continue work there. Emptied cesspool at No 2 FIELD AMBULANCE, ECOLE Jules Ferry	

(73989) W4141—463. 400,000. 9/14. H.&J.Ltd. Forms/C. 2118/10.

Instructions regarding War Diaries and Intelligence Summaries are contained in F. S. Regs., Part II. and the Staff Manual respectively. Title pages will be prepared in manuscript.

WAR DIARY
or
INTELLIGENCE SUMMARY.
(*Erase heading not required.*)

Army Form C. 2118.

Hour, Date, Place	Summary of Events and Information	Remarks and references to Appendices.
August 5. 1915 BETHUNE	and completed urine pit in rear of Sergeants Mess. Contents of cesspools removed to tipping ground and covered in.	
	Work of cleaning up area used as tipping ground at Boulevard Voltaire BETHUNE completed	
PITHEAD (PRIEURÉ ST PRY)	Routine work continued at PITHEAD and surroundings	
	2167 L CPL MORELAND returned from hospital	
August 6. 1915. VERQUIN.	Sent squad of 10 men under Cpl WORKMAN to VERQUIN CROSS ROADS to report to Officer R.E. as a digging party for new incinerators to be erected by R.E.s on VERQUIN. Visited locality with A.D.M.S. and saw Mayor who discussed with A.D.M.S. measures being taken in connection with new proposed Sanitary scheme for this Reserve billeting area	
BETHUNE	Sent party of 6 men under SERGT HATHAWAY to BETHUNE to meet 4 lorries detailed by R.E.s to go to BEUVRY to load bricks required for works at VERQUIN.	

Army Form C. 2118

Instructions regarding War Diaries and Intelligence Summaries are contained in F. S. Regs., Part II. and the Staff Manual respectively. Title Pages will be prepared in manuscript.

WAR DIARY
or
INTELLIGENCE SUMMARY
(Erase heading not required.)

Place	Date	Hour	Summary of Events and Information	Remarks and references to Appendices
VERMELLES	6 8/15	-	Sent party to VERMELLES under SERGT PARKER to supervise Sanitary arrangements for new Soldiers Institute - and other Sanitary conditions in area requiring alteration.	
ANNEZIN	6 8/15	-	Accompanied A.D.M.S. and D.A.D.M.S. to ANNEZIN. Inspected sites for proposed new system of latrines for this reserve billet. Inspected billets of 1st Bn NORTHAMPTON REGT finding Sanitary state of one of A Co's in a very unsatisfactory condition. A.D.M.S. saw C.O. and pointed out defects which the latter promised to have remedied before unit left for trenches.	
PITHEAD PRIEURE ST PRY	6 8/15		Discussed with A.D.M.S. and D.A.D.M.S. steps to be taken to carry out new proposed scheme of Sanitation throughout Division Area. This scheme will include the return of SANITARY SECTION men at present attached to Units to the SECTION. The partition of the Division Area into Sanitary Districts each to be patrolled by a Sanitary Inspector from the SECTION, some of whom will be billetted in their districts. Provision of a pail system throughout Division Area and for the erection of special types of incinerators for burning contents of latrine pails.	
VERMELLES	7 8/15	-	Sent squad from SANITARY SECTION under SERGT PARKER to VERMELLES. Filled in deep well at SOUTH WALES BORDERERS billet for Cookers. Cleared away manure from yard covered greater part of yard with fresh earth and chloride of lime.	

Army Form C. 2118

Instructions regarding War Diaries and Intelligence Summaries are contained in F. S. Regs., Part II. and the Staff Manual respectively. Title Pages will be prepared in manuscript.

WAR DIARY
or
INTELLIGENCE SUMMARY
(Erase heading not required.)

Place	Date	Hour	Summary of Events and Information	Remarks and references to Appendices
VERQUIN	7/8/15	✓	Sent squad from SANITARY SECTION to VERQUIN to assist Sappers in the building of incinerators for burning contents of latrine pails.	
ANNEZIN	7/8/15	✓	Sent squad from SECTION to ANNEZIN under SERGT HATHAWAY to build incinerators for ~~to~~ burning contents of latrine pails in lines of DIVISION AMMUNITION COLUMN. Accompanied A.D.M.S. in his inspection of billets of 1ST BN BLACK WATCH and saw M.O. i/c and ADJUTANT and discussed steps to be taken to deal with sanitation of billets. Arranged for 6 latrine pails to be supplied for Officers latrines. Inspected Sections 2 and 3 of DIV. AMM. COL. finding incinerators had been erected by SANITARY SECTION suitable for dealing with excreta.	
VERQUIGNEUL	7/8/15		Inspected billets of No 2 SIEGE BATTERY R.G.A and No 2 MOTOR MACHINE GUN SECTION at VERQUIGNEUL, finding condition very unsatisfactory. Saw O/C's in charge of both units and pointed out necessary steps to be taken to clean up billets and surroundings. Arranged to supply assistance from SANITARY SECTION in the way of brooms, sprays disinfectants etc. O/C's of both units promised to take necessary steps.	
LABOURSE	7/8/15	-	Inspected LABOURSE district and found that at South end of village the transport lines of 2ND BN KINGS ROYAL RIFLE CORPS and surroundings was in a very dirty state. Arranged to send squad from SANITARY SECTION to clean up. Inspected site for proposed brick water-trough at LABOURSE and called on BRIGADE MAJOR I.D.A. Pointed out that the R.E's were the proper people to carry out the work and that SANITARY SECTION would assist as far as possible. [initials] WEATHER WARM and CLOUDY	

Instructions regarding War Diaries and Intelligence Summaries are contained in F. S. Regs., Part II. and the Staff Manual respectively. Title Pages will be prepared in manuscript.

WAR DIARY
or
INTELLIGENCE SUMMARY
(Erase heading not required.)

Army Form C. 2118

Place	Date	Hour	Summary of Events and Information	Remarks and references to Appendices
VERQUIN.	8 8/15	✓	Sent Squad from SANITARY SECTION to VERQUIN to assist R.E in erecting new permanent incinerators. Visited area finding work proceeding satisfactorily	
NOYELLES	8 8/15	✓	Visited NOYELLES in response to complaint of C.O. 2ND BN R MUNSTER FUSILIERS that billets taken over by his unit from 1st BN R. WELSH FUSILIERS were left in a very dirty state. Found on inspection that billets had been cleaned up since receipt of message but one billet had not been touched so as to allow of condition being inspected by SANITARY OFFICER. The surroundings of this billet were in a very filthy state. Offensive refuse, tins, food, etc lying about and attracting swarms of flies. Reported to A.D.M.S. on return. Called at Hdqrs 3RD BRIGADE with reference to statement that S.O. had authorised collection of manure by 26TH BRIGADE R.F.A to lie close to Chateau grounds. Saw Staff Captain and informed him no such authority given.	
LABOURSE	8 8/15	✓	Inspected billet of 2ND BN KINGS ROYAL RIFLE CORPS in Schools at LABOURSE and found ~~that~~ upper attic occupied by 60 men was not sufficiently ventilated. Reported to A.D.M.S. on return and suggested that at a small cost this very excellent billet could be greatly improved	
PITHEAD RIEURE ST PRY	8 8/15		11813 Pte GRAHAM 1st BN SCOTS GUARDS attached to SANITARY SECTION absent without leave found by M.M.P drunk at 7pm in vicinity of BETHUNE on evening of 7TH instant was brought back under escort.	

[signature]

Army Form C. 2118

Instructions regarding War Diaries and Intelligence Summaries are contained in F. S. Regs., Part II. and the Staff Manual respectively. Title Pages will be prepared in manuscript.

WAR DIARY
or
INTELLIGENCE SUMMARY
(Erase heading not required.)

Place	Date	Hour	Summary of Events and Information	Remarks and references to Appendices
VERQUIN	9/8/15	7 a.m.	Sent squad from SANITARY SECTION under SERGT HATHAWAY to clean out ditch at South entry to VERQUIN. Squad from SECTION under CPL WORKMAN sent to VERQUIN to assist Sappers in building special incinerators. Visited VERQUIN and inspected billets of 1st BN CAMERON HIGHLANDERS with special reference to arrangements for the establishment of a permanent pail latrine system for the whole of the billets. Inspected part of the billets of 1st BN SCOTS GUARDS and saw M.O. i/c and arranged to complete inspection of these billets tomorrow with view to the establishment of a permanent system of pail latrines.	
BETHUNE	9/8/15		Sent CPL MORELAND to BETHUNE to report to CAPT IRVINE R.A.M.C. for duty in connection with the arrangements for providing a pail system and suitable incinerators for use of the Units billeted there. Sent in seats made by SANITARY SECTION for pail latrine system at ORPHANAGE BETHUNE.	
PITHEAD PRIEURE (ST PRY)	9/8/15		Arranged with A.D.M.S. for the proposed Sanitary scheme of partition of Division Area into 5 Sanitary Districts, each to be patrolled by a Sanitary Inspector from the SANITARY SECTION. The scheme includes provision of a latrine pail system and a suitable type of incinerator for burning contents of pails. Sanitary Inspectors near firing line to live in their districts or close thereto.	

Army Form C. 2118

Instructions regarding War Diaries and Intelligence Summaries are contained in F. S. Regs., Part II. and the Staff Manual respectively. Title Pages will be prepared in manuscript.

WAR DIARY
or
INTELLIGENCE SUMMARY
(Erase heading not required.)

Place	Date	Hour	Summary of Events and Information	Remarks and references to Appendices
PITHEAD (PRIEURE) ST PRY	9/8/15	✓	The groupings of districts is as follows:—	
			No 1 ANNEZIN and BETHUNE — LCE CPL MORELAND	
			No. 2 GARDEN CITY and FOUQUIERES — LCE CPL TETLOW	
			No 3. VERQUIN and VAUDRICOURT — LCE CPL CLAYDON	
			No 4 LABOURSE, SAILLY LABOURSE and VERQUIGNEUL } Lce Cpl Jenkins	
			No 5 ANNEQUIN, CAMBRIN NOYELLES & VERMELLES } LCE SERGT PARKER	
			2138 PTE SNELLING rejoined SECTION from leave of absence from England	
			[initials]	
VERQUIN	10/8/15	7am	Sent Squad to VERQUIN under CPL WORKMAN to assist sappers in bricklaying work for new incinerators.	
			Visited and completed inspection of billets of 1st BN SCOTS GUARDS on VERQUIN	

Army Form C. 2118

Instructions regarding War Diaries and Intelligence Summaries are contained in F. S. Regs., Part II. and the Staff Manual respectively. Title Pages will be prepared in manuscript.

WAR DIARY
or
INTELLIGENCE SUMMARY
(Erase heading not required.)

Place	Date	Hour	Summary of Events and Information	Remarks and references to Appendices
VERQUIN	10/8/15		and supervised preparations for the carrying out of pail latrine system there	
VERQUIGNEUL	10/8/15		Sent party to VERQUIGNEUL under L Cpl HOWES to continue work of treating manure midden at billet of No 2 MOTOR MACHINE GUN SECTION. Midden pumped out, manure removed to fields and earth and lime covering applied. Party assisted by fatigue party of 10 men from Unit.	
BETHUNE	10/8/15		Lce Cpl MORELAND sent to BETHUNE to work under orders of CAPT IRVINE. RAMC Party sent to look after condition of manure tipping ground off PRIEURE ST PRY ROAD	
GARDEN CITY	10/8/15		Party under Lce Cpl TETLOW sent to GARDEN CITY to assist LONDON SCOTTISH in carrying out Sanitation of Camp	
PITHEAD (PRIEURE ST PRY)	10/8/15		Load of lime, and fly traps sent to 2ND BN R MUNSTER FUSILIERS at NOYELLES 11813 PTE GRAHAM remanded for attendance of witnesses until 9am tomorrow 11894 PTE EDWARDS, 1ST BN SOUTH WALES BORDERERS attached to SECTION was detailed to report to OC. 23RD FIELD CO. R.E. for Sanitary duties 4149 PTE PLANE, 2ND BN R SUSSEX REGT, attached to SECTION was detailed to report to OC. 1ST BN LONDON SCOTTISH for Sanitary duties	

G.H.

Army Form C. 2118

Instructions regarding War Diaries and Intelligence Summaries are contained in F. S. Regs., Part II. and the Staff Manual respectively. Title Pages will be prepared in manuscript.

WAR DIARY
or
INTELLIGENCE SUMMARY
(Erase heading not required.)

Place	Date	Hour	Summary of Events and Information	Remarks and references to Appendices
VERQUIN	11/8/15	7am	Sent squad from SANITARY SECTION under CPL WORKMAN to VERQUIN to continue work with R.E's in erecting incinerators.	
			Sent party under L. CPL. CLAYDON to VERQUIN to prepare sites for latrine pails. Visited district finding work proceeding satisfactorily	
BETHUNE	11/8/15	7am	Sent party under SERGT HATHAWAY to BETHUNE to empty out cesspool in vicinity of No 2 FIELD AMBULANCE with vidange Cart	
BETHUNE and ANNEZIN	11/8/15		Lce Cpl MORELAND sent to BETHUNE and ANNEZIN to continue work under CAPTAIN IRVINE RAMC in selecting etc sites for latrines	
FOUQUIERES GARDEN CITY	11/8/15		Lce Cpl TETLOW sent to FOUQUIERES and GARDEN CITY to assist in Sanitary work there.	
PITHEAD (PRIEURE ST PRY)	11/8/15		Took Summary of evidence for F G C M in charge against 11813 PTE GRAHAM 1ST BN SCOTS GUARDS, attached for duty with SANITARY SECTION and forwarded documents to A.A. & Q.M.G. 1ST DIV.	
			Routine work at PITHEAD and 2ND ECHELON continued.	GJL
VERQUIN	12/8/15	7am	Sent squad under CPL WORKMAN to continue work with R.E's at VERQUIN	
			Sent party under L. CPL. CLAYDON to continue work of preparing sites etc for pail latrines	

Army Form C. 2118

Instructions regarding War Diaries and Intelligence Summaries are contained in F. S. Regs., Part II. and the Staff Manual respectively. Title Pages will be prepared in manuscript.

WAR DIARY
or
INTELLIGENCE SUMMARY
(Erase heading not required.)

Place	Date	Hour	Summary of Events and Information	Remarks and references to Appendices
VERQUIN	12 8/15		Inspected and supervised work being carried out at VERQUIN in connection with new pail latrine system	
VERQUIN BETHUNE ANNEZIN FONTENELLE FARM	12 8/15		Accompanied A.D.M.S. in his inspection of work being carried out by R.E.S. and SANITARY SECTION at VERQUIN, ORPHANAGE BETHUNE, ANNEZIN and FONTENELLE FARM (CONVALESCENT COY)	
PITHEAD	12 8/15		The following men joined the SANITARY SECTION today and have been taken on the attached strength 31 PTE COOK J. 1ST BN GLOSTER REGT 16207 " POOLE T do 14638 " BEER G 1ST BN S. WALES BORDERERS	GH
VERQUIN	13 8/15	7am	Sent party under CORPLS WORKMAN and CLAYDON to continue work at VERQUIN visited district finding work proceeding satisfactorily	
BETHUNE and ANNEZIN	13 8/15		Sent L/CPL MORELAND to BETHUNE and ANNEZIN to continue work there under orders of CAPT IRVINE R.A.M.C.	

Army Form C. 2118

Instructions regarding War Diaries and Intelligence Summaries are contained in F. S. Regs., Part II. and the Staff Manual respectively. Title Pages will be prepared in manuscript.

WAR DIARY
or
INTELLIGENCE SUMMARY
(Erase heading not required.)

Place	Date	Hour	Summary of Events and Information	Remarks and references to Appendices
FOUQUIERES GARDEN CITY	13/8/15		Sent L/Cpl TETLOW to FOUQUIERES and GARDEN CITY to continue work there under orders of the ADMS	
NOYELLES	13/8/15		Sent L/Sergt PARKER to proceed to NOYELLES to make plan of billets there for the preparation and selection of suitable sites for pail latrine system. Plan submitted to DADMS.	
VERQUIGNEUL	13/8/15		Visited and inspected lines of No 2 MOTOR MACHINE GUN SECTION at VERQUIGNEUL and saw C.O. and discussed further steps to be taken to improve sanitation of billets and surroundings. There was undoubtedly a marked improvement since my previous visit a few days ago and C.O. promised to take other steps suggested and asked for necessary equipment from SANITARY SECTION for the purpose, which I promised to give him.	
PITHEAD (PRIEURE ST PRY)			C.O of 1st DIVISIONAL TRAIN called at my office with reference to the arrangements to be carried out to clean up roadways etc in front of refilling points. Arranged that S.O. should clean up that part of roadway from Control post to level crossing at BETHUNE. This agreed to. Routine work carried out at PIT HEAD and surroundings	

GH

Instructions regarding War Diaries and Intelligence Summaries are contained in F. S. Regs., Part II. and the Staff Manual respectively. Title Pages will be prepared in manuscript.

WAR DIARY *or* INTELLIGENCE SUMMARY

(Erase heading not required.)

Army Form C. 2118

Place	Date	Hour	Summary of Events and Information	Remarks and references to Appendices
VERGUIN	14/8/15	7am.	Sent squad from SECTION to assist R.E's at VERGUIN. Squad under CPL WORKMAN	
			Sent squad from SECTION to VERGUIN under L CPL CLAYDON to continue work of preparing sites for latrine pails system.	
VERMELLES	14/8/15		Sent party with lorry to VERMELLES to obtain waste materials for building incinerators under CPL HOWES.	
FOUQUIERES / BETHUNE	14/8/15		Sent squad from SECTION to clean up roadway from Control Post FOUQUIERES to Railway Crossing BETHUNE, under SERGT HATHAWAY.	
ANNEZIN	14/8/15		Detailed L CPL MORELAND and 2 men from SANITARY SECTION as escort for 11113 PTE GRAHAM at F.G.C.M. at ANNEZIN.	
			Attended as prosecutor F.G.C.M. at ANNEZIN for trial of PTE GRAHAM.	
FOUQUIERES GARDEN CITY	14/8/15		Accompanied A.D.M.S. in his inspection of GARDEN CITY at FOUQUIERES. Saw CO and M.O. i/c and with them inspected camp in detail – Satisfactory improvement apparent since my last visit. Most of the sanitary details having been attended to. Visited also No 3 FIELD AMBULANCE finding conditions generally satisfactory.	
			Sent L.CPL. TETLOW to GARDEN CITY and FOUQUIERES to continue work there	
PITHEAD	14/8/15		Routine work continued at PITHEAD	
			Wire fly blinds fitted at G.O.C's.	
			Weather Dry and warm with cool breeze blowing	[initials]

Army Form C. 2118

Instructions regarding War Diaries and Intelligence Summaries are contained in F. S. Regs., Part II. and the Staff Manual respectively. Title Pages will be prepared in manuscript.

WAR DIARY
or
INTELLIGENCE SUMMARY
(Erase heading not required.)

Place	Date	Hour	Summary of Events and Information	Remarks and references to Appendices
VERQUIN	15/8/15	7am	Squad from SECTION sent under CPL WORKMAN to assist R.E's at VERQUIN	
			Sent Squad under L.CPL. CLAYDON to VERQUIN to continue work of preparing sites for permanent latrines incinerators etc	
CAMBRIN & VERMELLES	15/8/15		Sent party with Lorry to CAMBRIN and VERMELLES under L.CPL HOWES to obtain building materials for incinerators etc. Also to bring back 6 barrels of cement from 23RD FIELD CO. RE. at LABOURSE.	
PITHEAD			SECTION had a half holiday.	
			The following N.C.O's and men of the SANITARY SECTION serving with Units rejoined the SECTION today.	
			1646 L.CPL. (Acting CPL) HOBBS from 1st BN CAMERON HIGHRS	
			2207 PTE (Actg L.CPL) BROADHEAD from 2ND BN WELCH REGT	
			1262 do (do) HOLLIMAN from 5th BN R SUSSEX REGT	
			2209 do (do) LAWRENCE from 1st BN L N.LANCASHIRE REGT	
			1565 do (do) PHENNA from 2ND BN R MUNSTER FUSILIERS	
			1408 PTE LUFF from 2ND BN R SUSSEX REGT	
			1613 do READING from 9TH BN. KINGS LIVERPOOL REGT	
				[illegible]
VERQUIN	16/8/15	7am	Sent squad from SECTION under L CPL CLAYDON to VERQUIN to continue work of preparing sites for permanent latrines. Also 4 men under CPL WORKMAN to assist RE's in bricklaying work. Visited VERQUIN finding work proceeding satisfactorily	

Army Form C. 2118

Instructions regarding War Diaries and Intelligence Summaries are contained in F. S. Regs., Part II. and the Staff Manual respectively. Title Pages will be prepared in manuscript.

WAR DIARY
or
INTELLIGENCE SUMMARY
(Erase heading not required.)

Place	Date	Hour	Summary of Events and Information	Remarks and references to Appendices
BETHUNE	16/8/15		Sent party of 3 men under L CPL MORELAND to continue work at BETHUNE under orders of CAPT IRVINE RAMC.	
FOUQUIERES	16/8/15		Sent party of 4 men under L CPL TETLOW to continue work of building incinerators at lines of NORTHUMBERLAND HUSSARS	
LABOURSE	16/8/15		Visited LABOURSE and inspected sites for permanent latrines and suitable incinerators at billets of the Battalion billeted there. Saw M.O. i/c and arranged for the work to be started there tomorrow.	
PITHEAD	16/8/15		Sent party under L. CPL. HOWES to continue work of cleaning up surroundings at PITHEAD, PRIEURE ST PRY and the roadway Faubourg ST PRY BETHUNE.	
			1607 PTE (Acting LCE CPL) MARTINS rejoined SECTION today from Sanitary duty with 1st BN GLOUCESTER REGT	
			16707 PTE POOLE 1st BN GLOUCESTER REGT attached to SECTION was today detailed to report to OC LOWLAND FIELD Co for Sanitary duty.	
			[initials]	
VERQUIN	17/8/15	7am	Sent squad to VERQUIN under CPL WORKMAN to assist R.E's in the erection of special incinerators there	
			Sent squad of 12 men under L CPL CLAYDON to continue work of preparing sites for latrines at VERQUIN. Visited locality finding work proceeding satisfactorily	
BETHUNE ANNEZIN	17/8/15		Sent party under L CPL MORELAND to continue work under orders of CAPT IRVINE RAMC at BETHUNE and ANNEZIN	

Army Form C. 2118

Instructions regarding War Diaries and Intelligence Summaries are contained in F. S. Regs., Part II. and the Staff Manual respectively. Title Pages will be prepared in manuscript.

WAR DIARY
or
INTELLIGENCE SUMMARY
(Erase heading not required.)

Place	Date	Hour	Summary of Events and Information	Remarks and references to Appendices
FOUQUIERES	17/8/15		Sent party under L CPL TETLOW to continue work at lines of NORTHUMBERLAND HUSSARS and other parts of the district	
LABOURSE	17/8/15		Sent party under CPL HOBBS to LABOURSE to prepare sites etc for permanent latrines within billeting area	
ANNEQUIN	17/8/15		Visited ANNEQUIN to inquire into cases of Enteric fever amongst civilian population. Found at a farm house on CAMBRIN ROAD (F 30a 5 8 BETHUNE MAP) a man suffering from Enteric. History of 2 previous members of family having suffered from the disease since January last. Cows kept and milk and butter sold to neighbours. No precautions were being taken to prevent spread of infection. Reported specially to A.D.M.S. on return.	
NOYELLES.	17/8/15		Visited NOYELLES with D.A.D.M.S. and inspected sites etc for permanent latrines	
PITHEAD	17/8/15		1622 PTE (acting L CPL) WRAY today rejoined Section from 1st BN NORTHAMPTON REGT	[initials]
VERQUIN	18/8/15	7am	Sent Squad under L. CPL. CLAYDON to continue work at VERQUIN of preparing sites for latrines. Visited district finding work proceeding as quickly as possible. Some delay resulting from the seats being made by R.E's not being delivered. Sent party under Cpl WORKMAN to VERQUIN to assist R.E in building incinerators	

Army Form C. 2118

Instructions regarding War Diaries and Intelligence Summaries are contained in F. S. Regs., Part II. and the Staff Manual respectively. Title Pages will be prepared in manuscript.

WAR DIARY
or
INTELLIGENCE SUMMARY
(Erase heading not required.)

Place	Date	Hour	Summary of Events and Information	Remarks and references to Appendices
BETHUNE	18/8/15		Sent L. Cpl MORELAND with party to BETHUNE to report for duty under CAPT IRVINE RAMC. Accompanied A.D.M.S. on his inspection of ORPHANAGE, BETHUNE. Found 10th Bn GLOUCESTER REGT had just come in and the CO complained of finding the Sanitary condition of the billet unsatisfactory when he arrived there being only one latrine pail available. That he had had to borrow latrine pails from 1st Bn GLOUCESTER REGT, that rooms were dirty and had no brooms brushes or pails to clean up. Arranged to enquire at once into the question of the pails and to send a squad from SANITARY SECTION with equipment to assist in cleaning up billet etc. Sent party of 6 men under Sergt HATHAWAY and L Cpl HOWES at 2 pm	
FOUQUIERES GARDEN CITY	18/8/15		Sent L. Cpl TETLOW with party to FOUQUIERES and GARDEN CITY to continue work there in connection with latrines etc.	
ANNEQUIN CAMBRIN	18/8/15		Visited ANNEQUIN and CAMBRIN to investigate cases of Typhoid Fever amongst civilian population. Special report to A.D.M.S.	
LABOURSE	18/8/15		Sent Cpl HOBBS to LABOURSE to continue work of laying out sites etc for latrines; incinerators etc.	
PITHEAD	18/8/15		1652 Cpl DAWES reported for duty today from 26th BRIGADE RFA	

Instructions regarding War Diaries and Intelligence Summaries are contained in F. S. Regs., Part II. and the Staff Manual respectively. Title Pages will be prepared in manuscript.

WAR DIARY
or
INTELLIGENCE SUMMARY
(Erase heading not required.)

Army Form C. 2118

Place	Date	Hour	Summary of Events and Information	Remarks and references to Appendices
VERQUIN.	19/8/15	7am	Sent Squad from SANITARY SECTION to VERQUIN under LCPL CLAYDON to continue work. Visited locality finding work proceeding satisfactorily. Party under CPL WORKMAN to VERQUIN to assist R.E's. in building incinerators.	
BETHUNE ANNEZIN	19/8/15		LCPL MORELAND with party of 3 men to BETHUNE and ANNEZIN for duty under CAPT IRVINE RAMC.	
FOUQUIERES GARDEN CITY	19/8/15		L CPL TETLOW to FOUQUIERES and GARDEN CITY with 2 men for duty with CAPT BELL RAMC	
LABOURSE	19/8/15		CPL HOBBS with 6 men to LABOURSE to prepare sites etc for permanent latrines. Visited LABOURSE finding work of preparing sites for latrines and building of incinerators proceeding satisfactorily. Found 6TH BN LONDON REGT, 47TH DIVISION occupying this billeting area of 1ST DIVN. Roads and billets in a dirty state. Saw C.O. and M.O. i/c pointing out that it was the duty of the Unit occupying the billeting area to carry out the Sanitation. The M.O. stated he had no brooms etc so I sent on loan a supply of brooms etc. 1378 CPL Jenkins returned to Section from duty with 25TH BRIGADE R.F.A. 1608 PTE (acting LCPL) Draycott returned to Section from duty with 39TH BRIGADE R.F.A.	[initials]
VERQUIN	20/8/15	7am.	Sent squad to VERQUIN under LCE CPL CLAYDON to continue work of preparing sites etc for permanent latrines. Visited VERQUIN finding work proceeding satisfactorily	

Instructions regarding War Diaries and Intelligence Summaries are contained in F. S. Regs., Part II. and the Staff Manual respectively. Title Pages will be prepared in manuscript.

WAR DIARY
or
INTELLIGENCE SUMMARY
(Erase heading not required.)

Army Form C. 2118

Place	Date	Hour	Summary of Events and Information	Remarks and references to Appendices
BETHUNE and ANNEZIN	20/8/15		L. CPL MORELAND with 3 men to BETHUNE and ANNEZIN for Sanitary duty under CAPT IRVINE RAMC.	
GARDEN CITY	20/8/15		L. CPL TETLOW and 2 men to GARDEN CITY for duty under CAPT BELL RAMC	
LABOURSE	20/8/15		CPL HOBBS with 6 men to LABOURSE to continue work of preparing sites etc for permanent latrines	
			Visited LABOURSE finding work proceeding satisfactorily.	
SAILLY LABOURSE	20/8/15		Visited SAILLY LABOURSE and inspected billeting area for selection of suitable sites for permanent pail latrine system.	
VERQUIN	20/8/15		Accompanied A.D.M.S. in his inspection of works being carried out at VERQUIN.	
SAILLY LABOURSE	20/8/15		Inspected Hdqrs 43RD BRIGADE RFA finding large heap of manure lying in horse lines full of fly larvae. Saw SERGT MAJOR in absence of an officer and told him that such heap of manure should not have been allowed to accumulate and that it must be sprayed with cresol and removed forthwith.	
PITHEAD	20/8/15		2969 PTE LIDDLE 1ST BN BLACK WATCH attached to SANITARY SECTION for duty was today detailed to report to OC LONDON SCOTTISH for Sanitary duty.	

Instructions regarding War Diaries and Intelligence Summaries are contained in F. S. Regs., Part II. and the Staff Manual respectively. Title Pages will be prepared in manuscript.

WAR DIARY
or
INTELLIGENCE SUMMARY
(Erase heading not required.)

Army Form C. 2118

Place	Date	Hour	Summary of Events and Information	Remarks and references to Appendices
BETHUNE ANNEZIN	21/8/15		CPL DAWES with party t BETHUNE and ANNEZIN t continue work under orders of CAPTAIN IRVINE RAMC	
FOUQUIERES			L. CPL TETLOW with party t continue work under orders of CAPTAIN BELL RAMC	
VERQUIN			L CPL CLAYDON with squad from SECTION t VERQUIN t continue work of preparing latrine sites, making urine pits, erecting suitable incinerators etc	
LABOURSE			CPLS HOBBS and JENKINS t LABOURSE with squad t continue work there of laying out sites etc for permanent pail system of latrines.	
SAILLY LABOURSE			SERGT HATHAWAY with party from SECTION pumping manure middens at SAILLY LABOURSE. Visited and inspected SAILLY LABOURSE Saw M.O. i/c 1st BN S WALES BORDERERS and inspected with him suitable sites for permanent pail latrines and incinerators	
LABOURSE			Visited LABOURSE and found work proceeding satisfactorily. Saw ADJUTANT 23RD FIELD Co R.E and suggested he should arrange for latrine seats for his COMPANY t be prepared and the work carried out by his own men t which he agreed	
BETHUNE			Visited ORPHANAGE in reply t request of TOWN COMMANDANT BETHUNE that a complaint of insanitary state of billet has been made. Saw M.O. i/c 8TH ROYAL BERKSHIRE REGT, unit occupying billet and inspected with him the whole of the rooms occupied and the sanitary conveniences. With the exception that some of the rooms and passages and stairs were badly in need of scrubbing, the condition generally of this billet was reasonably satisfactory. Reported verbally t A.D.M.S. on return.	

Army Form C. 2118

Instructions regarding War Diaries and Intelligence Summaries are contained in F. S. Regs., Part II. and the Staff Manual respectively. Title Pages will be prepared in manuscript.

WAR DIARY
or
INTELLIGENCE SUMMARY
(Erase heading not required.)

Place	Date	Hour	Summary of Events and Information	Remarks and references to Appendices
PITHEAD	21/8/15		CPL WORKMAN with squad from SECTION cleaning up roadways billets and surroundings from PITHEAD to BETHUNE.	
			2207 PTE BROADHEAD RAMC awarded 10 days F.P. No. 2 for offence prejudicial to good order and discipline.	
			2167 L CPL MORELAND left for England having been granted 7 days leave of absence	
			Weather Fine and Warm	
VERQUIN.	22/8/15		Sent L CPL CLAYDON with Squad to continue work at VERQUIN.	
			Visited and inspected work being carried out at VERQUIN finding everything satisfactory	
LABOURSE	-		Sent CPL JENKINS with Squad to continue work at LABOURSE	
ANNEZIN			Sent CPL DAWES with party to continue work at ANNEZIN under orders of CAPT IRVINE RAMC	
VERMELLES			Sent lorry to VERMELLES with CPL HOBBS to obtain building materials to continue work of building incinerators etc in the DIVISIONAL AREA.	
SAILLY LABOURSE			Established depot for building materials at SAILLY LABOURSE	
PITHEAD	.		Sent CPL WORKMAN with party to clean up roadways and billeting area in BETHUNE	
			WEATHER Fine and showery at times	

Instructions regarding War Diaries and Intelligence Summaries are contained in F. S. Regs., Part II. and the Staff Manual respectively. Title Pages will be prepared in manuscript.

WAR DIARY
or
INTELLIGENCE SUMMARY
(Erase heading not required.)

Army Form C. 2118

Place	Date	Hour	Summary of Events and Information	Remarks and references to Appendices
VERQUIN	23/8/15		Sent squad from SECTION under L CPL CLAYDON to continue work at VERQUIN.	
LABOURSE			Sent squad under CPL JENKINS to continue work at LABOURSE	
GARDEN CITY			Sent L CPL TETLOW and party to continue work at GARDEN CITY under orders of CAPT BELL RAMC	
BETHUNE ANNEZIN			Sent CPL DAWES with party to continue work at BETHUNE and ANNEZIN under orders of CAPT IRVINE RAMC	
PITHEAD			Obtained on Imprest a/c 200 fcs from FIELD CASHIER	
			Obtained additional supply of cement from REs (6 barrels)	GW
			WEATHER FINE	
VERQUIN	24/8/15		Sent CPL CLAYDON with squad to continue work at VERQUIN	
			Accompanied ADMS in his inspection of works being carried out by SECTION at VERQUIN and LABOURSE. Found work proceeding satisfactory	
LABOURSE			CPLS JENKINS and HOBBS ~~to continue~~ with 8 men to continue work at LABOURSE	
ANNEZIN			CPL DAWES with party of 4 men to ANNEZIN to continue work under orders of CAPTAIN IRVINE RAMC.	
GARDEN CITY CAMP			L CPL TETLOW with 2 men to continue work at GARDEN CITY CAMP	
SAILLY LABOURSE			SERGT HATHAWAY with 4 men and pump to pump out flooded manure middens at billets of 26TH FIELD Co. RE and TRANSPORT of 1ST BN GLOUCESTER REGT.	

Instructions regarding War Diaries and Intelligence Summaries are contained in F. S. Regs., Part II. and the Staff Manual respectively. Title Pages will be prepared in manuscript.

WAR DIARY
or
INTELLIGENCE SUMMARY
(Erase heading not required.)

Army Form C. 2118

Place	Date	Hour	Summary of Events and Information	Remarks and references to Appendices
PITHEAD	24/8/15		CPL WORKMAN with 6 men to continue work of cleaning roadways and surroundings of billets. FAUBOURG ST PRY and BETHUNE 12 barrels cement received from R.E's 60078 PTE PEARCE R.A.M.C. reported himself from No 2 FIELD AMBULANCE and is attached to the SANITARY SECTION for temporary duty 2128 ACTG LCE SERGT PARKER yesterday returned off leave from England WEATHER Fine and Cool.	
VERQUIN.	25/8/15		Sent L.CPL CLAYDON with squad to VERQUIN to continue work there Visited and inspected work being carried out at VERQUIN and supervised the preparation of suitable sites etc for permanent latrines at the minehead for use of troops billeted in this area of the village. Saw OC and M.O. i/c 8TH BN ROYAL BERKSHIRE REGT and discussed steps to be taken to maintain Sanitary State of the billets and surroundings. Lent brooms spray etc to this unit until they have received their own supply Saw M.O. i/c LONDON SCOTTISH with regard to Sanitary State of billets of his Unit and discussed steps to be taken to secure proper precautions for the working of the new incinerator and latrine pail system and other necessary matters Found that 18 pails of the 40 supplied to 1ST BN. LOYAL NORTH LANCASHIRE REGT which billeted at VERQUIN were missing. Wired to M.O. i/c with reference to their whereabouts.	

Army Form C. 2118

Instructions regarding War Diaries and Intelligence Summaries are contained in F. S. Regs., Part II. and the Staff Manual respectively. Title Pages will be prepared in manuscript.

WAR DIARY
or
INTELLIGENCE SUMMARY
(Erase heading not required.)

Place	Date	Hour	Summary of Events and Information	Remarks and references to Appendices
BETHUNE ANNEZIN	25/8/15		Cpl DAWES with party of 4 men to BETHUNE and ANNEZIN to continue work under orders of CAPTAIN IRVINE RAMC.	
GARDEN CITY and FOUQUIERES			L CPL TETLOW with 2 men to GARDEN CITY and FOUQUIERES to continue work under CAPT BELL RAMC	
LABOURSE			CPL JENKINS with Squad from SECTION to LABOURSE to continue work there.	
VERMELLES			CPL HOBBS with party of 4 men and lorry to draw building materials from VERMELLES for use of SANITARY SECTION.	
PITHEAD			CPL WORKMAN with party to continue work of cleaning roads etc on Faubourg St Pry and billeting area BETHUNE Routine work carried out at PITHEAD Weather. Fine and warm	[initials]
VERQUIN	26/8/15		Sent squad from SECTION under L CPL CLAYDON to VERQUIN to continue work there	
LABOURSE			Sent squad to LABOURSE under CPL JENKINS to continue work there Visited and inspected work at VERQUIN and LABOURSE	
BETHUNE ANNEZIN			Sent party under CPL DAWES to ANNEZIN and BETHUNE to continue work there under orders of CAPT IRVINE RAMC	
GARDEN CITY CAMP			Sent party under L CPL TETLOW to continue work at GARDEN CITY CAMP under orders of CAPT BELL RAMC	

Instructions regarding War Diaries and Intelligence Summaries are contained in F. S. Regs., Part II. and the Staff Manual respectively. Title Pages will be prepared in manuscript.

WAR DIARY
or
INTELLIGENCE SUMMARY
(Erase heading not required.)

Army Form C. 2118

Place	Date	Hour	Summary of Events and Information	Remarks and references to Appendices
BETHUNE	26/8/15		Squad under CPL WORKMAN to continue work in billeting area and roadways at BETHUNE	
PITHEAD			Routine work at PITHEAD	
			4800 PTE FORD detailed for special duty at GARDEN CITY CAMP	[initials]
VERQUIN	27/8/15		Sent Squad to VERQUIN under L.CPL CLAYDON to continue work there	
LABOURSE			Squad to LABOURSE to continue work under CPL JENKINS.	
			Visited and inspected work of Sanitation being carried out at VERQUIN and LABOURSE	
BETHUNE } ANNEZIN }			Sent CPL DAWES with party to continue work at BETHUNE and ANNEZIN under orders of CAPT IRVINE RAMC	
GARDEN CITY CAMP			Party under L.CPL. TETLOW to GARDEN CITY CAMP under orders of CAPT BELL RAMC.	
BETHUNE } FOUQUIERES }			Squad under CPL WORKMAN to clean up roadways etc at billeting area BETHUNE and FOUQUIERES.	[initials]
VERQUIN.	28/8/15		Sent Squad under SERGT PARKER and L. CPL CLAYDON to VERQUIN to continue work there. Some delay in finishing latrine sites owing to R.E. not having time to make any more seats. Arranged for timber to be obtained for this purpose and the seats to be made by the SANITARY SECTION.	
			Fatigue party of 12 men and N.C.O. with horse and limber obtained from 8th Bn R BERKSHIRE REGT to assist SANITARY SECTION at VERQUIN.	

Army Form C. 2118

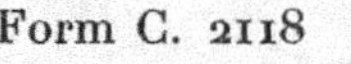

Instructions regarding War Diaries and Intelligence Summaries are contained in F. S. Regs., Part II. and the Staff Manual respectively. Title Pages will be prepared in manuscript.

WAR DIARY
or
INTELLIGENCE SUMMARY
(Erase heading not required.)

Place	Date	Hour	Summary of Events and Information	Remarks and references to Appendices
LABOURSE	28 8/15		Sani Cpl JENKINS to LABOURSE with Squad from SECTION to continue work of preparing and finishing latrine sites etc.	
BETHUNE / ANNEZIN			Cpl DAWES with party to ANNEZIN and BETHUNE to continue work there. Latrine pails brought back to Store from Rue du Faubourg d'Arras. No units occupying billets there.	
FOUQUIERES / GARDEN CITY CAMP			L CPL TETLOW with party to FOUQUIERES and GARDEN CITY CAMP to continue work.	
VERMELLES			CPL HOBBS with party and motor lorry to VERMELLES to obtain bricks etc for SECTION	
PITHEAD			Routine work continued at PITHEAD and surroundings.	
			930 PTE BIGNELL attached to SANITARY SECTION from 2ND BN R SUSSEX REGT, detailed for incinerator duty at BETHUNE and attached for rations and discipline to NO 1 FIELD AMBULANCE	
			60078 PTE PEARCE RAMC temporarily attached to SANITARY SECTION today rejoined his unit No 2 FIELD AMBULANCE	
			G.H.J.	
ANNEQUIN	29 8/15		Visited ANNEQUIN to investigate case of Cerebro Spinal Meningitis in A Co No 2 Platoon 1st Bn GLOUCESTER REGT. Saw M.O. i/c and inspected billet and contacts and made necessary arrangements for isolation, disinfection etc	
VERQUIN			Sani squad from SANITARY SECTION to VERQUIN to continue work there under SERGT PARKER	
			Fatigue party of 12 men + NCO with horse and limber obtained from 5th BN R BERKSHIRE REGT to assist SANITARY SECTION at VERQUIN	

Army Form C. 2118

Instructions regarding War Diaries and Intelligence Summaries are contained in F. S. Regs., Part II. and the Staff Manual respectively. Title Pages will be prepared in manuscript.

WAR DIARY
or
INTELLIGENCE SUMMARY
(Erase heading not required.)

Place	Date	Hour	Summary of Events and Information	Remarks and references to Appendices
ANNEZIN } BETHUNE }	29/8/15		Party to ANNEZIN and BETHUNE under CPL DAWES to continue work.	
LABOURSE			CPL JENKINS with party to LABOURSE to continue work.	
FOUQUIERES } GARDEN CITY CAMP }			L CPL TETLOW with party to FOUQUIERES and GARDEN CITY CAMP to continue work.	
SAILLY LABOURSE			CPL HOBBS with motor lorry to collect timber from R.E and take it to Sawmills BETHUNE for cutting to proper sizes for use of SECTION. Also to deliver buckets to various working parties of SANITARY SECTION.	
PITHEAD			Routine work continued.	
			3849 PTE STRINGER. 1st BN LONDON SCOTTISH notified ENTERIC FEVER	G.J.
VERQUIN.	30/8/15		Senr SERGT PARKER and CPL JENKINS with squad from SANITARY SECTION to VERQUIN to continue work there.	
BETHUNE } ANNEZIN }			Senr CPL DAWES to ANNEZIN and BETHUNE to continue work there with party from SANITARY SECTION	
FOUQUIERES } GARDEN CITY }			L CPL TETLOW to FOUQUIERES and GARDEN CITY CAMP to continue work under orders of CAPT BELL RAMC	
PITHEAD			Routine work continued at PITHEAD and surroundings.	
			CPL HOBBS left today for ENGLAND having been granted leave of absence.	
			1562 CPL DAWES of SANITARY SECTION reported by APM. 2ND DIVN as being found in Estaminet at BETHUNE during prohibited hours. Charge investigated and case adjourned until tomorrow	G.J.

Army Form C. 2118

Instructions regarding War Diaries and Intelligence Summaries are contained in F. S. Regs., Part II. and the Staff Manual respectively. Title Pages will be prepared in manuscript.

WAR DIARY
or
INTELLIGENCE SUMMARY
(Erase heading not required.)

Place	Date	Hour	Summary of Events and Information	Remarks and references to Appendices
VERQUIN	3/8/15		Sergt PARKER and Lce Cpl CLAYDON with squad to VERQUIN to complete work of fixing permanent latrine system there.	
LABOURSE			Cpl JENKINS with squad from SECTION to LABOURSE to continue work of fixing latrines etc there.	
ANNEZIN			Cpl DAWES to ANNEZIN with party from SECTION to continue work of sanitation there	
BETHUNE PRIEURE ST. PRY			Party under Cpl WORKMAN to work round billet, roadway to BETHUNE and 2ND ECHELON HDQRS.	
			Cpl Dawes RAMC. admonished for being found in an estaminet drinking during prohibited hours	
			[initials]	

1st Division

121/7087

S

Sept '15.

Summarised but not copied

No 13. Sanitary Section

Vol V

Sep 1. 15

Army Form C. 2118.

Instructions regarding War Diaries and Intelligence Summaries are contained in F. S. Regs., Part II. and the Staff Manual respectively. Title pages will be prepared in manuscript.

WAR DIARY
or
INTELLIGENCE SUMMARY.

(Erase heading not required.)

Place	Date	Hour	Summary of Events and Information	Remarks and references to Appendices
			WAR DIARY OF CAPT G Q LENNANE RAMCT OC NO 13 SANITARY SECTION FROM SEPTEMBER 1ST TO SEPTEMBER 30TH (VOLUME 6)	

2353 Wt. W2544/1454 700,000 5/15 D. D. & L. A.D.S.S./Forms/C. 2118.

Instructions regarding War Diaries and Intelligence Summaries are contained in F. S. Regs., Part II. and the Staff Manual respectively. Title Pages will be prepared in manuscript.

WAR DIARY
or
INTELLIGENCE SUMMARY
(Erase heading not required.)

Army Form C. 2118

Place	Date	Hour	Summary of Events and Information	Remarks and references to Appendices
AUCHEL	1 9/15		Sent party under L CPL MORELAND to AUCHEL to clean up billets and store for D.A.D.O.S. 1st DIV	
VERQUIN			SERGT PARKER with L CPL CLAYDON and squad from SECTION to VERQUIN to complete work of fixing permanent latrines etc pail system.	
LABOURSE			CPL JENKINS with party to LABOURSE to continue fixing system of permanent pail latrines there	
ANNEZIN			CPL DAWES with party to ANNEZIN to continue work of fixing permanent latrine etc system there.	
GARDEN CITY CAMP			Motor lorry and party supplying bricks for work at GARDEN CITY CAMP	
PITHEAD			CPL WORKMAN and party continuing routine work at Pithead and Rue du Faubourg Sn Pry.	[illegible]
			Strength of Section 28 Attached 26 54	
ANNEZIN	2 9/15		CPL DAWES to ANNEZIN to inspect billets there. Reported that with exception of one billet the Sanitary condition was found to be satisfactory	
LABOURSE			CPL JENKINS with party to LABOURSE to inspect billets there. Reported certain insanitary conditions which he found there and remedied.	
PITHEAD			CPL WORKMAN with squad from SECTION engaged on routine work at PITHEAD and surroundings	[illegible]
			Strength of Section 28 Attached 26 Total 54	

Army Form C. 2118

Instructions regarding War Diaries and Intelligence Summaries are contained in F. S. Regs., Part II. and the Staff Manual respectively. Title Pages will be prepared in manuscript.

WAR DIARY
or
INTELLIGENCE SUMMARY
(Erase heading not required.)

Place	Date	Hour	Summary of Events and Information	Remarks and references to Appendices
PITHEAD PRIEURE ST PRY	3/9/15		1417 SERGT EDWARDS appointed as Acting STAFF SERGEANT	
			SECTION under orders to evacuate billet at PITHEAD and march at 5pm by LABEUVRIERE ROAD west of CLARENCE RIVER to MARLES-LES-MINES to take over billets allotted to them there	
MARLES-LES-MINES			SECTION arrived at MARLES-LES-MINES at 6.30pm with lorry and equipment complete	
			Billet at PITHEAD ~~before~~ evacuated and these and surroundings left in a Sanitary state and an indemnity received from mine manager to the effect that no damage had been committed during the period billets were occupied by SANITARY SECTION	
VERQUIN, FOUQUIERES, GARDEN CITY CAMP, ANNEZIN, BETHUNE, LABOURSE			Sanitary districts as follows, VERQUIN, FOUQUIERES and GARDEN CITY CAMP, ANNEZIN and BETHUNE, and LABOURSE inspected by Sanitary Inspectors from SANITARY SECTION before area evacuated by 1ST DIVISION TROOPS and reported as being in a Sanitary state.	
			STRENGTH of SECTION 28 Attached 26 54	

[signature]

Instructions regarding War Diaries and Intelligence Summaries are contained in F. S. Regs., Part II. and the Staff Manual respectively. Title Pages will be prepared in manuscript.

WAR DIARY
or
INTELLIGENCE SUMMARY
(Erase heading not required.)

Army Form C. 2118

Place	Date	Hour	Summary of Events and Information	Remarks and references to Appendices
MARLES-LES-MINES	4 9/15		Case of Mumps notified in the person of 15792 PTE WILSON 10TH BN GLOSTER REGT. Usual precautions taken. 1 doz Contagious disease notices for placing billets "Out of Bounds" sent to M.O.'s of this Unit. Also a supply to M.O.'s 1st BN BLACK WATCH who notified a case of Scarlet Fever amongst civilian population in the neighbourhood of his Unit's billets.	
			SERGT PARKER with party engaged in erecting incinerators at SECTION billet	
			SERGT HATHAWAY with party fixing permanent pail latrine system for SECTION billet at MARLES	
			CPL WORKMAN with party engaged in cleaning out billet of 2ND ECHELON MESS at MARLES.	
			CPLS DAWES and JENKINS with party cleaning up roadways etc in village of MARLES.	
			Strength of Section 28	
			Attached 27	
			55	[initials]

Army Form C. 2118

Instructions regarding War Diaries and Intelligence Summaries are contained in F. S. Regs., Part II. and the Staff Manual respectively. Title Pages will be prepared in manuscript.

WAR DIARY
or
INTELLIGENCE SUMMARY
(Erase heading not required.)

Place	Date	Hour	Summary of Events and Information	Remarks and references to Appendices
MARLES-LES-MINES	5 9/15		Cleaned up billets and surroundings at MARLES-LES-MINES. 3 horses and carts engaged. Horses lent by TRANSPORT 2ND BN R MUNSTER FUSILIERS and NO 141 FIELD AMBULANCE. Carts obtained from MAIRIE.	
			Routine work at billets carried out.	
GOSNAY			Visited HDQRS 1st DIV at GOSNAY finding Sanitary conditions fairly satisfactory.	
			Strength of Section 26 attached 26 54	GJL
FERFAY	6 9/15		Squad from SECTION under SERGT PARKER to FERFAY to clean up billets and surroundings of 1st INF. BRIGADE UNITS and 1st DIVISIONAL TRAIN. Latrines, brick incinerators etc built. Reported that work done by Sanitary Squad of 1st BN BLACK WATCH would be improved by use of cement. Roadways were cleaned up by 1st BRIGADE UNITS.	GJL
FERFAY AMES LIERES LESPRESSES			Visited area occupied by 1st BRIGADE units, 10th BN GLOUCESTERS at FERFAY 9th BN ROYAL BERKSHIRES at AMES. 1st BN BLACK WATCH at FERFAY 1st BN CAMERON HIGHLANDERS at LIERES 1st BN LONDON SCOTTISH at LESPRESSES finding Sanitary conditions on the whole satisfactory.	
			Saw M.O. 1st BN CAMERON HIGHLANDERS in reference to cleansing of vermin and gave necessary advice as to the procedure to be carried out in his unit. Reported to ADMS on return.	

Instructions regarding War Diaries and Intelligence Summaries are contained in F. S. Regs., Part II. and the Staff Manual respectively. Title Pages will be prepared in manuscript.

WAR DIARY
or
INTELLIGENCE SUMMARY
(Erase heading not required.)

Army Form C. 2118

Place	Date	Hour	Summary of Events and Information	Remarks and references to Appendices
AUCHEL	6 9/15		Squad from SANITARY SECTION under L Cpl MORELAND to AUCHEL to inspect billets – Cleared out billets yards, drains and channels, sprayed and disinfected same. Pits dug for refuse. Covered in latrines etc. Squad assisted by Sanitary Squad of 2ND BN R. MUNSTER FUSILIERS. Streets all swept up in billeting area	
			Visited No 141 FIELD AMBULANCE	
			Saw O.C. 1ST DIVISIONAL TRAIN	
MARLES-LES-MINES			Routine work carried out at MARLES-LES-MINES. Streets cleaned and billets inspected	
			930 PTE BIGNELL, 2ND BN R SUSSEX REGT and 7311 PTE ARCHER 1ST BN GLOUCESTER REGT both attached to the SANITARY SECTION for duty were today detailed to report to O.C No 4 COMPANY 1ST DIVISIONAL TRAIN for Sanitary duty.	
			Strength of Section 28 Attached 24 52	[initials]
ALLOUAGNE	7 9/15		Visited and inspected billets and lines of 1ST D.A.C at ALLOUAGNE finding conditions somewhat unsatisfactory. Saw Co & M.O. & and went round lines with the M.O. pointing out certain insanitary conditions requiring to be remedied – e.g. want of incinerators, unsatisfactory state of latrines etc to which he promised to give his attention	

Instructions regarding War Diaries and Intelligence Summaries are contained in F. S. Regs., Part II. and the Staff Manual respectively. Title Pages will be prepared in manuscript.

WAR DIARY
or
INTELLIGENCE SUMMARY
(Erase heading not required.)

Army Form C. 2118

Place	Date	Hour	Summary of Events and Information	Remarks and references to Appendices
ALLOUAGNE	7 9/15		Visited and inspected lines of No 2 FIELD AMBULANCE finding conditions satisfactory. New pail latrines and incinerators for excreta being erected.	
LOZINGHEM			Visited HQRS 1ST BN L. N. LANCASHIRE REGT at LOZINGHEM and saw M.O. i/c in reference to undue prevalence of illness in the Unit. Reported result of investigation to A.D.M.S. in return	
MARLES-LES-MINES			Party under L CPL TETLOW engaged in erecting seats for latrine pails at lines of MOTOR MACHINE GUN SECTION – assisted by fatigue party from M.M.GUN SECTION.	
			Section engaged in cleaning up roadways and billets and surroundings at MARLES-LES-MINES.	
			11813 PTE GRAHAM, 1ST BN SCOTS GUARDS attached to SANITARY SECTION placed under close arrest for drunkenness and fighting in his billet.	
			2324 PTE NEVILLE RANCT placed under open arrest for fighting in his billet.	
			Strength of Section 28 Attached 24 52	GH
FERFAY	7 9/15		Visited HQRS 1ST BRIGADE at FERFAY. Inspected billets of 1ST BN CAMERON HIGHLANDERS	
LIERES			at LIERES and 10TH BN GLOUCESTER REGT at FERFAY and BLACK WATCH 1ST BN at FERFAY unable to see M.O's i/c of these units but found conditions fairly satisfactory.	
ALLOUAGNE			Visited ALLOUAGNE and inspected lines of LOWLAND FIELD Co which I found to require	

Instructions regarding War Diaries and Intelligence Summaries are contained in F. S. Regs., Part II. and the Staff Manual respectively. Title Pages will be prepared in manuscript.

WAR DIARY
or
INTELLIGENCE SUMMARY
(Erase heading not required.)

Army Form C. 2118

Place	Date	Hour	Summary of Events and Information	Remarks and references to Appendices
ALLOUAGNE	8/9/15		attention. In the absence of Officer i/c San Sergt i/c and pointed out matters requiring immediate attention. Arranged to send squad from SECTION to assist in cleaning up billets and surroundings.	
			Visited and inspected LAUNDRY and disinfecting apparatus at DIVISIONAL TRAIN. Finding conditions fairly satisfactory	
MARLES-LES-MINES			SECTION at work in MARLES cleaning up roadways and billets, and surroundings of 2ND ECHELON MESS. Also lines of MOTOR MACHINE GUN SECTION and MOTOR TRANSPORT AMMUNITION COLUMN.	
			Heard charge against 11713 PTE GRAHAM and adjourned case until tomorrow.	
			3567 PTE CRAIG 1ST BN BLACK WATCH attached to the SECTION for duty was today detailed to report to CAMP COMMANDANT 1ST DIV for Sanitary duty.	
			Strength of Section 28 Attached 23 51	G.L.
ALLOUAGNE	9/9/15		Sent Squad from SANITARY SECTION to ALLOUAGNE under SERGT PARKER and CPL MORELAND to clean up lines of LOWLAND FIELD Co R.E. Erected incinerator for burning refuse 26TH BDE RFA AMM COL lines. Erected incinerator and dug refuse pit under direction of M.O. i/c. Built incinerator on lines of No 1 SECTION 1ST DAC. Squad from SANITARY SECTION were assisted by Sanitary fatigue men from these various units.	

Army Form C. 2118

Instructions regarding War Diaries and Intelligence Summaries are contained in F. S. Regs., Part II. and the Staff Manual respectively. Title Pages will be prepared in manuscript.

WAR DIARY
or
INTELLIGENCE SUMMARY
(Erase heading not required.)

Place	Date	Hour	Summary of Events and Information	Remarks and references to Appendices
ALLOUAGNE	9/9/15		Visited ALLOUAGNE and inspected work being carried out.	
MARLES-LES-MINES			Various parties from the SANITARY SECTION engaged in Sanitary work at MARLES-LES-MINES 2ND ECHELON - BILLETS for MOTOR MACHINE GUN SECTION. Cleaning up roadways and disposing of excreta etc.	
			Strength of Section 28 Attached 23 51	[initials]
PHILOSOPHE	10/9/15		Squad from SANITARY SECTION under L Cpl MORELAND sent to PHILOSOPHE to carry out Sanitary work at advanced dressing station Bearers No 1 FIELD AMBULANCE. Relaying drain channels, cleaning out drains. Disinfecting latrines, clearing refuse from cellars. Cleaning streets, surrounding dugouts and thoroughly disinfecting and spraying all necessary places.	
MARLES-LES-MINES			Party under LCE SERGT PARKER putting up 2 separate pail latrine systems digging, preparing urine pits, making latrine seats and arranging for the disposal of contents of latrine pails for the 15TH BRIGADE AMM Col (250 men) at MARLES-LES-MINES.	
			Routine work continued at MARLES-LES-MINES - roadways. billets of 2ND ECHELON,	

Army Form C. 2118

Instructions regarding War Diaries and Intelligence Summaries are contained in F. S. Regs., Part II. and the Staff Manual respectively. Title Pages will be prepared in manuscript.

WAR DIARY
or
INTELLIGENCE SUMMARY
(Erase heading not required.)

Place	Date	Hour	Summary of Events and Information	Remarks and references to Appendices
MARLES-LES-MINES	10/9/15		MILITARY POLICE and MOTOR MACHINE GUN SECTION cleared. Heard charge against 11813 PTE GRAHAM 1ST BN SCOTS GUARDS attached to No 13 SANITARY SECTION of drunkenness and fighting in his billet. Dismissed charge of drunkenness. Awarded accused 21 days F.P. No. 1 for fighting in his billet. Visited LILLERS to obtain materials, paint, for work of SECTION. Strength of Section 28 Attached 23 51	G.J.
MARLES-LES-MINES	11/9/15		Routine work continued at MARLES-LES-MINES. Various parties from SECTION at work cleaning up roadways, billets and surroundings. Disposing of excreta and refuse – and other useful sanitary work. Making notice boards for Field Ambulance use etc. Received 2 stretchers for use of SANITARY SECTION. Received report from OC SANITARY SECTION 15TH DIV, complaining of condition in which he found latrines and incinerators at VERQUIN – Forwarded report with covering letter to A.D.M.S. for necessary action. 2424 PTE THOMAS 1ST BN GLOUCESTER REGT attached to the SECTION for duty was today admitted to Hospital. Strength of SECTION 28 attached 22 = Total 50.	G.J.

Army Form C. 2118

Instructions regarding War Diaries and Intelligence Summaries are contained in F. S. Regs., Part II. and the Staff Manual respectively. Title Pages will be prepared in manuscript.

WAR DIARY
or
INTELLIGENCE SUMMARY
(Erase heading not required.)

Place	Date	Hour	Summary of Events and Information	Remarks and references to Appendices
LIERES	12/9/15		With A.D.V.S. visited and inspected Transport Lines of 1st Bn CAMERON HIGHLANDERS at LIERES and arranged for the burial of horse suspected to have died from infectious disease	
MAZINGARBE PHILOSOPHE			Accompanied A.D.M.S. to MAZINGARBE to HQRS 3RD INFANTRY BRIGADE and to PHILOSOPHE to inspect Sanitary requirements for Advanced Dressing Station there. Arranged to send a squad from SANITARY SECTION with equipment tomorrow to carry out necessary work.	
MARLES-LES-MINES			Routine work continued at MARLES-LES-MINES Strength of Section ~~28~~ 28 Attached ~~22~~ 22 ~~50~~ 50	G.J.
GOSNAY	13/9/15		Visited and inspected lines of NORTHUMBERLAND HUSSARS at GOSNAY which were fairly satisfactory but required incinerator and more suitable site for latrines. Arranged to send party from SECTION to assist unit in carrying out necessary work	
MARLES-LES-MINES			2208 PTE ALLWRIGHT RAMC.T. SAN. SECTION today admitted to Hospital diagnosed P.U.O. 7326 PTE DUGGAN, E attached to SECTION from 2ND BN R MUNSTER FUSILIERS left on 7 days leave to England Strength of Section 27 Attached 22 49	G.J.

Army Form C. 2118

Instructions regarding War Diaries and Intelligence Summaries are contained in F. S. Regs., Part II. and the Staff Manual respectively. Title Pages will be prepared in manuscript.

WAR DIARY
or
INTELLIGENCE SUMMARY
(Erase heading not required.)

Place	Date	Hour	Summary of Events and Information	Remarks and references to Appendices
ECQUESDECQUES	14 9/15		Sent SGT HATHAWAY and CPL JENKINS to ECQUESDECQUES to clean up billets and surroundings of 2ND BN KINGS ROYAL RIFLE CORPS – Assisted by Sanitary Squad of this Unit built incinerator, dug refuse pit, cleared up roadways and ditches etc etc. Visited locality with A.D.M.S. and found work proceeding satisfactorily	
LAPUGNOY		7 am	Sent party with lorry to LAPUGNOY to receive 60 stretchers and deliver them to Advanced Dressing Station PHILOSOPHE	
		5 30pm	Under instructions of ADMS went to LAPUGNOY RAILWAY SIDING and obtained from O.C Hospital Train 23 stretchers to be delivered in the morning to O.C Advanced Dressing Station PHILOSOPHE	
LOZINGHEM			Visited LOZINGHEM and investigated 2 cases of Enteric Fever reported amongst civil population by M.O. i/c 1ST BN L N LANCASHIRE REGT. Placed both cases occurring in 2 houses "Out of Bounds" to troops.	
MARLES-LES-MINES			Took over medical inspection at request of ADMS. and medically inspected 4 men – 3 reporting sick from 15TH BDE AMM. COL R.G.A and 1 from MOTOR MACHINE GUN SECTION	
			Reported 4800 PTE FORD, 2ND BN R MUNSTER FUSILIERS attached to SANITARY SECTION as an absentee, not having returned from leave to England – to A.P.M	
			Routine work continued at MARLES-LES-MINES.	
			Strength of Section 27 Attached 22 49	[initials]

Instructions regarding War Diaries and Intelligence Summaries are contained in F. S. Regs., Part II. and the Staff Manual respectively. Title Pages will be prepared in manuscript.

Army Form C. 2118

WAR DIARY
or
INTELLIGENCE SUMMARY
(Erase heading not required.)

Place	Date	Hour	Summary of Events and Information	Remarks and references to Appendices
PHILOSOPHE	15 9/15	✓	Sent L CPL MORELAND with motor lorry to deliver 33 Stretchers to M.O. i/c Advanced Dressing Station PHILOSOPHE	
MARLES-LES-MINES			Sent SECTION'S lorry to LILLERS (1ST D.S.C.) to be repaired and obtained loan of lorry from D.A.D.O.S. 1st DIV	
			Parties from SANITARY SECTION engaged in cleaning up billets and surroundings of MOTOR MACHINE GUN SECTION - 15TH BDE AMM COL RGA - 2ND ECHELON billets, roadways etc	
			7400 PTE BOURA RAMC NO 1 FIELD AMBULANCE notified as suffering from Enteric Fever 15679 " BENNETT 10TH BN GLOSTERS " " " Paratyphoid B	
			Medical inspection of 3 men of 15 BDE AMM COL RGA	
			4800 PTE FORD 2ND BN R MUNSTER FUSILIERS attached to SAN SECTION returned to duty from leave to England - 1 day late	
			Strength of Section 27 Attached 22 = 49	[initials]
MARLES-LES-MINES	16 9/15	9am	Medical Inspection - 15TH BDE AMM COL RGA 2 men HDQRS STAFF 1ST DIV. 1 man	
			Adjourned charge of overstaying his leave against PTE FORD of 2ND BN R MUNSTER FUSILIERS attached to SAN SECTION	
			CPL WORKMAN and party cleaning up billets and surroundings of MOTOR MACHINE GUN SECTION	
			SERGT HATHAWAY and party cleaning up billet of SECTION and surroundings and disposing of latrine pail contents etc	
			L CPL HOWES and party at M M POLICE billets	
			L CPL TETLOW and party cleaning up 2ND ECHELON billet and surroundings etc	

Army Form C. 2118

Instructions regarding War Diaries and Intelligence Summaries are contained in F. S. Regs., Part II. and the Staff Manual respectively. Title Pages will be prepared in manuscript.

WAR DIARY
or
INTELLIGENCE SUMMARY
(Erase heading not required.)

Place	Date	Hour	Summary of Events and Information	Remarks and references to Appendices
MARLES-LES-MINES	16 9/15		SERGT PARKER and party cleaning up billets and surroundings of 15 BDE AMM COL RGA and roadways at upper end of MARLES	
			CPL JENKINS and party constructing Sullage pit for surface drainage at MARLES-LES-MINES	
			L. CPL CLAYDON and 2 men engaged in making direction boards etc for Advanced Dressing Station, Regimental Aid Posts etc	
			Strength of Section 27 Attached 22 49	GJ
PHILOSOPHE	17 9/15		Sent L CPL ~~Clarkson~~ MORELAND with Motor ambulance to PHILOSOPHE to deliver notice boards, stretchers etc to M O i/c Advanced Dressing Station	
MARLES-LES-MINES		9am	Medical Inspection	
		2pm	Medical Board at A.D.M.S. office to examine candidates for Commissions	
			SECTION engaged in routine work of cleaning billets roadways etc at MARLES-LES-MINES	
			11670 PTE WILSON of 1ST BN S. WALES BORDERERS attached to SANITARY SECTION reported to A P M as absent without leave	
			4800 PTE FORD of 2ND BN R MUNSTER FUSILIERS attached to SECTION awarded 7 days CC for When on Active Service Overstaying his leave 1 day.	

Army Form C. 2118

Instructions regarding War Diaries and Intelligence Summaries are contained in F. S. Regs., Part II. and the Staff Manual respectively. Title Pages will be prepared in manuscript.

WAR DIARY
or
INTELLIGENCE SUMMARY
(Erase heading not required.)

Place	Date	Hour	Summary of Events and Information	Remarks and references to Appendices
MARLES-LES-MINES	17 9/15		The following 6 men attached to the 2ND BN R MUNSTER FUSRS for Sanitary duty today rejoined SANITARY SECTION 13390 PTE KILROY, 1ST BN S. WALES BORDERERS 15191 " EVANS do 1353 " SMITH 2ND BN WELCH REGT. 6884 " JONES do 10267 " NOLAN do 12014 " STOKES do Strength of Section 27 Attached 28 55	
PHILOSOPHE	19 9/15		Squad of 12 men and 2 NCOs from SANITARY SECTION sent to PHILOSOPHE to carry out necessary Sanitary work at Advanced Dressing Station there. Trench Stretchers, Staffs for notice boards, latrine pails delivered to M.O. i/c.	
FERFAY and BELLERY			Visited FERFAY and BELLERY to investigate outbreak of Mumps in the 10TH BN. GLOSTER REGT. Saw ~~A~~O.C. and M.O. i/c and with the latter medically inspected No 1 COMPANY in which most of the cases occurred. Also inspected MACHINE GUN SECTION, 2 cases, and No 10 PLATOON, No 3 COMPANY at FERFAY. Segregated 5 men as suspects and discussed with M.O. steps to be taken to prevent further spread of disease. Medically inspected 11 Contacts of 10 PLATOON No 3 Co at FERFAY and segregated 1 suspect. Also advised that remaining 10 contacts should be removed from billet and bivouaced. Arranged for disinfection by SANITARY SECTION of all billets and other Sanitary measures. Reported action to A.D.M.S. and suggested further precautionary steps, eg. bivouacing the whole of No 1 Co for his consideration.	
MARLES-LES-MINES			The following men of the 2ND BN ROYAL MUNSTER FUSILIERS attached to the SANITARY	

Army Form C. 2118

Instructions regarding War Diaries and Intelligence Summaries are contained in F. S. Regs., Part II. and the Staff Manual respectively. Title Pages will be prepared in manuscript.

WAR DIARY
or
INTELLIGENCE SUMMARY
(Erase heading not required.)

Place	Date	Hour	Summary of Events and Information	Remarks and references to Appendices
MARLES-LES-MINES	18 9/15		SECTION for duty, today Sent back to their units for Sanitary duty 4800 PTE FORD 4545 " KEHELY 4729 " PORT 5393 " BARRY Strength of Section 27 Attached 24 51	GD
FERFAY BELLERY	19 9/15		On instructions of A.D.M.S. visited FERFAY and BELLERY and medically inspected 10TH BN GLOSTER REGT 3 COMPANIES at FERFAY and 1 COMPANY and MACHINE GUN SECTION at BELLERY with M.O. i/c. Found No 10 PLATOON Contacts and Suspects (14) at FERFAY in bivouacs and apparently free from infection. No 1 COMPANY and MACHINE GUN SECTION at BELLERY bivouaced. Contacts and Suspects in one field and remainder of COMPANY and MACHINE GUN SECTION in another field. All men appeared to be healthy and free from infection. No further cases of MUMPS reported since 17th inst. Reported to A.D.M.S. on return	
AUCHEL			Enquired into case of Enteric Fever reported from Ammunition Park at AUCHEL – Saw OC who promised to send report form to M.O. who reported case to IV CORPS. Report form subsequently forwarded for the purpose	
MARLES-LES-MINES			Received orders to move SANITARY SECTION to VERQUIN by 2 p.m. tomorrow. Orders subsequently cancelled by telephone message from HQRS 1ST DIV. at 10 p.m. Strength of Section 27 Attached 24 = 51	GD

Instructions regarding War Diaries and Intelligence Summaries are contained in F. S. Regs., Part II. and the Staff Manual respectively. Title Pages will be prepared in manuscript.

WAR DIARY
or
INTELLIGENCE SUMMARY
(Erase heading not required.)

Army Form C. 2118

Place	Date	Hour	Summary of Events and Information	Remarks and references to Appendices
FERFAY and BELLERY	20/9/15		Accompanied A.D.M.S. to FERFAY and BELLERY to inspect contacts and suspects from mumps in 10TH BN GLOSTER REGT – Also visited 8TH BN R BERKSHIRE REGT to enquire into case of Enteric Fever notified by M.O. i/c.	
LAPUGNOY			Visited LAPUGNOY and called at MAIRIE to enquire into case of diphtheria in civilian house reported by D.D.M.S. IV CORPS. Was informed at MAIRIE that case was one of fatal Enteric Fever and was shown Death Certificate of French Doctor who attended case. Proceeded to house indicated and saw inmate who answered to name reported by D.D.M.S. who stated she had been well from throat complaint for 15 days past and that no one had died or had suffered from Enteric Fever in her house. Reported to D.D.M.S. on return for further instructions	
MARLES-LES-MINES			Medically examined with A.D.M.S. attached men of SANITARY SECTION as to their physical fitness for service with their respective units.	
			Medical Inspection of sick men, 15 BDE AMM COL. RGA 4 men, MOTOR MACHINE SECTION, 2 men and SANITARY SECTION 1 man.	
			Heard charge against 11670 Pte WILSON, 1st BN SOUTH WALES BORDERERS attached to SANITARY SECTION, of being absent without leave for 23 hours. Awarded prisoner 14 days Field Punishment No 1	
			Heard charge against 14016 Pte BILSON, 1st BN L NORTH LANCASHIRE REGT attached to SANITARY SECTION of being absent without leave 5 hours and of being improperly dressed on Sept 18 1915. awarded 7 days F.P. No 2.	
			Strength of Section 27 Attached 24 51	C.A.P.

Army Form C. 2118

Instructions regarding War Diaries and Intelligence Summaries are contained in F. S. Regs., Part II. and the Staff Manual respectively. Title Pages will be prepared in manuscript.

WAR DIARY
or
INTELLIGENCE SUMMARY
(Erase heading not required.)

Place	Date	Hour	Summary of Events and Information	Remarks and references to Appendices
LAPUGNOY	21/9/15		Visited LAPUGNOY with French Interpreter and obtained further particulars at Mairie as to infected area and number of Homes in the Rue Haute. Placed out of bounds notices on infected houses (5) and later saw M.O. i/c 1st BN NORTHAMPTON REGT part of which unit was occupying this area. Also drew his attention to the fact that I found soldiers of his unit drinking unsterilized water from a village pump. He promised to give the matter his immediate attention. Reported specially to A.D.M.S. on return.	
MARLES-LES-MINES		9am	Medical Inspection 15TH BDE AMM COL RGA 3 men, 2 of whom sent to No 141 FIELD AMBULANCE	
			SANITARY SECTION 1 man.	
			Parties from SANITARY SECTION cleaning up bivouacs and surroundings of 2ND BN KINGS ROYAL RIFLE CORPS and 2ND BN R SUSSEX REGT at MARLES-LES-MINES	
			Routine work carried out	
			Motor Lorry sent to LILLERS for repairs to spring	
			Heard charge against 2709 PTE WILLIAMS, 1ST BN GLOSTER REGT attached to SANITARY SECTION. Awarded 7 days C.C. for smoking on parade	
			1353 PTE SMITH C 2ND BN WELCH REGT attached to SECTION admitted to Hospital	
			Strength of Section 27	
			Attached 23	
			50	[signature]

Army Form C. 2118

Instructions regarding War Diaries and Intelligence Summaries are contained in F. S. Regs., Part II. and the Staff Manual respectively. Title Pages will be prepared in manuscript.

WAR DIARY
or
INTELLIGENCE SUMMARY
(Erase heading not required.)

Place	Date	Hour	Summary of Events and Information	Remarks and references to Appendices
GOSNAY	22 9/15		Visited and inspected with OC. 1st FIELD AMBULANCE sanitary arrangements at GOSNAY. Found sanitary state of this unit excellent.	
VAUDRICOURT			Visited lines of 23RD FIELD Co R.E. at VAUDRICOURT	
VERQUIN			Visited and inspected latrines and incinerators at VERQUIN.	
LAPUGNOY			Party sent to LAPUGNOY under L CPL MORELAND to clean up bivouacs and surroundings of 1ST BN NORTHAMPTONSHIRE REGT and 8TH BN R BERKSHIRE REGT.	
MARLES-LES-MINES		9am	Medical Inspection.	
			7326 PTE DUGGAN 2ND BN R MUNSTER FUSILIERS attached to SANITARY SECTION returned from leave to England	
			Strength of Section 27 Attached 23 50	[initials]
LAPUGNOY	23 9/15		Party under CPL WORKMAN at work at LAPUGNOY cleaning up bivouacs of 1ST BN NORTHAMPTON REGT and 8TH BN R BERKSHIRE REGT.	
MARLES-LES-MINES			SANITARY SECTION under orders to evacuate billets at MARLES LES MINES and march to VERQUIN to take over billets allotted to them there	
			Routine work carried out at MARLES.	
		9am	Medical Inspection	
			Handed over medical and sanitary charge of details of IV CORPS troops viz.	

Army Form C. 2118

Instructions regarding War Diaries and Intelligence Summaries are contained in F. S. Regs., Part II. and the Staff Manual respectively. Title Pages will be prepared in manuscript.

WAR DIARY
or
INTELLIGENCE SUMMARY
(Erase heading not required.)

Place	Date	Hour	Summary of Events and Information	Remarks and references to Appendices
MARLES LES-MINES	23/9/15		15 BDE AMM COL RGA. 1st BDE AMM COL and MOTOR MACHINE GUN SECTION & CAPT WOOD RAMC	
		12 noon	SANITARY SECTION evacuated billets at 12 noon and marched to VERQUIN, where they arrived and took over billets at 3.30pm	
VERQUIN			HDQRS offices cleaned out by SANITARY SECTION assisted by a fatigue party from No 1 FIELD AMBULANCE.	
			Strength of Section 27 attached 23 50	GH
VERQUIN	24/9/15		Received orders to attach 1 NCO and men from the SANITARY SECTION RAMC.T for duty to each of the following	
			No 1 FIELD AMBULANCE at NOEUX-LES-MINES — CPL DAWES; PTES SNELLING, LUFF, REASING, WRAY, WHITE	
			BEARERS No 1 FIELD AMBULANCE at PHILOSOPHE — L SERGT PARKER; PTES HOLLIMAN, PHENNA, KEARNES, BROADHEAD, DRACOTT	
			No 2 FIELD AMBULANCE at VERQUIN — SERGT HATHAWAY; PTES LAWRENCE, NEVILLE, DOWNHAM, MARTIN, RIVERS	
			To The SENIOR CHAPLIN, 1st DIV. — L CPL CLAYDON.	

Instructions regarding War Diaries and Intelligence Summaries are contained in F. S. Regs., Part II. and the Staff Manual respectively. Title Pages will be prepared in manuscript.

WAR DIARY
or
INTELLIGENCE SUMMARY
(Erase heading not required.)

Army Form C. 2118

Place	Date	Hour	Summary of Events and Information	Remarks and references to Appendices
VERQUIN	24/9/15		2208 PTE ALLWRIGHT rejoined SECTION from Hospital today	
			Squad from SANITARY SECTION engaged in cleaning out and disinfecting Schools at VERQUIN for No 2 FIELD AMBULANCE.	
			Routine work continued at VERQUIN.	
			1378 CPL JENKINS of SECTION today admitted to Hospital	
			Strength of Section ~~28~~ 27 Attached ~~25~~ 23 ~~49~~ 50	GJ
NOEUX-LES-MINES MAZINGARBE PHILOSOPHE	25/9/15	5.30am	Accompanied A.D.M.S. to NOEUX-LES-MINES-MAZINGARBE and PHILOSOPHE	
			Sent motor lorry with L CPL MORELAND to collect wounded at PHILOSOPHE and bring them to No 2 FIELD AMBULANCE	
VERQUIN		4.30am	Squad from SECTION at work at 4.30am getting ready lower School at VERQUIN for No 2 FIELD AMBULANCE	
			Party at work cleaning up H.QRS. and surroundings	
			Visited and supervised party from SANITARY SECTION detailed for duty with No 2 FIELD AMBULANCE	
NOEUX-LES-MINES		6pm	Visited NOEUX-LES-MINES at 6pm. and saw O.C. No 1 FIELD AMBULANCE, and reported to D.A.D.M.S. on return	
VERQUIN			On duty at No 2 FIELD AMBULANCE until morning. Supplied 25 blankets from SANITARY SECTION for use of wounded	
			2205 PTE ALLWRIGHT detailed for duty with No 25 SANITARY SECTION. 14TH DIVISION	
			STRENGTH of SECTION 26 attached 23 = 49	GJ

Army Form C. 2118

Instructions regarding War Diaries and Intelligence Summaries are contained in F. S. Regs., Part II. and the Staff Manual respectively. Title Pages will be prepared in manuscript.

WAR DIARY
or
INTELLIGENCE SUMMARY
(Erase heading not required.)

Place	Date	Hour	Summary of Events and Information	Remarks and references to Appendices
PHILOSOPHE	26/9/15		Sent motor lorry with L.CPL MORELAND and load of straw to PHILOSOPHE - and to collect wounded. Two loads of wounded removed to 141 FIELD AMBULANCE at GOSNAY	
			Sent a party of 7 extra men attached to SANITARY SECTION to PHILOSOPHE to report to O.C. BEARERS No 1 FIELD AMBULANCE for Sanitary duty etc.	
VERQUIN			Detailed party of 10 men and N.C.O at request of O.C. No 2 FIELD AMBULANCE to dig graves in VERQUIN churchyard for men who died of wounds in No 2 F Ambulance	
			Visited and supervised work of Sanitary Squad at No 2 FIELD AMBULANCE.	
			On duty as M.O. at No 2 FIELD AMBULANCE at request of O.C. from 3pm until 1.30 am	
NOEUX-LES-MINES			Visited Sanitary Squad at No 1 FIELD AMBULANCE NOEUX-LES-MINES. Saw O.C. who informed me that he required no further assistance at present	
			Strength of Section 26 Attached 23 49	[initials]
PHILOSOPHE	27/9/15		On instructions received from A D M S sent on 3 extra attached men of SANITARY SECTION to PHILOSOPHE for sanitary duty with Advanced Dressing Station	
			Sent motor lorry to remove wounded from PHILOSOPHE Advanced Dressing Station to No 2 FIELD AMBULANCE	
VERQUIN ~~NOEUX-LES-MINES~~			Supervised work of Squad from SANITARY SECTION at No 2 FIELD AMBULANCE	
GOSNAY			On instructions of A D M S reported for duty as M.O with No 141 FIELD AMBULANCE at GOSNAY from 1pm to 6pm	
			Strength of Section 26 attached 23 = 49	[initials]

Army Form C. 2118

Instructions regarding War Diaries and Intelligence Summaries are contained in F. S. Regs., Part II. and the Staff Manual respectively. Title Pages will be prepared in manuscript.

WAR DIARY
or
INTELLIGENCE SUMMARY
(Erase heading not required.)

Place	Date	Hour	Summary of Events and Information	Remarks and references to Appendices
PHILOSOPHE	28/9/15		Sent lorry to PHILOSOPHE for duty with No 1 and 2 FIELD AMBULANCE BEARER party	
VERQUIN			Squad from the SANITARY SECTION at work clearing up schools at VERQUIN after evacuation by No 2 FIELD AMBULANCE in readiness to receive No 1/1, FIELD AMBULANCE advancing from GOSNAY	
			Party of attached men of SANITARY SECTION returned from duty with No 1 and 2 FIELD AMBULANCE BEARERS at PHILOSOPHE and rejoined the SECTION.	
			Routine work continued at VERQUIN	
			Investigated case of Enteric Fever at VERQUIN reported by Mayor - at a house of a civil inhabitant and posted infectious disease notice on the door and arranged for inoculating other members of the family	
			Strength of Section 26 Attached 23 49	
			[signature]	
VERQUIN	29/9/15		SECTION under orders to evacuate billets at VERQUIN and march to NOEUX-LES-MINES to take up billets allotted to them there	
			Routine work continued at VERQUIN up to their time of leaving.	
			SERGT HATHAWAY and 5 men of SANITARY SECTION detailed for duty with No 2 FIELD AMBULANCE rejoined SECTION today	
NOEUX-LES-MINES			The SANITARY SECTION left VERQUIN at 5pm and arrived at NOEUX-LES-MINES at 7pm and occupied billets of No 1/1 FIELD AMBULANCE for the night.	
			1417 Acts Staff Sergt W Edwards placed under arrest for neglect of Duty	

Instructions regarding War Diaries and Intelligence Summaries are contained in F. S. Regs., Part II. and the Staff Manual respectively. Title pages will be prepared in manuscript.

WAR DIARY
or
INTELLIGENCE SUMMARY.
(Erase heading not required.)

Army Form C. 2118.

Place	Date	Hour	Summary of Events and Information	Remarks and references to Appendices
VERQUIN	29/9/15		11940 Cpl Workman 2nd Welch Regt. 14251 Pte Beavan 1st Bn S Wales Borderers 11813 Pte Graham 1st Bn Scots G ds 15359 Smith do 11670 " Wilson 1st Bn S.W. Borderers 14638 " Bees do 13467 " Brady do 4016 Bilson 1st Bn L N Lancs Regt 14191 " Duggan do 15191 " Evans 1st Bn S Wales Borderers were today detailed to report for duty to CAMP COMMANDANT 4TH CORPS for duty with the 4TH CORPS INFANTRY TROOPS DETACHMENT Strength of Section 26 Attached 13 = 39	GJ
NOEUX-LES-MINES	30/9/15		Obtained billets for SECTION with great difficulty owing to number of troops in area. Sent party to clear drain at No 141 FIELD AMBULANCE Tried to obtain baths for 1st DIVISION TROOPS at NOEUX-LES-MINES Saw Director of Mines who after some persuasion granted use of FOSSES No 1 and 3 Twelve Baths. Made arrangements with owner of brewery at Noeux-Les-Mines to supply hot water and approx facilities for the installation of baths in the brewery yards. Bought 21 tubs and obtained use of [illegible] Borrowed tent for No 141 FIELD AMBULANCE and used in addition a corner of the washing-up shed in brewery. This will afford bathing	

2353 Wt W2544/1454 700,000 5/15 D. D. & L. A.D.S.S./Forms/C. 2118.

Army Form C. 2118.

Instructions regarding War Diaries and Intelligence Summaries are contained in F. S. Regs., Part II. and the Staff Manual respectively. Title pages will be prepared in manuscript.

WAR DIARY
or
INTELLIGENCE SUMMARY.
(Erase heading not required.)

Place	Date	Hour	Summary of Events and Information	Remarks and references to Appendices
NOEUX-LES-MINES	30/9/15		accomodation for about 1000 troops daily. Routine work continued at NOEUX-LES-MINES. Strength of Section 26 Attached 13 = 39	GY

2353 Wt. W2544/1454 700,000 5/15 D. D. & L. A.D.S.S./Forms/C. 2118.

Army Form C. 2118.

Instructions regarding War Diaries and Intelligence Summaries are contained in F. S. Regs., Part II. and the Staff Manual respectively. Title Pages will be prepared in manuscript.

WAR DIARY
or
INTELLIGENCE SUMMARY

(Erase heading not required.)

Place	Date	Hour	Summary of Events and Information	Remarks and references to Appendices
NOEUX-LES-MINES	OCTOBER 1915 1 – 6	–	Routine Work. 2108 a/L/cpl Claydon promoted to rank of Corporal from 2nd inst.	
MAZINGARBE	7 – 8	–	Routine Work. Capt Macleod assumed temporary command of the Section on the 7th inst vice Capt Lennane sick.	
NOEUX-LES-MINES & MAZINGARBE	9 – 15	–	Routine work at Noeux les Mines & Mazingarbe. 2566 Pte Weston 2nd London Sanitary Coy R A M C T arrived as a reinforcement on 12-10-15.	
ALLOUAGNE	16 – 18	–	Routine Work.	
BURBURE	19	–	Section moved to Burbure.	
AUCHEL	20	–	Section moved to Auchel. Capt W J E Bell R A M C assumed temporary command of the Section vice Capt Macleod sick. 2658 Pte J C Castle 2nd London Sanitary Coy. R A M C T arrived as a reinforcement.	
do	20 – 31	–	Routine Work. Capt Lennane R A M C T took over command of the Section on the 30th inst	

2449 Wt. W14957/M90 750,000 1/16 J.B.C. & A. Forms/C.2118/12.

Army Form C. 2118.

Instructions regarding War Diaries and Intelligence Summaries are contained in F. S. Regs., Part II. and the Staff Manual respectively. Title Pages will be prepared in manuscript.

WAR DIARY
or
INTELLIGENCE SUMMARY

(Erase heading not required.)

Place	Date	Hour	Summary of Events and Information	Remarks and references to Appendices
AUCHEL	1 11/15 to 5 11/15	–	Routine work at AUCHEL Sergt EDWARDS was admitted to hospital on the 4th inst.	
MARLES-LES-MINES	6 11/15 to 15 11/16	–	Routine work No 2128 A/Sgt W R PARKER promoted to the rank of Sergeant from the 14th inst.	
NOEUX-LES-MINES	16 11/16 to 30 11/16	–	Routine work. 2167 LCpl MORELAND was admitted to hospital on 25 11/16 074456 Pte A R THOMAS, A.S.C. M.T. joined the Section vice M/3 1566 Pte ROBINSON A.S.C M.T. transferred to 282 Coy M.T. A.S.C. on 27th inst.	
do	1 12/15 to 31 12/15	–	Routine work at Noeux les Mines, Mazingarbe and Philosophe. 1 N.C.O. and six men were detailed for sanitary duty at Mazingarbe, where they were billeted as from 12th inst. No 2708 Pte C F PEILE. 2nd London Sanitary Coy. R A M C T arrived as a reinforcement on the 22nd inst.	

2449 Wt. W14957/M90 750,000 1/16 J.B.C. & A. Forms/C.2118/12.

Jan. – May 1916

No. 13. Sanitary Section

Army Form C. 2118.

Instructions regarding War Diaries and Intelligence Summaries are contained in F. S. Regs., Part II. and the Staff Manual respectively. Title Pages will be prepared in manuscript.

WAR DIARY
or
INTELLIGENCE SUMMARY
(Erase heading not required.)

Place	Date	Hour	Summary of Events and Information	Remarks and references to Appendices
NOEUX-LES-MINES	1 1/16 to 15 1/16	–	Routine work at Noeux les Mines, MAZINGARBE and PHILOSOPHE. 2 NCOs. and 6 men were detached for duty at MAZINGARBE and PHILOSOPHE.	
LILLERS	16 1/16 to 31 1/16	–	Routine work at LILLERS, and neighbourhood. Capt W. J. E. Bell assumed temporary command of the Section on the 18th inst vice Capt Lennane on sick leave.	
LILLERS	1 2/16 to 15 2/16	–	Routine work at LILLERS and neighbourhood The Section was divided into 3 parties (each in charge of an N.C.O.) which were attached to Nos 1. 2. + 141 Field Ambulances respectively from 6th to 8th inst for Divisional Exercises.	
BRACQUEMONT NOEUX-LES-MINES	16 2/16 to 29 2/16		Routine work at NOEUX-LES-MINES (BRACQUEMONT) LES BREBIS and district. 2 N.C.Os. and 6 men were billeted at LES BREBIS for duty in that area. Capt M.K. Acheson. R.A.M.C. took over temporary command of the Section from 17th to 22nd inst when Capt Lennane returned from sick leave.	

2449 Wt. W14957/M90 750,000 1/16 J.B.C. & A. Forms/C.2118/12.

Army Form C. 2118.

Instructions regarding War Diaries and Intelligence Summaries are contained in F. S. Regs., Part II. and the Staff Manual respectively. Title Pages will be prepared in manuscript.

WAR DIARY
or
INTELLIGENCE SUMMARY
(Erase heading not required.)

Place	Date	Hour	Summary of Events and Information	Remarks and references to Appendices
BRACQUEMONT NOEUX-LES-MINES	1 3/16 to 31 3/16	–	Routine work at BRACQUEMONT, LES BREBIS and district.	
			2128 Sgt Parker was promoted to the rank of Staff Sergeant as from 15 1/16.	
			732 Sgt HATHAWAY reverted, at his own request, to rank of Corporal 27 3/16.	
			1562 Cpl DAWES was promoted to the rank of Sergeant 27 3/16.	
			732 Sgt HATHAWAY was admitted to Hospital on the 31st inst.	
			14 T U men of various units were attached to the Section, from 1st Provisional Coy during the month, for Sanitary duty.	
do	1 4/16 to 30 4/16	–	Routine work	
			Capt. L.T. Poole R.A.M.C. took temporary command of the Sect from 13th to 18th inst vice Capt. Lennane on leave	
			2126 Pte W. WITHAM 2nd Lon Sanitary Co R.A.M.C.T arrived as a reinforcement on the 20th inst.	
			2708 Pte C.F. PEILE appointed a/LCpl (without pay) on 30th inst	
			Attached Men. 4 P.B men attached as from 4th inst. for sanitary duty	
			10 T.U " " during month do	
do	1 5/16 to 31 5/16	–	Routine work	
			Capt L.T. POOLE R.A.M.C. assumed temporary command of the Section from 19th to 30th inst vice Capt. Lennane on leave	
			1646 LCpl K.W. Hobbs was appointed to acting rank of Corporal with pay as from 9-4-16	
			2180 Pte KEARNES was admitted to Hospital on the 22nd inst	
			2155 LCpl H. TETLOW do do 29th "	
			Attached Men. 6 P.B. men were attached for Sanitary duty	
			12 T.U. " " "	
			16 R.A.M.C " " " from 26th inst	

[illegible signature]

Instructions regarding War Diaries and Intelligence Summaries are contained in F. S. Regs., Part II. and the Staff Manual respectively. Title Pages will be prepared in manuscript.

WAR DIARY
or
INTELLIGENCE SUMMARY
(Erase heading not required.)

Army Form C. 2118.

Vol 6 To 15

Place	Date	Hour	Summary of Events and Information	Remarks and references to Appendices
June 1916 July 1916			WAR DIARY OF CAPT G. Q. LENNANE R.A.M.C.T. O.C. No 13 SANITARY SECTION 1ST DIVISION ~~FROM 1ST OCTOBER 1915~~ 1st JUNE 1916 TO 31ST JULY 1916 VOLUME 7	

2449 Wt. W14957/M90 750,000 1/16 J.B.C. & A. Forms/C.2118/12.

Instructions regarding War Diaries and Intelligence Summaries are contained in F. S. Regs., Part II. and the Staff Manual respectively. Title Pages will be prepared in manuscript.

WAR DIARY
or
INTELLIGENCE SUMMARY
(Erase heading not required.)

Army Form C. 2118.

Place	Date	Hour	Summary of Events and Information	Remarks and references to Appendices
BRACQUEMONT NOEUX-LES-MINES	1 6/16 to 30 6/16	–	Routine work at BRACQUEMONT LES BREBIS and district. 3018 Pte C. F. FROST 2nd London Sanitary Coy R.A.M.C.T. arrived as a reinforcement on the 15th inst. 2342. Pte W. H. MORFETT. do do do 23rd inst. Attached Men. 6 P B men were attached for Sanitary Duty 15 T U do do 15 R.A.M.C do do up to 28th inst. 13 R.A.M.C do do 25th to 28th inst.	
BRACQUEMONT	1 7/16 to 3 7/16	–	Routine work. (Strength Section 27 – "PB" Men 4 – "T.U." Men 15.)	
BRUAY	4 7/16	–	Section moved to BRUAY. all Sanitary services in district being handed over to S.O. 40th Division.	
"	5 7/16	–	4 P.B. men were returned to 40th Divisional Coy All surplus stores and equipment in excess of mobilisation table were dumped at Ordnance Stores 15 T.U. attached men were returned to 1st Divisional Coy.	
LILLERS.	6 7/16	–	Section marched to LILLERS and entrained. Section lorry (i/c of an N.C.O.) joined the 1st D.S.C.	
FLESSELLES	7 7/16	–	" arrived at CANDAS and marched to FLESSELLES.	
ST GRATIEN	8 7/16	–	March continued to St GRATIEN where the Sect. remained until the afternoon of the 10th inst. The Sanitary condition of the village & billets were inspected and reported on & efforts were made to improve same.	

2449 Wt. W14957/M90 750,000 1/16 J.B.C. & A. Forms/C.2118/12.

Instructions regarding War Diaries and Intelligence Summaries are contained in F. S. Regs., Part II. and the Staff Manual respectively. Title Pages will be prepared in manuscript.

WAR DIARY
or
INTELLIGENCE SUMMARY
(Erase heading not required.)

Army Form C. 2118.

Place	Date	Hour	Summary of Events and Information	Remarks and references to Appendices
DERNANCOURT	10 7/16	–	Section marched to DERNANCOURT.	
			1 N.C.O. & 3 men were detailed for duty with the Brigade in reserve at Albert.	
			" 4 " " " Cleansing Contalmaison Chateau, and relieved after four days by a similar party who completed the work.	
			A report on the insanitary conditions found at St. Gratien was sent to the A.D.M.S. on the 12th inst.	
			1646 a/Cpl Hobbs was promoted to substantive rank of Corporal vice 732 Cpl Hathaway.	
			1632 a/L/Cpl Palmer was promoted to substantive rank of Lance Corporal	
			2207 Pte BROADHEAD left for England to take up employment as a Marine Fitter on 19th inst.	
ALBERT	20 7/16		Headquarters of Section moved to Albert.	
			1 N.C.O. & 6 men detailed for duty with No 1 Field Ambulance.	
			1 " 7 " " " " 2 " "	
			Remainder of the Section employed on routine work at Albert.	
ST GRATIEN	26 7/16		Section moved to St Gratien. Parties as above remaining with the Field Ambulances to which they were attached.	
			Routine work at St Gratien carried on by remainder of Section until the 29th inst.	
MONTIGNY	29 7/16		Section moved to Montigny and at once proceeded to set up baths at Baizieux, Henencourt & Millencourt	
			N.C.O. & 2 men were detailed for duty in charge of 1st Brigade Baths. Baizieux	
			" 2 " " " " 2nd " " Henencourt	
	to		" 6 " remained attached to No 1 Field Ambulance at Millencourt	
			5 men remained attached to No 2 Field Ambulance.	
			Remainder of Section employed on routine work at Montigny & Behencourt.	
	31 7/16		Disposition of Section as on 29th inst.	[signature] Capt O.C. [illegible] San. Section

2449 Wt. W14957/M90 750,000 1/16 J.B.C. & A. Forms/C.2118/12.

Aug 1916

S

1st Div

No. 13 Sanitary Section

Instructions regarding War Diaries and Intelligence Summaries are contained in F. S. Regs., Part II. and the Staff Manual respectively. Title Pages will be prepared in manuscript.

WAR DIARY
or
INTELLIGENCE SUMMARY
(Erase heading not required.)

Army Form C. 2118.

Vol 16

Place	Date	Hour	Summary of Events and Information	Remarks and references to Appendices
			WAR DIARY OF CAPT. G. Q LENNANE_RAMCT O.C. No 13 SANITARY SECTION 1ST DIVISION 1ST TO 31ST AUGUST 1916 VOLUME 8	

2449 Wt. W14957/M90 750,000 1/16 J.B.C. & A. Forms/C.2118/12.

Army Form C. 2118.

Instructions regarding War Diaries and Intelligence Summaries are contained in F. S. Regs., Part II. and the Staff Manual respectively. Title Pages will be prepared in manuscript.

WAR DIARY
or
INTELLIGENCE SUMMARY
(Erase heading not required.)

Place	Date	Hour	Summary of Events and Information	Remarks and references to Appendices
MONTIGNY	1 8/16		Disposition of Section:- No 2 Field Ambulance. 5 men temporarily attached for Sanitary duty; " 1 " " 1. NCO + 6 men. " ; 1st Bdy Baths, Baizieux 1 NCO + 2 men in charge; 2nd " Henencourt 1 " + 2 " " ; Remainder at Section H.Qrs Montigny. Strength 24, A.S.C.M.T. 2 = 26	
			Management of Foden Steam Disinfector taken over by Section in accordance with A.D.M.S. 1st Div. No 7R/M/12 of 28/7/16	
"	2 8/16		Disposition of Sect. as yesterday. 6 men from 1st Divisional Coy working on Fatigue at Montigny.	
			Inspection made of part of 1st Brigade area.	
"	3 8/16		Inspection made of portion of 2nd Brigade area, MILLENCOURT WOODS and report on same sent to A.D.M.S.	
			6 T.U. men from 1st Div Coy attached to Section for duty.	
			Disposition of Section as yesterday.	
"	4 8/16		Inspection continued in 2nd Brigade area.	
			Disposition of Section as yesterday	
"	5 8/16		Inspection made of grounds at Behencourt chateau + report on same sent to A.D.M.S.	
			Report on sanitary condition of 2nd Brigade area sent to A.D.M.S.	
			Disposition of men as yesterday.	
"	6 8/16		Inspection made of 3rd Brigade area.	
			Disposition of Section as yesterday.	
"	7 8/16		Report to A.D.M.S. on sanitary condition of 3rd Brigade area.	
"	8 8/16		Fatigue party of N.C.O. + 15 men from Div. Coy + 7 prisoners from A.P.M. clearing up chateau grounds Behencourt.	
			Ten additional T.U. men from Div. Coy. attached to Section and detailed for duty {5 in 2nd Brigade area, 5 " 3rd " "}	
			Disposition of section as yesterday.	
			Fatigue party ~~clean~~ at Behencourt Chateau as yesterday.	

2449 Wt. W14957/M90 750,000 1/16 J.B.C. & A. Forms/C.2118/12.

Army Form C. 2118.

WAR DIARY
or
INTELLIGENCE SUMMARY
(Erase heading not required.)

Instructions regarding War Diaries and Intelligence Summaries are contained in F. S. Regs., Part II. and the Staff Manual respectively. Title Pages will be prepared in manuscript.

Place	Date	Hour	Summary of Events and Information	Remarks and references to Appendices
MONTIGNY	9/8/16.		Disposition of men & routine work as yesterday Inspection of & report sent to A.D.M.S. re 1st D.S.C. water supply at Behencourt. Interview with Corps Camp Commandant re Div. Baths at Henencourt. Arranged with Bdy HQrs to allot baths to 3rd Corps H.Q. whole day on 10th crip to run on 13th. Inspected baths at Baizieux Henencourt & Millencourt.	
"	10/8/16		Disposition of section same. Later 5 O.Rs returned from No 2 Field Ambulance Fatigue of 5 prisoners on road cleaning and 20 men from Div Coy. cleaning up Chateau grounds Behencourt No 1367 Pte W Tillcock, 1st London Sanitary Coy. arrived as a reinforcement	
"	11/8/16		Disposition of Section - 2 NCOs & 6 men at HQrs - NCO & 2 men 1st Bdy Baths - NCO & 2 men 2nd Bdy Baths NCO & 6 men No 1 Field Ambulance NCO & 3 men 1st Brigade area. Fatigue party of 16 men ~~[illegible]~~ cleaning up streets &c in Behencourt Inspections made of 1st 2nd & 3rd Bdy areas and baths Visited Henencourt re cases of diarrhoea. 2nd Bdy. Samples of water taken from tank & Bdy water carts. 2 tents & drain rods drawn from Ordnance.	
"	12/8/16		Disposition of Section as yesterday. Fatigue of 20 men from Div Coy cleaning up in Henencourt Woods	
"	13/8/16		do do Inspection made of new area.	
"	14/8/16		do do 2nd Bdy Baths at Henencourt dismantled transported to Albert & re erected. Three Sect men sent to assist in dismantling baths at Henencourt & proceeded with same to Albert. Five T U men returned from 2nd Brigade and rejoined Divisional Coy.	
ALBERT	15/8/16		Sect Headqrs moved from Montigny to Albert. All parties returned to Section at Albert 3 attached T. U. men rejoined the Divisional Coy. No 1613 Pte Reading was admitted to Hospital.	[initials]

2449 Wt. W14957/M90 750,000 1/16 J.B.C. & A. Forms/C.2118/12.

Instructions regarding War Diaries and Intelligence Summaries are contained in F. S. Regs., Part II. and the Staff Manual respectively. Title Pages will be prepared in manuscript.

WAR DIARY
or
INTELLIGENCE SUMMARY
(Erase heading not required.)

Army Form C. 2118.

Place	Date	Hour	Summary of Events and Information	Remarks and references to Appendices
ALBERT	16/8/16		Strength. Section 26. Attached from 1st Divisional Coy. 8. Employed on routine work in 1st Div. area. Baths set up and 749 men of 49th Brigade (Australians) bathed. 2126 Pte WITHAM detailed for duty (as a draughtsman) at Headquarters. No 1632 LCpl Palmer appointed acting Corporal without pay.	
"	17/8/16		Inspection made of Brigade Transport, and 1st D.A.C area & report on same sent to A.D.M.S. N.C.O. + 2 men with fatigue party of 24 at work in BECOURT WOOD. " + 6 men in charge of Baths 588 men bathed. Remainder of section routine work & making latrine seats & 732. Pte A Mason. 1st Lon San. Coy arrived as a reinforcement. Section recommenced drawing disinfectants in bulk & issuing same as required to units in Divisional area.	
"	18/8/16		Section Lorry i/c an N.C.O. carrying wounded for No 1 Field Ambulance Work continued in Becourt Wood, fatigue party of 24 provided for the afternoon. 3 R.E. carts carting bricks for incinerators 1 N.C.O. + 6 men i/c of baths. 556 men bathed.	
"	19/8/16		Section Lorry carrying wounded for No 1 Field Ambulance. Becourt Wood. 1 NCO 5 men, and fatigue party of 24. 2 R.E. carts drawing materials. Baths. 1 NCO + 6 men. 286 men bathed.	
"	20/8/16		Lorry (i/c an NCO) returned from No 1 Field Ambulance Becourt Wood. N.C.O. + 5 men at work providing sanitary services. 2 RE carts drawing materials. Baths. N.C.O. + 5 men fitting up shelter & improving Baths.	
"	21/8/16		Plan received from 1st Division showing Sanitary Area allotted to Sanitary Section. No 18120 Pte Cowland 8th R Berks. temporarily attached to the Section. Baths. N.C.O. + 6 men. 347 men bathed. Becourt Wood. N.C.O. and 5 men at work. As this wood is excluded on the plan received yesterday the work here was discontinued after 2 deep trench latrines had been constructed (3 more were in course of construction) 2 incinerators were built, and refuse &c lying about the wood was collected & burnt.	

2449 Wt. W14957/M90 750,000 1/16 J.B.C. & A. Forms/C.2118/12.

Instructions regarding War Diaries and Intelligence Summaries are contained in F. S. Regs., Part II. and the Staff Manual respectively. Title Pages will be prepared in manuscript.

WAR DIARY
or
INTELLIGENCE SUMMARY
(Erase heading not required.)

Army Form C. 2118.

Place	Date	Hour	Summary of Events and Information	Remarks and references to Appendices
ALBERT	22/8/16	–	N.C.O. + 2 men Albert area	
			" " Forward area	
			5 " in charge of Baths 723 men bathed	
			2 " making latrine seats + urinals	
			Lorry to workshops for repairs another lorry supplied by workshops pending completion of repairs	
			No 6559 Pte M Carey. 2nd R. Munsters reported from the 1st Divisional Coy for duty with the Section	
"	23/8/16	–	With A.D.M.S. inspected area East of Becourt ~~Wood~~ Hill + 2nd Brigade Headquarters	
			Albert 1 N.C.O. + 3 men building incinerator	
			Front Area " 2 " " incinerator + latrines	
			Baths 1 N.C.O. + 7 men in charge 371 men bathed	
"	24/8/16		Transport Lines. N.C.O. and Pte Tillcock inspecting + supervising	
			Amiens Road Area Pte Mason inspecting	
			Baths. 1 N.C.O. and 7 men. 358 men bathed	
"	25/8/16		Inspection made of 43rd Brigade HQ 14th Division and directions given to improve sanitary services	
			N.C.O. and 1 man with fatigue party cleaning up Transport lines + round Lozenge Wood	
			Baths. N.C.O. + 7 men. 556 men bathed.	
	26/8/16		Inspection of forward area	
			Baths N.C.O. + 7 men. 544 men bathed	
			No 732 Pte A. Mason + No 1367 Pte W. Tillcock appointed acting Lance Corporals without pay.	

2449 Wt. W14957/M90 750,000 1/16 J.B.C. & A. Forms/C.2118/12.

Army Form C. 2118.

Instructions regarding War Diaries and Intelligence Summaries are contained in F. S. Regs., Part II. and the Staff Manual respectively. Title Pages will be prepared in manuscript.

WAR DIARY
or
INTELLIGENCE SUMMARY
(Erase heading not required.)

Place	Date	Hour	Summary of Events and Information	Remarks and references to Appendices
ALBERT	27/8/16		Inspection of area between Fricourt Farm and Becourt Wood & report made by S Sgt Parker. Baths. NCO & 6 men. 311 men bathed	
"	28/8/16		Inspection of Becourt Hill area. & report sent to A D M S re outbreak of diarrhoea in 73rd Bde ~~Transport~~ RFA Baths NCO & 5 men. 661 men bathed	
"			2648 Pte Castle was admitted to Hospital	
	29/8/16		Inspection of billets in Albert by S. Sgt Parker & report sent to Capt Joscelyn Bivouac at 117 Battery. R.F.A. Wagon lines disinfected after Scarlet Fever. Baths. NCO & 6 men. 662 men bathed	
"	30/8/16		Further inspection made by S. Sgt Parker of billeting area in Albert. Baths NCO & 6 men. 422 men bathed.	
"	31/8/16		Routine work. Inspection made of area at rear of 16-18 Rue de Cersonnieres & report by S Sgt Parker NCO & 6 men in charge of Baths. 507 men bathed making a total of 7641 since 16th inst. " 4 " making Latrine seats. Of which 208 have been issued to date in addition 56 "drum" pattern latrines have been completed Attended with A D M S. conference held by D D M S 3rd Corps	G. [illegible] Capt O.C. 1st Div. Sanitation

2449 Wt. W14957/M90 750,000 1/16 J.B.C. & A. Forms/C.2118/12.

Sept 1916

S

140/1788

Vol 17

CONFIDENTIAL

WAR DIARY

OF

CAPTAIN G. Q. LENNANE. R.A.M.C.T.

O.C. No 13 SANITARY SECTION. 1st DIVISION

FROM 1st TO 30th SEPTEMBER. 1916

VOLUME IX.

Instructions regarding War Diaries and Intelligence Summaries are contained in F. S. Regs., Part II. and the Staff Manual respectively. Title Pages will be prepared in manuscript.

WAR DIARY
or
INTELLIGENCE SUMMARY
(Erase heading not required.)

Army Form C. 2118.

Place	Date	Hour	Summary of Events and Information	Remarks and references to Appendices
ALBERT	1 9/16		Inspection made of BECOURT HILL area.	
			BECOURT HILL AREA. N.C.O. 3 section and 2 attached men building incinerators & latrines	
			FORWARD AREA. N.C.O. 2 men building incinerators latrines etc.	
			BATHS. N.C.O. and 8 men. Total number bathed 343.	
			Remainder of Section employed on routine work, inspecting, and drawing stores etc.	
	2 9/16		Routine work as yesterday, with the addition of a fatigue party of 30 men employed in Becourt Hill area	
			Baths. 81 men bathed.	
			Civilian latrine, discharging into stream, above baths reported to S.O. at Albert	
	3 9/16		Routine work. Baths. 355 men bathed.	
	4 9/16		Inspection made of Nothants and M G Corps billets in Albert and report on same sent to S.O. Albert.	
			Section employed on routine work, inspecting & working baths (681 men bathed)	
			2342 Pte W H MORFETT left for the Base having been pronounced unfit for further service at the front under authority of A.D.M.S. 1st Division No 7 R.M/331 of 3 9/16.	
			2126 Pte W Witten. returned for duty with the Section from Hqrs 1 Division.	
	5 9/16		Inspection made by S.O. of Transport Area.	
			Routine work as yesterday with addition of a fatigue party of 30 men employed in Transport Area.	
			NCO & 6 men i/c Baths. 549 men bathed.	
	6 9/16		2648 Pte Castle returned to duty from 141 Field Ambulance	
			NCO & 6 men i/c Baths 555 men bathed	
			Section employed on routine work. Fatigue party of 50 men employed in Becourt Hill area.	
	7 9/16		Routine work & fatigue party as yesterday. Baths 349 men bathed.	
	8 9/16		Do Do Do Do 629 Do	
			Inspection made by S.O. of 1 Div Train Hqrs Camp and Horse Lines and report sent to A.D.M.S.	
	9 9/16		Routine work as yesterday. Baths 623 men bathed.	[initials]

2449 Wt. W14957/M90 750,000 1/16 J.B.C. & A. Forms/C.2118/12.

Army Form C. 2118.

Instructions regarding War Diaries and Intelligence Summaries are contained in F. S. Regs., Part II. and the Staff Manual respectively. Title Pages will be prepared in manuscript.

WAR DIARY
or
INTELLIGENCE SUMMARY

(Erase heading not required.)

Place	Date	Hour	Summary of Events and Information	Remarks and references to Appendices
ALBERT	10 9/16		Routine work as yesterday_ Baths 129 men bathed, making a total of 12 435 since 16th August_ 13120_ Pte Cowland_ 8th R Berks, and temporarily attached, was recalled to his unit_ Baths handed over to Town Major Albert, in accordance with III Corps Orders_	
	11 9/16		Orders received that, under III Corps Administrative Instructions No 23_ dated 11 9/16, Section would be relieved in Right Division Area by the 47th Divisional Sanitary Section at noon on the 12th inst, and would proceed to Montigny and take over sanitation in "B" area_ W. of Albert. N.C.O. and one man proceeded to Montigny with lorry, moving stores &c. Remainder of Section employed on routine work in area_	
MONTIGNY	12 9/16		Section left Albert at 8.30 a.m. and marched to Montigny arriving at 1 p.m. employed transferring stores and clearing up at Headqrs and billet_	
	13 9/16		4 NCO's of the Sect each made inspection of the areas of Behencourt, Bresle, Lahoussoye, & Franvillers_ Section employed transferring stores, fitting up latrine accommodation at Headqrs & overhauling equipment Strength_ Section 26_ Attached from 1st Divisional Coy. 9_	
	14 9/16		Parties were detailed, to be billeted and rationed, for Sanitary Duties as follows:- Bresle_ 1 NCO 3 Section and 3 attached men Lahoussoye_ 1 " 3 " " 3 " " Franvillers_ 1 " 3 " " 2 " " Remainder of Section at Headquarters Montigny and employed on sanitary duties ~~at~~ there and at Behencourt and district_ & making a supply of latrine seats, urinals &c for issue to units billeted in the Sanitary Area_ R 4151_ Pte F Gossman_ 2 K.R.R. Corps reported for duty with the Section from 1st Div. Coy vice No 1973 Pte J Waters 1/6 Welsh recalled_	
	15 9/16		Disposition of Section as yesterday_ Fatigue party of 10 men from 1 Div. Coy clearing up at Behencourt_ 2 carpenters from 10th Glosters assisting with making latrine seats_ Bresle Fatigue party of 16 men employed clearing up &c	

Instructions regarding War Diaries and Intelligence Summaries are contained in F. S. Regs., Part II. and the Staff Manual respectively. Title Pages will be prepared in manuscript.

WAR DIARY
or
INTELLIGENCE SUMMARY

(Erase heading not required.)

Army Form C. 2118.

Place	Date	Hour	Summary of Events and Information	Remarks and references to Appendices
MONTIGNY	16/9/16		Disposition of Section as yesterday. Fatigue parties – 10 men from Div Coy. 50 " – 8th R Berks at Bresle.	
	17/9/16		Disposition of Section as yesterday. Fatigue parties – 12 men from 1st Div Coy. 60 " at Bresle.	
	18/9/16			
	19/9/16		Disposition of Section as yesterday. Fatigue parties. 12 men at Montigny. 9 " Franvillers	
	20/9/16		1st Division moved. Sanitary Section remaining in charge of "B" area. 4 additional men attached at Section Headquarters from 1st Div. Coy. 2788 Pte T. J. BRYANT 2nd London Sanitary Coy R.A.M.C.T. arrived as a reinforcement to the Section.	
	21/9/16		Disposition of Section as yesterday. Fatigue party of 9 men from Town Major Henencourt.	
	22/9/16		Do Do " " 30 men Franvillers, 9 men Henencourt.	
	23/9/16		Do Do 30 " Franvillers, 9 men Henencourt, 50 men Bresle. Inspection by Staff Sgt. of 15th Div Hqrs and arrangements made with S M to improve sanitary matters there.	
	24/9/16		Disposition of Section as yesterday. Fatigue parties. 30 at Franvillers, 40 " Bresle, 9 Henencourt.	
	25/9/16		Inspection by S. O. of Lavieville and report on same sent to A.D.M.S. 1st Division.	
	26/9/16		Disposition of Section as yesterday	
	27/9/16		Do Do Daily fatigue party of 12 men from 1st Divisional Coy arranged for.	
	28/9/16		Do Do	
	29/9/16		Do Do Lorry moving office of A.D.M.S., drawing stores & afterwards to 1st D.S.C. workshops for repairs. Conference at office of D.D.M.S. III Corps	
	30/9/16		Disposition of Section as yesterday. Strength 27. Attached men 16. Infectious disease – 1st Division – 1 to 30 Sept: Dysentery 13 cases. Scarlet Fever 2. Tuberculosis 1 case.	G. J. [illegible] Capt.

2449 Wt. W14957/M90 750,000 1/16 J.B.C. & A. Forms/C.2118/12.

Oct 1916

S

140/1788

Vol 18

CONFIDENTIAL.

WAR DIARY

OF

CAPT G. Q. LENNANE. R.A.M.C.T

O.C No 13 SANITARY SECTION. 1ST DIVISION.

FROM 1ST TO 31ST OCTOBER 1916.

VOLUME X.

Army Form C. 2118.

Instructions regarding War Diaries and Intelligence Summaries are contained in F. S. Regs., Part II. and the Staff Manual respectively. Title Pages will be prepared in manuscript.

WAR DIARY
or
INTELLIGENCE SUMMARY
(Erase heading not required.)

Place	Date	Hour	Summary of Events and Information	Remarks and references to Appendices
MONTIGNY	1/10/16		Routine work carried on during day. All subsections returned to Section HQrs in evening.	
	2/10/16		Stores and equipment overhauled, and with the exception of one lorry load, deposited at Railhead Frechencourt, in charge of N.C.O. and one man of Section, for transport by rail.	
			2187 Pte A. W. White was admitted to Hospital. Remainder of Section (24 NCOs & men) with lorry and 14 attached men proceeded to BAIZIEUX and were billeted for the night at Divisional Headquarters.	
MOYENNEVILLE	3/10/16		Section proceeded by bus, in accordance with 1st Division No 5410/22 Administrative Orders, to MOYENNEVILLE arriving at 8 p.m. and took over billet alloted to them there.	
	4/10/16		Section employed making latrines at Div. HQrs, inspecting area, water supplies &c.	
			1st Division No 5803 of 2/10/16, re discipline when in Rest Area, read out on parade.	
			1607 Pte Martin and 1603 Pte Tracott left for ten days leave. 2 cases German Measles reported in 10 Gloucesters	
	5/10/16		Inspection by S.O. of No 7 Area.	
	6/10/16		Sub sections detailed for sanitary duty as follows.	
			QUESNOY (1st Brigade Area) N.C.O. 3 Section and 3 attached men	
			ACHEUX (2nd " ") do do	
			FEUQUIERES (3rd " ") do do	
	7/10/16		Inspection by S.O. of Area.	
			Lorry proceeded to MERICOURT to draw Baths	
			24804 Pte J. Ables 1st Northants Regt. attached from 1 Divisional Coy. was admitted to 141 Field Ambulance	
	8/10/16		Baths installed at Miannay and Fressenneville for 1st and 3rd Brigades respectively.	
	9/10/16		Baths completed at Fressenneville and bathing commenced. Nine cases of Measles. 10th Gloucesters	
	10/10/16		Baths at Fressenneville placed in charge of a fatigue party of one N.C.O. and 6 men from 141 Field Ambulance under supervision of Sanitary Section (Vide A.D.M.S. 1 Division 1134 of 9/10/16) and baths at MIANNAY placed in charge of a similar party.	
	11/10/16		Party of Section fitting up baths at TOEUFLES for 2nd Brigade.	

2449 Wt. W14957/M90 750,000 1/16 J.B.C. & A. Forms/C.2118/12.

Instructions regarding War Diaries and Intelligence Summaries are contained in F. S. Regs., Part II. and the Staff Manual respectively. Title Pages will be prepared in manuscript.

WAR DIARY
or
INTELLIGENCE SUMMARY
(Erase heading not required.)

Army Form C. 2118.

Place	Date	Hour	Summary of Events and Information	Remarks and references to Appendices
MOYENNEVILLE	12/10/16		Inspection of Section and routine work as yesterday. Disinfection carried out of five 10th Gloucester Billets at Quesnoy after German Measles. 2187 Pte A. W. White rejoined from Hospital.	
	13/10/16		With D A + Q M G to TOEUFLES (2nd Brigade Baths) and MIANNAY (1st Brigade Baths). Saw M.O. 10th Gloucester Regt re outbreak of German Measles and suggested further precautions & preventive measures. To Abbeville to D.D of Stores re supply of bench boards for baths. Report for month of Sept. sent to A.D.M.S. 1st Division.	
	14/10/16		Baths at TOEUFLES fitted up and placed in charge of NCO and 6 men of No 1 Field Ambulance. Visited and inspected Tessenneville, Fenquieres, Acheux, Chépy, Valines and Divisional Laundry. Saw M.O. i/c 1st S.W.B. re cases of Dysentery and M.O. i/c 10th Glosters re outbreak of German Measles. Visited and inspected Quesnoy, Campagne, Miannay, Toeufles. Water supplies and water carts tested at Toeufles	
	15/10/16		Routine work. 1565 Pte Phenna and 2187 Pte White left on ten days leave.	
	16/10/16		Inspected 1st 2nd + 3rd Brigade areas. Investigated outbreak of German Measles 10th Gloster Regt. Inspected 3rd Brigade Baths, visited Abbeville and purchased stores required. Visited Sanitary Sub sections at Campagne and Acheux.	
	17/10/16		Inspected 1st Brigade Area. Quesnoy re German Measles outbreak in 10th Glosters. Campagne and Franlieu re billets of 8th R. Berks and No 2 Coy Divisional Train. Inspected Baths at Miannay and Toeufles also Divisional Laundry and Steam Disinfector. Lorry to 1st ASC Workshops for new tyres.	
	18/10/16		Inspected Baths at Toeufles and Miannay. Visited and inspected Sanitary areas at Acheux, Chépy, Valines, Hqrs 1st Brigade and 10th Glosters at Quesnoy. Disinfected billet after case of suspected Diphtheria at Miannay.	
	19/10/16		Visited 1st Brigade + Hqrs of 10th Gloucester Regt and [illegible] of segregated men report to A.D.M.S. Visited Acheux + Valines re Sanitary Matters. Visited Chépy Station re Timber &c.	

2449 Wt. W14957/M90 750,000 1/16 J.B.C. & A. Forms/C.2118/12.

Instructions regarding War Diaries and Intelligence Summaries are contained in F. S. Regs., Part II. and the Staff Manual respectively. Title Pages will be prepared in manuscript.

WAR DIARY
or
INTELLIGENCE SUMMARY
(Erase heading not required.)

Army Form C. 2118.

Place	Date	Hour	Summary of Events and Information	Remarks and references to Appendices
MOYENNEVILLE	20/10/16		Inspection and report to A.D.M.S. of 3rd Brigade M. G. Coy. area.	
			24804 Pte Ablis. 1st Northants Regt attached from 1st Divisional Coy. rejoined the Section from 141 Field Amb.	
	21/10/16		Visited and inspected 3rd Brigade area. Lorry returned from 1st D.S.C. Workshops.	
	22/10/16		Report on work carried out in Divisional Area sent to A.D.M.S. 1st Division.	
	23/10/16		Inspected 1st Brigade area. Baths. Campagne. Quesnoy. Segregation camp of 10th Glosters.	
			Parlue re case of German Measles in 8th R Berks. Report on same to A.D.M.S. 2 Platoons isolated. tents asked for. Afternoon. Parlue re German Measles. Fressenneville & Aigneville.	
	24/10/16		Parlue re outbreak of German Measles. and report on same sent to A.D.M.S. One case G. Measles reported in 8 R Berks.	
	25/10/16		Baths dismantled and with heavy stores &c deposited at GAMACHES Station in charge of N.C.O. and 2 men of Section. reference 1 Division Administrative Orders 5410/32.	
			Totals Bathed. FRESSENNEVILLE 3633. MIANNAY 3633. TOEUFLES 995. Total 8.261.	
	26/10/16		Visited with A.D.M.S. 8th R Berks re German Measles. visited No 1 Field Ambulance re German Measles	
			Visited and inspected site for I.D. Hospital Fressenneville. Visited with A.D.M.S. Isolation Camp 10th Gloucesters. Quesnoy. Visited + inspected Chépy. 1 L N Lancs Regt.	
			Examined with D.A.D.M.S. suspects German Measles. 1st Signal Coy. R.E. 53 cases of G Measles reported in 8 R Berks	
	27/10/16		Routine work in area and inspections of work in progress Seven cases of German Measles reported in 1st Signal Coy. + thirteen in 8 R Berks.	
	28/10/16		Inspection of all work in progress in area, disinfection of billets occupied by 1st Signals after German Measles. Two cases of German Measles reported in No 1 Field Ambulance.	

G.L.

2449 Wt. W14957/M90 750,000 1/16 J.B.C. & A. Forms/C.2118/12.

Army Form C. 2118.

Instructions regarding War Diaries and Intelligence Summaries are contained in F. S. Regs., Part II. and the Staff Manual respectively. Title Pages will be prepared in manuscript.

WAR DIARY
or
INTELLIGENCE SUMMARY
(Erase heading not required.)

Place	Date	Hour	Summary of Events and Information	Remarks and references to Appendices
MOYENNEVILLE	29/10/16		Sub-Sections returned to Section Headquarters in evening.	
			2187 Pte White + 1565 Pte Phemna reported off leave.	
			German Measles - three cases reported in 1st Signal Coy.	
	30/10/16		Lorry in charge N.C.O. of Section with stores and equipment left for BAIZIEUX at midnight.	
			Sketch plans showing sanitary services set up by Division in No 7 area sent to G.A + Q.M.G 1st Division.	
	31/10/16		Section proceeded by motor bus, along with 1st Divisional Headquarters to BAIZIEUX.	
			Strength of Section 27. Attached from 1st Divisional Coy 13.	

Summary of Infectious Disease during Month.

Paratyphoid A	1	case
" B	2	"
Dysentery	27	"
Diphtheria	1	
Mumps	1	"
German Measles	157	"

[signature] Capt.

2449 Wt. W14957/M90 750,000 1/16 J.B.C. & A. Forms/C.2118/12.

Nov. 1916

140/1846

Vol ~~20~~ 19

S

Confidential

WAR DIARY OF

CAPT C YATES FORD - R.A.M.C.

O.C. No 13 SANITARY SECTION - 1ST DIVISION -

FROM 1ST TO 30TH NOVR 1916 -

VOLUME ~~XI~~

Army Form C. 2118.

Instructions regarding War Diaries and Intelligence Summaries are contained in F. S. Regs., Part II. and the Staff Manual respectively. Title Pages will be prepared in manuscript.

WAR DIARY
or
INTELLIGENCE SUMMARY
(Erase heading not required.)

Place	Date	Hour	Summary of Events and Information	Remarks and references to Appendices
BAIZIEUX	1/11/16		Section employed inspecting and cleaning up at Headquarters overhauling stores &c.	
			1562 Sergt A. Dawes was admitted to Hospital.	
			36294 Pte W H Thomas. 2 Welsh Regt attached to San Sect from 1 Divisional Coy was awarded 14 days F P No 1 for absence without leave	
			Infectious Disease notified. 36672. Pte J. KEEN. 8 R. Berks. Para B.	
			3148 " C MacINTYRE. 1 Camerons. Para B.	
	2/11/16		Routine work as yesterday. Water supplies tested.	
	3/11/16		FRICOURT arranging to take over San. Sect Hqrs at Red Cottage from 50th Divisional San Sect.	
			Advance party of one N.C.O. and 9 men proceeded there in evening.	
			2108 Cpl T. B. CLAYDON. appointed acting sergeant with pay vice Sgt Dawes evacuated from Hospital 2/11/16.	
	4/11/16		FRICOURT making arrangements for working Right Forward Sector of III Corps Sanitary Area	
			Section moved to F.3.b.2.4 and took over office and dug outs from 50 Div. San Section leaving behind a detachment of 2 N.C.Os. and 4 men to look after sanitation at Div. Hqrs.	
			Infectious disease notified. 53540. Pte J.E. GITTENS. 2nd Welsh att'd 3rd M G Coy. German Measles.	
			Twenty eight additional cases of German Measles in 8 R. Berks Regt.	
			Billet occupied by 3rd M G Coy disinfected after German Measles.	
FRICOURT.	5/11/16		Preliminary inspections made in new area. Section employed arranging & overhauling stores &c.	
			Strength. Section 26. Attached from 1st Divisional Coy 11.	
	6/11/16		Attended conference of D.M.S. 4th Army at office of D.D.M.S III Corps. with reference to Sanitation in Right Forward Area.	
			Detachment of Sanitary Section left BAIZIEUX and Subsection of one N.C.O. 3 Section and 2 attached men billeted in Albert for sanitary duty there.	
			Infectious disease notified. 5 additional cases of German Measles in 8th R. Berks Regt	
			2 do do 10th Gloucester Regt	[initials]

2449 Wt. W14957/M90 750,000 1/16 J.B.C. & A. Forms/C.2118/12.

Army Form C. 2118.

Instructions regarding War Diaries and Intelligence Summaries are contained in F. S. Regs., Part II. and the Staff Manual respectively. Title Pages will be prepared in manuscript.

WAR DIARY
or
INTELLIGENCE SUMMARY
(Erase heading not required.)

Place	Date	Hour	Summary of Events and Information	Remarks and references to Appendices
FRICOURT	7/11/16		Inspected area around BAZENTIN-LE-PETIT. Infectious Disease notified. 53601 Pte MOLYNEAUX. 2nd Welsh Regt Diphtheria. 4 cases German Measles in 8th R Berks Regt.	
	8/11/16		Area divided into four sections each of which were placed in charge of trained N.C.Os. and men of the Section for daily inspection and report. Orders of day announced. ref. D.R.O. 308 of 29/10/16. award of Meritorious Service Medal to 2108 Cpl (a/Sergt) T.B. Claydon (L Gazette d/19/10/16)	
	9/11/16		Infectious disease notified. 2 cases of German Measles in 8 R Berks Regt. and one case in 3rd M G Coy Behencourt to D.D.M.S. III Corps and A.P.M. III Corps. R4151 Rfm Gossman. 2nd K R R Corps, attached from 1st Divisional Coy, awarded 28 days F.P No1 for quitting his fatigue party at 12.20 pm & failing to return. Infectious disease notified. one case of German Measles in 8 R Berks Regt do do 10 Gloucester Regt	
	10/11/16		Routine work and inspections in area. Infectious Disease notified. 53550 Pte Holt 2nd Welsh Regt German Measles 45699 " Moore. No 3 M.G. Coy do 1939 " Rivett. 1 Northants Regt Typhoid Fever. 40283 " Barber. 1 B. Watch Dysentery. 11961 " Green. 2 R Surrey Regt Dysentery.	
	11/11/16		Inspected camp of 6th Welsh Regt, Lowland R Es, Bottom Wood, "Rose" Water Point and water carts. Infectious Disease notified. T/16750. Dr Davis. 1st Divnl Train Para B 36651 Pte Gillett. 8th R Berks. Dysentery 26631 " Cannon. 1 L.N Lancs Dysentery. 2nd Lieut Low. 151 M.G. Coy. Scarlet Fever.	
	12/11/16		Routine work. visited and inspected Bazentin-le-Petit and surroundings. Investigated case of Scarlet Fever. Officer 151 M.G. Coy and report on same sent to A.D.M.S. 50th Division Seven cases German Measles notified. 3 in 2nd Welsh Regt. one in 3rd M.G. Coy and 3 in 1st Signal Coy R.E. 1565 Pte S.H PHENNA appointed a/L.Cpl. without pay.	[initials]

2449 Wt. W14957/M90 750,000 1/16 J.B.C. & A. Forms/C.2118/12.

Army Form C. 2118.

Instructions regarding War Diaries and Intelligence Summaries are contained in F. S. Regs., Part II. and the Staff Manual respectively. Title Pages will be prepared in manuscript.

WAR DIARY
or
INTELLIGENCE SUMMARY

(Erase heading not required.)

Place	Date	Hour	Summary of Events and Information	Remarks and references to Appendices
FRICOURT	13/11/16		Inspected camp occupied by 1st Brigade and report on same sent to A.D.M.S. 1st Division	
			Sketch plans and lists of camps and sanitary services in area sent to D.D.M.S. III Corps.	
			Fatigue party of 26 men from 151 Infantry Bde. employed cleaning up and making new latrines in Bazentin area.	
			Lorry to 1st D.S.C. Workshops for repairs.	
	14/11/16		2209 Pte Lawrence detailed for sanitary duty at Officers School. Henencourt.	
			Fatigue party of 23 men employed in Bazentin area.	
	15/11/16		Inspection of Mametz Wood area with Sergt Claydon. Report to A.D.M.S. 50th Division re case of diphtheria in 50th Div Signal Coy.	
			Fatigue party of 26 men employed in Bazentin area.	
			Infectious disease notified. R 203650 Rfn FROUD. 2nd K.R.R. Corps. Enteric Group.	
			17518 Pte McDonald. 1st Camerons. Para B.	
			R. 15674 Rfn. Curry 2 K.R.R. Corps. Dysentery	
			1174 Pte Rice 3 M.G. Coy Tuberculosis	
			216779 Charlesworth A.S.C.M.T. Tuberculosis	
	16/11/16		Routine work in area. Fatigue party of 27 men employed cleaning up & making latrines at BAZENTIN.	
	17/11/16		Do. Do. Do. 26 Do.	
	18/11/16		Do. Do. 24 Do.	
			Infectious disease notified. German Measles. No 1 M.G. Coy 6 cases (one N.Y.D.)	
			" 3 " " 2 "	
			1st R. Highrs 2 "	
			No 141 Field Ambulance 1 " N.Y.D.	
			Lorry returned from 1st D.S.C. Workshops	

2449 Wt. W14957/M90 750,000 1/16 J.B.C. & A. Forms/C.2118/12.

Army Form C. 2118.

Instructions regarding War Diaries and Intelligence Summaries are contained in F. S. Regs., Part II. and the Staff Manual respectively. Title Pages will be prepared in manuscript.

WAR DIARY
or
INTELLIGENCE SUMMARY
(Erase heading not required.)

Place	Date	Hour	Summary of Events and Information	Remarks and references to Appendices
FRICOURT	19/11/16		Fatigue party of 26 men employed in BAZENTIN area.	
			Reference D.D.M.S. III Corps No. 671/16 the following men left for duty with the Sanitary Officer Albert and are accordingly struck off the strength of the Section:-	
			No. 1607 Pte MARTIN R. No. 2126 Pte WITHAM W. No. 2024 Pte NEVILLE G.	
			Arrangements made for taking over charge of Baths at BAZENTIN under 1st Division No. 5542/39 and party detailed accordingly.	
			Infectious Disease Notified German Measles. 1 case in 1st R. Hughes	
	20/11/16		do. do. 2nd Welsh Regt.	
			Sub section of 2 N.C.Os. one Section and three attached men left for sanitary duty in Bazentin area.	
			One N.C.O. left to take charge of Baths at Bazentin.	
			Fatigue parties employed in Bazentin area. 26 men from 151st Infantry Brigade and 32 from 2nd Welsh Regt.	
			Infectious Disease notified:- 36856 Pte Austin J. 1st Gloucesters. Dysentery.	
			43140 Jolley A. 1st Northants Diphtheria.	
			Capt. C.Y. Ford R.A.M.C. called and went through work in progress with a view to taking temporary charge of Section.	
	21/11/16		Capt. C.Y. Ford assumed temporary command of the Section vice Capt. G.D. Lamane on leave.	
			Fatigue parties in Bazentin area. 24 men 151st Infantry Brigade and 32 from 1st Gloucester Regt.	
			Appointment of 2108 Cpl Claydon T.B. (A/Sgt with pay from 3/11/16) confirmed in rank (Sgt Substantive) from 9/11/16	
			Infectious Disease notified German Measles. one case in 1st Camerons	
			do. three cases " 3rd M.G. Coy	
			Baths at BAZENTIN taken over under 1 Div No. 5542/39. 187 men of 2 R Munster Fusiliers & 3 men from 1st Divisional Coy detailed by "Q" 1st Division No. 797 of 19/11/16 to assist working same	

2449 Wt. W14957/M90 750,000 1/16 J.B.C. & A. Forms/C.2118/12.

Instructions regarding War Diaries and Intelligence Summaries are contained in F. S. Regs., Part II. and the Staff Manual respectively. Title Pages will be prepared in manuscript.

WAR DIARY
or
INTELLIGENCE SUMMARY
(Erase heading not required.)

Army Form C. 2118.

Place	Date	Hour	Summary of Events and Information	Remarks and references to Appendices
FRICOURT	22/11/16		Visited and inspected Divisional Baths and areas round Bazentin and Mametz Wood – Fatigue Parties in Bazentin area as yesterday.	
	23/11/16		Visited and inspected Divisional Training School at Fréchencourt –	
			Infectious disease notified – 14984 Pte Corner 1st Glosters – German Measles	
			340 " Campbell 22 Aus: Infy, Dysentery	
	24/11/16		Fatigue parties as yesterday 11177 Sgt Marklove – 1st S.W.B. – Suspected Diphtheria	
			Visited with A.D.M.S. Divisional Baths, Bazentin Area and Bazentin-le-grand.	
			Inspected 1st Divisional Headquarters –	
			Fatigue parties as yesterday.	
	25/11/16		Visited, with D.D.M.S. III Corps. Bazentin Area & Div. Baths.	
			Infectious disease notified – No 11931. Pte Pyzall. 2nd Sussex. German Measles –	
			Fatigue parties as yesterday –	
	26/11/16		Attended conference at Office of D.D.M.S. III Corps – Area now being administered by No 13 Sanitary Section to include Becourt Camp and area to right of Becourt and	
			Fatigue party of 20 men and 2 NCOs from 1st Brigade at work in Bazentin – Lozenge Wood Road –	
	27/11/16		Visited Divisional Headquarters, Becourt Camp, and Bazentin area –	
			Infectious disease notified – 4 cases N.Y.D. Dysentery – in 10 Glosters. 1st L.N. Lancs – 2nd R.M.F. 479 [illegible] Coy R.E.	
			2 " N.Y.D. German Measles in 10th Glosters.	
	28/11/16		Inspected areas occupied by 2nd Brigade in Mametz Wood with A.D.M.S. 1st Division.	
			Fatigue parties employed in Bazentin area 25 men from 1st Infy Bde & 10 from 1st R Highrs	
			2138 Pte C.A. Snelling appointed a/L/Cpl without pay and detailed to proceed tomorrow 29th inst for sanitary duty under the Town Major at Becourt Camp	

2449 Wt. W14957/M90 750,000 1/16 J.B.C. & A. Forms/C.2118/12.

Army Form C. 2118.

Instructions regarding War Diaries and Intelligence Summaries are contained in F. S. Regs., Part II. and the Staff Manual respectively. Title Pages will be prepared in manuscript.

WAR DIARY
or
INTELLIGENCE SUMMARY

(Erase heading not required.)

Place	Date	Hour	Summary of Events and Information	Remarks and references to Appendices
FRICOURT	29/11/16		Drying room at Baths, BAZENTIN placed at disposal of 2nd Bde for next three days for drying their kind and rain soaked clothing after coming out of trenches. Infectious Disease notified. German measles 9 cases in 10th Gloucester Regt (all N.Y.D.) Dysentery (Flex.) 1 " " 1 M.G. Coy.	
	30/11/16		Fatigue Party of 16 in Bazentin area. Visited and inspected Mametz and Bazentin areas. Section employed on routine work in area, and with fatigue party erecting 6-spray baths at F.33.24. Revised plan of Corps Sanitary Areas received from D.D.M.S. III Corps. No 838/16. and work adjusted accordingly. Fatigue party of 30 men and 2 NCOs in Bazentin area. 2 additional men temporarily attached to Sub Sect at Bazentin from 1st Gloucester Regt. Baths Bazentin. Total Bathed 21st to 30th Nov. 3060. Provided with filter bed for treating village water with Chloride of Lime. Infectious Disease. Summary for November:- German Measles 68 cases (40 in 8th R. Berks) Fauler Paratyphoid B 4 " Dysentery 7 " Tuberculosis 2 " Typhoid Fever 1 " Diphtheria 2 " Enteric Group 1 " 85 " G. Yates Ford Capt. R.A.M.C. O.C. 13 S.S. 1st Div	

Dec 1916

140/1900.

Vol 20

Confidential.

WAR DIARY OF

Capt. C. Yates Ford. R.A.M.C

O.C. No. 13 Sanitary Section. 1st Division

FROM 1st TO 31st DECEMBER. 1916.

VOLUME XII

Instructions regarding War Diaries and Intelligence Summaries are contained in F. S. Regs., Part II. and the Staff Manual respectively. Title Pages will be prepared in manuscript.

WAR DIARY
or.
INTELLIGENCE SUMMARY
(Erase heading not required.)

Army Form C. 2118.

Place	Date	Hour	Summary of Events and Information	Remarks and references to Appendices
FRICOURT.	1 12/16		Visited and inspected BAZENTIN area – No 1646 Cpl HOBBS left for III Corps Rest Station to erect Clayton disinfector. Fatigue party of 30 men BAZENTIN area chiefly employed erecting Hospital for Trench Feet Cases –	G.Y.F.
	2 12/16		Albert re supply of biscuit boxes. Visited Becourt Camp and Bazentin with D.D.M.S. Fatigue party of 30 men at Bazentin, erecting kitchen latrines and ablution places at Trench Feet Hospital – Infectious disease notified – Para B – one case in 1st Northants Regt; Dysentery – " " 1st M.G. Coy; Dysentery – " " 1st S.W. Borderers; Pneumonia Lobar – " " 1st L.N. Lancs	"
	3 12/16		Visited Bomb School and Div. Officers School at FRECHENCOURT. Inspected sanitary and water arrangements, kitchens and billets, and found same in highly satisfactory state under direction of M.O. i/c Capt. Orme Keep. Inspected Bazentin-le-Petit area and found work progressing satisfactorily – Fatigue party of 30 men at work in this area. Infectious disease notified – one case of dysentery in 2nd Welsh Regt and one in 1st S.W.B.	"
	4 12/16		Visited and inspected Bazentin and Mametz Wood areas – Fatigue party of 30 men at work in Bazentin area – | Rfn Greenwood sent to No 4 Coy 1st Div Train for sanitary duty temporarily	"
	5 12/16		Bazentin – 1st Brigade Hdqrs selecting latrine site etc. Fatigue party of 30 men – Baths at Fricourt working – 120 men of 6th Welsh Regt bathed – Report and War Diary for November sent to A.D.M.S.	"
	6 12/16		Interview with Brigadier – 1st Brigade re standardising means of ablution and water supply in area – inspected 1st Bde. area, sanitary services now nearly complete – visited A.D.M.S. III Corps to discuss this matter – Fatigue party of 40 in Bazentin area. Infectious disease notified – 3 cases dysentery in 1 L.N. Lancs, 2nd R.M.F. & 46/39 Bde. S/14408 Pte Clark 1st R Hyhs temporarily attached to section	" G.Y.F.

2449 Wt. W14957/M90 750,000 1/16 J.B.C. & A. Forms/C.2118/12.

Instructions regarding War Diaries and Intelligence Summaries are contained in F. S. Regs., Part II. and the Staff Manual respectively. Title Pages will be prepared in manuscript.

WAR DIARY
or
INTELLIGENCE SUMMARY
(Erase heading not required.)

Army Form C. 2118.

Place	Date	Hour	Summary of Events and Information	Remarks and references to Appendices
			3 men from 10 Gloster Regt temporarily attached to Sub Section at Bazentin.	
FRICOURT	7/12/16		Visited Bazentin area. Inspected new camp areas of 1. 2. & 3 Brigades and marked out sites for latrines, incinerators and ablution benches with engineer in charge. Fatigue Party Bazentin area. 20 men.	
	8/12/16		Inspected 1. 2 & 3 Brigade areas. Arranged for carrying out series of experiments in drying room Bazentin to find out the most economical and efficient process of generating heat in order to make same more efficient. Fatigue party 20 men. 730 L/Cpl Mason was admitted to No 1 Field Ambulance.	
	9/12/16		BAZENTIN. Experiments at drying room, found method installed by five hours, test proved inefficient. Series of ablution benches being erected in new camps. an approved pattern having been installed at Brigade HdQrs as a model for Units to follow. 1632 Pte Wray. R.A.M.C.T. and 8029 Pte Barnes (attached from 2nd Welsh) left for England on ten days leave. 3839 Pte HOARE. 2nd Sussex. notified Dysentery (Flex) Fatigue party of 40 men Bazentin area.	
	10/12/16		Re arrangement made re inspecting area. and an additional man detailed to join sub section at Bazentin to assist in Forward area. Fatigue Party of 40 men Bazentin Area.	
	11/12/16		Carried on experiments in drying rooms at new camps in Bazentin District, an improved method now in force whereby these sheds have become efficient. Inspection and arrangements to improve sanitation made of 1st Divisional Reinforcement Camps. Five men, for work in ironing room at Bazentin Baths, reported from Division. 20 Fatigue men at work Bazentin Area. 8594 Pte Wickenden. 2nd R. Sussex notified Dysentery (Flex)	

2449 Wt. W14957/M90 750,000 1/16 J.B.C. & A. Forms/C.2118/12.

Army Form C. 2118.

Instructions regarding War Diaries and Intelligence Summaries are contained in F. S. Regs., Part II. and the Staff Manual respectively. Title Pages will be prepared in manuscript.

WAR DIARY
or
INTELLIGENCE SUMMARY

(Erase heading not required.)

Place	Date	Hour	Summary of Events and Information	Remarks and references to Appendices
FRICOURT	12/12/16		Inspected various new camps Bazentin and Mametz Wood. Bath house. ironing tent and Barbers Shop. with D.D.M.S. and A.D.M.S One man from 10th Gloucesters reported for duty as a Barber at Bazentin Baths Fatigue party of 20 men Bazentin Area.	
	13/12/16		Section men fixed latrines &c at 1st Div. Reinforcement Camp. Two men from 1st L.N. Lancs reported for duty as Ironers at Bazentin Baths. Infectious disease notified. three cases of Dysentery in 1st L.N. Lancs. Fatigue party 40 men Bazentin area	
	14/12/16		Visited Mametz Area and arranged for a fatigue party to put same in a sanitary condition Fatigue party of 40 men Bazentin Area. Man from 1st M.G. Coy. reported for duty at Baths Bazentin. making total number attached from 1st Division. 14. in addition to 3 men who report daily for duty from 1st Divisional Coy. and Sub Section of Fire section and three attached men. In all 25 NCOs & men. Case of suspected C.S.M. reported in 6th Welsh. & investigated.	
	15/12/16		New department for ironing clothing and destroying vermin and Barbers shop ~~for~~ opened at Bazentin Baths. Sanitation of newly formed camps at Bazentin nearly completed. Attended Conference with D.D.M.S. III Corps. Fatigue party of 20 men Bazentin Area. Infectious disease notified. Dysentery. 1st L.N. Lancs. 3 cases. 1st S.W.B. 1 " 2nd M.G. Coy 1 "	[illegible]

2449 Wt. W14957/M90 750,000 1/16 J.B.C. & A. Forms/C.2118/12.

Army Form C. 2118.

Instructions regarding War Diaries and Intelligence Summaries are contained in F. S. Regs., Part II. and the Staff Manual respectively. Title Pages will be prepared in manuscript.

WAR DIARY
or
INTELLIGENCE SUMMARY
(Erase heading not required.)

Place	Date	Hour	Summary of Events and Information	Remarks and references to Appendices
FRICOURT	16/12/16		Inspected Bazentin area. Baths, &c. Fatigue party of 20 men Bazentin area. Infectious disease notified. One case of dysentery in 1st L.N. Lancs.	
	17/12/16		Visited and inspected Bazentin area &c. Fatigue Party of 3 NCO's and 49 O.R. i/c an officer from 2nd Welsh Regt. at work cleaning up northern portion of Mametz Wood. and party of 40 employed on routine work in Bazentin area. Samples of water from shell holes sent to No 11 Mobile Laboratory Allonville. 1632 Cpl W.H. Palmer admitted to Field Ambulance. 2128 Staff Sergt Parker left on ten days leave.	
	18/12/16		Accompanied A.D.M.S. to BAZENTIN. Conference with R.E.s re drying rooms and possibility of converting Horsfall destructor into a combined incinerator and drying room. Decided this scheme to be undertaken at once at central point in Bazentin-le-Petit. Suggestion of disposal of water from ablution benches by means of deep, 15ft square, pits to chalk to be tried at Bazentin le Petit and High Wood areas. Arrangements made at Baths for provision of hot drinks, tea, cocoa &c to men after bathing. Fatigue party of 40 men cleaning up in Mametz Wood. 27607 Pte CRICK. 2nd K.R.R. Corps notified dysentery (Flex.)	
	19/12/16		Inspected Becourt area and arranged for transport of Horsfall destructor to Bazentin Bazentin. Fatigue party of 20 men cleaning up in Mametz Wood. Hot tea provided at Baths for troops after Bathing.	[initials]

2449 Wt. W14957/M90 750,000 1/16 J.B.C. & A. Forms/C.2118/12.

Army Form C. 2118.

Instructions regarding War Diaries and Intelligence Summaries are contained in F. S. Regs., Part II. and the Staff Manual respectively. Title Pages will be prepared in manuscript.

WAR DIARY
or
INTELLIGENCE SUMMARY
(Erase heading not required.)

Place	Date	Hour	Summary of Events and Information	Remarks and references to Appendices
FRICOURT	20/12/16		Inspected new camp areas at Bazentin. Hot drinks now being supplied at Bazentin Baths, 200 cups of tea being served in an hour. Attended conference with D.D.M.S. in afternoon.	
			Infectious disease notified. one case Dysentery 1st Northants	
			do. do. 1st L.N. Lancs.	
	21/12/16		Bazentin. Fatigue party of 20 men. Store for clothing erected at Baths.	
	22/12/16		1632 Cpl Palmer returned for duty from III Corps Rest Station.	
			Infectious disease notified. one case Dysentery. 1st Northants.	
	23/12/16		2708 LCpl Peile. left to take charge of baths at Bazentin	
			Infectious disease notified. Dysentery 10 cases	
			Scarlet Fever 1 "	
	24/12/16		Following reinforcements reported for duty with the Section:-	
			1343. Pte H HARGREAVES. 1st London Sanitary Coy.	
			1344. " H. G. BAKER. do.	
			1359. " A H CALVERLEY. do.	
			1336. " H L GIPPS. do.	
	25/12/16		Infectious disease notified. 1st Northants Regt one case of Dysentery	
			8th R. Berks. " do.	
	26/12/16		do. do. 1st D. A. C. do.	
			1st L N Lancs Regt. do.	

2449 Wt. W14957/M90 750,000 1/16 J.B.C. & A. Forms/C.2118/12.

Army Form C. 2118.

Instructions regarding War Diaries and Intelligence Summaries are contained in F. S. Regs., Part II. and the Staff Manual respectively. Title Pages will be prepared in manuscript.

WAR DIARY
or
INTELLIGENCE SUMMARY
(Erase heading not required.)

Place	Date	Hour	Summary of Events and Information	Remarks and references to Appendices
FRICOURT	27/12/16		Routine work and inspections in area.	
			Infectious disease notified. Dysentery eight cases. Lobar Pneumonia one case.	
	28/12/16		Routine work and inspections in area	
	29/12/16		Infectious disease notified. Dysentery two cases. in 1st L N Lancs.	
			one case. " 1st Gloucesters.	
	30/12/16		do. do. Dysentery two cases. Measles one case.	
	31/12/16		Routine work and inspections in area.	
			Total of Bathing Returns for month. Bazentin Baths. 14106 men bathed	
			Fricourt Baths. 847 " "	
			Infectious Disease. Summary for month:-	
			Para B 1 case	
			Dysentery 49 "	
			Lobar Pneumonia 2 "	
			Scarlet Fever 1 "	
			Measles 1 "	
			54 cases.	
				[illegible initials]

2449 Wt. W14957/M90 750,000 1/16 J.B.C. & A. Forms/C.2118/12.

Jan. 1917

140/941

Vol 21

Confidential –

WAR DIARY OF

Capt. L R TOSSWILL. R.A.M.C.T.

O.C. No 13 Sanitary Section 1st Division

From 1st to 31st January 1917 –

Volume XXI

Instructions regarding War Diaries and Intelligence Summaries are contained in F. S. Regs., Part II. and the Staff Manual respectively. Title Pages will be prepared in manuscript.

WAR DIARY
or
~~INTELLIGENCE~~ SUMMARY

(Erase heading not required.)

Army Form C. 2118.

Place	Date	Hour	Summary of Events and Information	Remarks and references to Appendices
FRICOURT	1/1/17		Visited and inspected BAZENTIN Area, New Camps. Baths &c.	
			Strength and distribution of Section:-	
			FRICOURT .... 20 N.C.Os and Men. and 9 attached men.	
			BAZENTIN .... 5 do. 17 do.	
			BECOURT CAMP .... 1 N.C.O. i/c of Town Majors P.B. Men.	
			DIV. TRAINING SCHOOL 1 " " Sanitary Squad.	
	2/1/17		Routine work and inspections in area. Baths at Bazentin cleaned up ready for handing over.	
			Following men returned to Divisional Coy. 26144. Pte Abrahams. 1st S.W. Borderers	
			36294 " Thomas W.H 2nd Welsh Regt.	
			2209 Pte Lawrence H. left for England on leave.	
	3/1/17		Lorry and drivers to workshops for repairs. Routine work and inspections in area.	
	4/1/17		Command of Section taken over by Capt L.R. TOSSWILL. R.A.M.C.T vice Capt C.Y. FORD RAMC	
			Baths at Bazentin taken over by 50th Division	
	5/1/17		Visited Div. Hdqrs. Bazentin Area, Baths, New Camps &c.	
	6/1/17		Routine work and inspections in area.	
	7/1/17		Visited Bazentin Area, inspected camps, baths &c. Continued wet weather renders the provision of sanitary services a matter of considerable difficulty, especially with regard to digging of pits for latrines, urinals &c.	
			No. 15364 Pte HANKS. attached from 1st Gloucester Regt returned to his Unit.	LRT.

2449 Wt. W14957/M90 750,000 1/16 J.B.C. & A. Forms/C.2118/12.

Army Form C. 2118.

Instructions regarding War Diaries and Intelligence Summaries are contained in F. S. Regs., Part II. and the Staff Manual respectively. Title Pages will be prepared in manuscript.

WAR DIARY
or
~~INTELLIGENCE~~ SUMMARY
(Erase heading not required.)

Place	Date	Hour	Summary of Events and Information	Remarks and references to Appendices
FRICOURT	8/1/17		Visited Bazentin Area. Lorry and drivers returned from workshops.	
	9/1/17		Inspected Water Points in Area. Weather unsettled. Some rain	
			30113 Pte C F FROST. left for England. authority D A G C R No 41843/11/B of 7/1/17	
	10/1/17		Routine work & inspections in area. Weather fine.	
	11/1/17		Visited and inspected High Wood Area and High Wood Camps.	
			13 men attached from 1st Division at Bazentin returned to their Units.	
			Arranged with Q 50 Division for daily fatigue party of 20 men for work in Bazentin Area.	
			Weather wet and cold. slight snow.	
	12/1/17		Inspected BECOURT CAMP with A D M S 1st Division. Weather showery.	
	13/1/17		Visited Fricourt Camp re case of Diphtheria in 1st Camerons. and reported overcrowding in huts	
			Report to A. D. M. S. 50th Division. re High Wood E + W. Camps.	
			" " " 1st " " Becourt Camp, with request for ruling that pails	
			shall be used in Latrines only when. (1) Contents are incinerated	
			(2) Nature of soil prevents digging of deep trenches.	
			Fatigue party of 20 men from 50 Divn at work in Bazentin Area. Weather fine few showers	
	14/1/17		Investigated outbreak of Dysentery in 1st Northants Regt and report to A D M S. 1st Division	
			Inspected MAMETZ WOOD Area and reports to D D M S III Corps re condition of vacated	
			Camps at X 23 d central and accumulation of horse manure on Contalmaison Road.	WT
			Weather Showery	

2449 Wt. W14957/M90 750,000 1/16 J.B.C. & A. Forms/C.2118/12.

Instructions regarding War Diaries and Intelligence Summaries are contained in F. S. Regs., Part II. and the Staff Manual respectively. Title Pages will be prepared in manuscript.

WAR DIARY
or
~~INTELLIGENCE SUMMARY~~
(Erase heading not required.)

Army Form C. 2118.

Place	Date	Hour	Summary of Events and Information	Remarks and references to Appendices
FRICOURT	15/1/17		Courses of Instruction in Sanitation (Reference D.M.S. 4th Army No 23/94 of 30/12/16) commenced – 23 N.C.Os. and men from sanitary squads of various units in the Division attended and were billeted and rationed by the Sanitary Section –	
	16/1/16		Second days Instruction given to the 23 NCOs + men who then rejoined their Units. Routine work and inspections carried out in area. Weather fine, but snow fell during night.	
	17/1/16		do. do. do. Slight snow + thaw in afternoon –	
	18/1/17		Visited new area – & inspected portions of same – 1262 Pte HOLLIMAN left for England on 10 days leave – weather very cold, slight falls of snow + sleet –	
	19/1/17		Routine work and arranging re Move &c. Visited HEILLY re disinfecting chamber. Baths at Fricourt dismantled – Total bathed during month to date 1568 –	
	20/1/17		Visited new area, and sent forward advance party of 2 N.C.Os. and 2 men who took over billet at Chingwolles – Two lorries supplied by D.A.D.O.S. 1st Division employed transporting stores – weather cold + unsettled –	
	21/1/17		Routine work in area, + transporting stores &c – weather very cold.	
	22/1/17		do. do – Subsection from BAZENTIN rejoined Section Headquarters – weather very cold, hard frost –	
	23/1/17		Section vacated billet at Fricourt and moved to BAIZIEUX – Stores not required were handed over to 1st Anzac Sanitary Section – weather fine, hard frost	LRT.

2449 Wt. W14957/M90 750,000 1/16 J.B.C. & A. Forms/C.2118/12.

Instructions regarding War Diaries and Intelligence Summaries are contained in F. S. Regs., Part II. and the Staff Manual respectively. Title Pages will be prepared in manuscript.

WAR DIARY
or
~~INTELLIGENCE SUMMARY~~
(Erase heading not required.)

Army Form C. 2118.

Place	Date	Hour	Summary of Events and Information	Remarks and references to Appendices
BAIZIEUX	24/1/17		Visited new area. Section employed overhauling sites &c. Hard frost.	
	25/1/17		Inspection made of 1st Div. Headqrs & Headqrs Billets. One N.C.O. & 4 men proceeded to join advance party in new area. 1369 Pte W. H. SLOBOM. 1st London Sanitary Coy. R.A.M.C.T. reported as a reinforcement. Hard frost.	
	26/1/17		Section moved to CHUIGNOLLES. leaving at BAIZIEUX a sub section of 1 N.C.O. & 7 men in accordance with D.R.O. No. 430 of 24/1/17	
CHUIGNOLLES	27/1/17		Preliminary inspections in new area. Hard frost.	
	28/1/17		Inspected baths &c. in Forward Area. Dompierre. Fontaine les Cappy &c.	
	29/1/17		Arranged with Capt Ford R.A.M.C. re construction of baths at CHUIGNES. Arranged with A.D.M.S. and D.A.D.M.S. 1st Div re incineration of excreta in CHUIGNOLLES.	
	30/1/17		Routine work. Inspected CHUIGNOLLES and fixed upon sites for Sanitary services. 2209 L/Cpl Lawrence reported from sanitary duty at 1st Divisional Training School.	
	31/1/17		Inspected CHUIGNES in company of Town Major and fixed upon sites for latrines &c. Weather fine. Hard frost. Reported to A.D.M.S. 1st Division re water supply in new area.	

L. R. Tosswill Capt RAMCT
O.C. 13th Sanitary Section
31/1/17.

2449 Wt. W14957/M90 750,000 1/16 J.B.C. & A. Forms/C.2118/12.

Feb. 1917

Confidential -

140/1994

Vol 23

WAR DIARY OF

O.C. No. 13 SANITARY SECTION - 1ST DIVISION

From 1st to 28th February 1917 -

VOLUME XIV

Army Form C. 2118.

Instructions regarding War Diaries and Intelligence Summaries are contained in F. S. Regs., Part II. and the Staff Manual respectively. Title Pages will be prepared in manuscript.

WAR DIARY
or
INTELLIGENCE SUMMARY
(Erase heading not required.)

Place	Date	Hour	Summary of Events and Information	Remarks and references to Appendices
CHUIGNOLLES	1 2/17		Section employed preparing latrines and collecting stores in new area. Weather very cold. hard frost.	
	2 2/17		Visited MORCOURT and CERISY with reference to water supply of 1st Division troops temporarily billeted there. Section employed as yesterday.	
	3 2/17		Reported to A.D.M.S. at MERICOURT. Visited CHUIGNES re removal of stores for sanitary work. Subsection left at BAIZIEUX rejoined Section Headquarters at CHUIGNOLLES. Section preparing latrines &c. Hard frost continues.	
	4 2/17		Visited MERICOURT re arrangements in new area and interview with D.D.M.S at CERISY. Tested water supply at MORCOURT. 2138 L/Cpl C.A. SNELLING left for duty at III Corps Head quarters. Section employed preparing latrines, incinerators, drawing bricks, erecting huts &c. Hard frost.	
	5 2/17		Visited DOMPIERRE, ASSEVILLIERS and BOIS DE BOULOGNE re water supply in forward area. Section employed as before. Hard frost.	
	6 2/17		Obtained ash bins for conveyance of excreta to incinerators. Fatigue party of 8 men and 2 limbers employed daily from today emptying latrine pails in public latrines at CHUIGNOLLES. Section employed in providing public sanitary services and moving stores to new billet. Hard frost continues.	
	7 2/17		Visited CHUIGNES re site of latrines and advised Town Major re sanitary arrangements.	WT

2449 Wt. W14957/M90 750,000 1/16 J.B.C. & A. Forms/C.2118/12.

Instructions regarding War Diaries and Intelligence Summaries are contained in F. S. Regs., Part II. and the Staff Manual respectively. Title Pages will be prepared in manuscript.

WAR DIARY
or
INTELLIGENCE SUMMARY

(Erase heading not required.)

Army Form C. 2118.

Place	Date	Hour	Summary of Events and Information	Remarks and references to Appendices
CHUIGNOLLES	8/2/17		Subsection of 1 N.C.O. and 4 men proceeded to CHUIGNES for sanitary duty in that area. 1646 Cpl K.W. Hobbs. left to take over temporary charge of baths at CHUIGNES. Huts at Camp 52 vacated by Tonkinese Troops, disinfected and A.D.M.S. notified. 3 men (Town Major's Billet Wardens) attached for rations. Weather fine, hard frost.	
	9/2/17		Visited waggon lines of 25th 26th & 39th Brigades R.F.A. Fatigue parties of 34 employed clearing up streets &c in Chuignolles. 4 Men from 1st Camerons and one man from 8th R.Berks temporarily attached to assist with carpenters & bricklayers work. Weather fine hard frost.	
	10/2/17		Visited CHUIGNES and Telegraph Camp occupied by 2nd R.M.F. Visited Abrevoir on Chuignes Road with D.E. and III Corps Water Engineer. Fatigue party of 40 men employed clearing up in Chuignolles. 40075 L/Cpl Lambert. 1st R.Hights temporarily attached for duty. Weather fine hard frost.	
	11/2/17		D.R.O. 456 re damage to growing crops read out on parade. Fatigue party of 40. digging drain for baths, cleaning up in village &c Lorry supplied by Division drawing materials from Engineers dump. 37178 L/Cpl Watkinson. 8 R.Berks temporarily attached from 1st Divisional Coy.	
	12/2/17		Four men from 1st Divisional Coy attached for duty as Town Major's men for removal and incineration of excreta from public latrines. 2 men from 1st L N Lancs temporarily attached for duty. Fatigue party of 20 men. clearing up village &c. Weather fine. hard frost.	WS

2449 Wt. W14957/M90 750,000 1/16 J.B.C. & A. Forms/C.2118/12.

Instructions regarding War Diaries and Intelligence Summaries are contained in F. S. Regs., Part II. and the Staff Manual respectively. Title Pages will be prepared in manuscript.

WAR DIARY
or
INTELLIGENCE SUMMARY

(Erase heading not required.)

Army Form C. 2118.

Place	Date	Hour	Summary of Events and Information	Remarks and references to Appendices
CHUIGNOLLES	13²/17		Orders re lights after 8 p.m. (1st Div 6640) read out on parade. Fatigue party of 40 men road cleaning and helping in yard. 6559 Pte CASEY. 2nd R.M.F. proceeded to Sub. Section at Chuignes for duty. Weather fine, hard frost.	
	14²/17		Supply tank for drinking & cooking water fixed near Headquarters. Visited CHUIGNES and FONTAINE-LES-CAPPY. G R Os and Local Orders re fire read out on parade. Weather fine, frost continues Baths in working order.	
	15²/17		Visited AMIENS to purchase - sanitary stores Bathing commenced for R.Es. 83 men bathed and clean clothing issued to same. Fatigue party of 20 employed cleaning out billets. Weather fine. frost not so severe.	
	16²/17		D. Hq moved into Chuignolles. Section employed fixing latrines &c. Fatigue party 40 men cleaning out billets, sweeping roads helping with baths &c. G S waggon employed daily from today drawing stores &c Weather fine. frost much less severe.	
	17²/17		200 gallon tank for supply of chlorinated water fixed at well of Billet No 70. Visited CHUIGNES and FONTAINE-LES-CAPPY. Saw French Chef de genie at Proyart with D.E. Combined incinerator and drying room (No 1) in use. allotment of coal for same (1st Div Q 259) one cwt daily (from today) for each incinerator. Fatigue party of 20 clean up village &c Thaw and heavy rain during night.	[initials]

2449 Wt. W14957/M90 750,000 1/16 J.B.C. & A. Forms/C.2118/12.

Army Form C. 2118.

Instructions regarding War Diaries and Intelligence Summaries are contained in F. S. Regs., Part II. and the Staff Manual respectively. Title Pages will be prepared in manuscript.

WAR DIARY
or
INTELLIGENCE SUMMARY
(Erase heading not required.)

Place	Date	Hour	Summary of Events and Information	Remarks and references to Appendices
CHUIGNOLLES	18²/17		Visited ASSEVILLERS – TELEGRAPH CAMP and BECQUINCOURT Fatigue party of 40 men. clearing up streets & helping in yard, baths &c. 2566 Pte J W. WESTRON was admitted to Hospital. Thaw continued	
	19²/17		Visited Corps Sanitary Officer at Corps Headquarters G. S. wagon complete reported for duty from 1st D.A.C. and is temporarily attached to Section. 1646 Cpl HOBBS. returned from temporary duty at 1st Divisional Baths CHUIGNES. 1369 Pte SLOBOM joined sub section at CHUIGNES for duty. Fatigue party of 40 men employed clearing up streets, billets, filling in old French latrines &c. Thaw continued and some rain.	
	20²/17		Visited FONTAINE-LES-CAPPY and TELEGRAPH CAMP to investigate cases of Infectious disease reported there and at each place saw contacts with cases. At Telegraph Camp found that one of contacts (Pte CLARKES. 1st S.W.B) was suffering from Rose Measles. Fatigue party 40 men clearing streets. improving drainage, &c. Two tanks sunk in ground for storage and tank fitted to G. S. wagon for conveyance of water to baths, a water cart not being available. Rain almost all day.	

LWS

2449 Wt. W14957/M90 750,000 1/16 J.B.C. & A. Forms/C.2118/12.

Army Form C. 2118.

Instructions regarding War Diaries and Intelligence Summaries are contained in F. S. Regs., Part II. and the Staff Manual respectively. Title Pages will be prepared in manuscript.

WAR DIARY
or
INTELLIGENCE SUMMARY
(Erase heading not required.)

Place	Date	Hour	Summary of Events and Information	Remarks and references to Appendices
CHUIGNOLLES	21 2/17		Inspected CHUIGNES. Visited Scabies Hospital at VILLERS-BRETONNEUX with DDMS. Section employed on routine work in area. Fatigue party cleaning up village for Town Major. Rain nearly all day.	
	22 2/17		Inspected CUISINES and FONTAINE-LES-CAPPY Camps. Visited CHUIGNES and fixed sites for permanent latrines and ablution benches. Fatigue party of 22 men cleaning up in village. 2566 Pte J. W. WESTRON rejoined from Hospital. Rain nearly all day.	
	23 2/17		Visited CHUIGNES & ASSEVILLERS also Hdqrs 25th Bde RFA near BECQUINCOURT. Fatigue party of 20 drawing bricks stores cleaning up yard etc. 3155 Pte S ROBERTS 1st L.N. Lancs. attd from 1st Divisional Coy. left for Transportation Depot BOULOGNE in accordance with ADMS 1st Div No 1927 of 22/2. Weather damp, slight frost at night.	
	24 2/17		Inspected billets of Supply Section at CHUIGNES Railhead and visited Corps Rest Station at CERISY with A.D.M.S. Tank for supply of chlorinated water fixed up at Billet No 59. Fatigue parties 68 men employed emptying latrine buckets, cleaning up streets, etc. 2 G.S. wagons and one limber drawing materials etc. Weather fine slight frost at night.	
	25 2/17		Inspected 1st Bde T'port Lines at CUISINES. Visited Corps Rest Station to advise re infectious accommodation & treatment. N.C.O. of Section sent to Maricourt with materials for latrines etc, & to see Town Major re accommodation required. Fatigue parties of 60 and 4 G.S. wagons. N.C.O. and one attached man sent to join Subsection at CHUIGNES. Weather fine and warm.	
	26 2/17		Making arrangements re case of C.S.M in 115 Bty 25 Bde RFA and accompanied G.O.C on inspection of billets in CHUIGNOLLES. Fatigue parties of 40 and 2 G.S wagons. Weather fine and warm.	

2149 Wt. W14957/M90 750,000 1/16 J.B.C. & A. Forms/C.2118/12.

Army Form C. 2118.

Instructions regarding War Diaries and Intelligence Summaries are contained in F. S. Regs., Part II. and the Staff Manual respectively. Title pages will be prepared in manuscript.

WAR DIARY
or
INTELLIGENCE SUMMARY.
(Erase heading not required.)

Place	Date	Hour	Summary of Events and Information	Remarks and references to Appendices
CHUIGNOLLES	27/2/17		Revised orders detailing fatigue parties (1st Division No 6745) in operation.– At CHUIGNOLLES – 12 men daily at 8.15 a.m. for sanitary duty. 4 " " " 8.15 a.m. and 2 p.m. together with 2 horses and driver for duty emptying latrine pails At CHUIGNES – 6 " " " 8.15 a.m. for sanitary duty. 4 " " " 8.15 a.m. & 2 p.m. together with 2 horses & driver for duty emptying latrine pails A waggon, fitted up for carrying latrine pails and contents to incinerators, in use at CHUIGNOLLES and another at CHUIGNES.	
	28/2/17		Inspected with A.D.M.S., Camps 5 & 6 and 1st D.A.C. Camp. MERICOURT-SUR-SOMME and Camp. 52 (1st D. Train) P.O.W. Camp and R.T.O's camp MERIGNOLLES. Section employed on routine work, fatigue parties as detailed yesterday, & three additional G.S. waggons drawing stores. Weather fine and mild.–	

Summary of Infectious Disease notified during month.–

Dysentery	10 cases
Paratyphoid B	2 "
do A	1 "
Mumps	2 "
Typhoid	1 "
T.B. (lung)	1 "
German Measles	3 "
Measles	3 "
C.S. Meningitis	1 "

In addition the following were notified as carriers.–

Para A.	3 cases.
Dysentery (Flex)	4. "

L. R. Tosswill Capt
O.C. 13th San. Section
1/3/17.

2353 Wt. W2544/1454 700,000 5/15 D. D. & L. A.D.S.S./Forms/C. 2118.

Mar. 1917

1st Div

Confidential

140/2043

Vol 23

WAR DIARY OF

O.C. No 13 SANITARY SECTION - 1ST DIVISION -

From 1st to 31st March 1917 -

Volume XV.

Army Form C. 2118.

WAR DIARY
or
INTELLIGENCE SUMMARY.
(Erase heading not required.)

Instructions regarding War Diaries and Intelligence Summaries are contained in F. S. Regs., Part II. and the Staff Manual respectively. Title pages will be prepared in manuscript.

Place	Date	Hour	Summary of Events and Information	Remarks and references to Appendices
CHUIGNOLLES	1 3/17		Visited Corps Hdqrs then drew supply of CHLORAMINE in CORBIE. then to Corps Rest Station at CERISY and left officers latrine as pattern. Strength. Section 27. Attached 24. Attached for rations only 8.	
	2 3/17		Inspected CHUIGNES in morning. In afternoon visited and inspected Div Training School at BLANGY TRONVILLE Thaw precautions off and lorry able to take the road.	
	3 3/17		Fatigue parties failed to report at appointed times. thereby causing delay + inconvenience. Weather fine but cold, snow fell during night.	
	4 3/17		Attended meeting of 4th Army Medical Society + discussion on dysentery. Weather fine + cold but snow melted rapidly.	
	5 3/17		Inspections in CHUIGNES.	
	6 3/17		Visited CHUIGNES and MERICOURT-SUR-SOMME and Camp 6 in morning. Afternoon to RAMC Dump at CERISY Party of 6 men sent to CUISINES camp to erect combined incinerator and drying room. Weather fine.	
	7 3/17		Visited Headquarters 4th Army with A.D.M.S. 3 additional "T.U" men attached to Section from 1st Divisional Coy Weather fine + cold.	

2353 Wt. W2544/1454 700,000 5/15 D. D. & L. A.D.S.S./Forms/C. 2118.

Instructions regarding War Diaries and Intelligence Summaries are contained in F. S. Regs., Part II. and the Staff Manual respectively. Title pages will be prepared in manuscript.

WAR DIARY
or
~~INTELLIGENCE~~ SUMMARY.

(Erase heading not required.)

Army Form C. 2118.

Place	Date	Hour	Summary of Events and Information	Remarks and references to Appendices
CHUIGNOLLES	8 3/17		Inspected billets in CHUIGNOLLES with A.D.M.S. R4151 Pte Gossman 2 K.R.R.C. "T.U" attd from 1 Div Coy pronounced FIT and returned to his Unit Fine slight frost	
	9 3/17		Inspected billets in CHUIGNOLLES with A.D.M.S. N.C.O. of Section, with fatigue party from 1st D.A.C. cleaning up Camp 6. Fine, slight snow & very cold	
	10 3/17		Inspected CHUIGNES and CUISINES hutments with A.D.M.S.	
	11 3/17		Inspection by N.C.O. of Section of Camps at MERIGNOLLES Station and letter setting out sanitary requirements sent to O.C. 1st Divisional Fatigue Party. Box Respirators issued to men, and tested with lacrymatory to ensure that they fit properly. Two men temporarily attached from 1st Camerons returned to their Unit. Weather fine & much warmer	
	12 3/17		Visited CHUIGNES re sanitary services arranged with R.E. Officer re disposal of ablution water from Baths	
	13 3/17		Visited camps of 1st Camerons BECQUINCOURT, Divisional Soup Kitchen and DIV. Gas School. Fatigue party of 20 from 1st D.A.C. cleaning out huts at No 6 Camp ½ N.C.O. of Section Weather fine & warmer	
	14 3/17		Lorry drew stores, latrine buckets &c from No 1 Field Ambulance CERISY Weather fine & warmer	[initials]

2353 Wt. W2514/1454 700,000 5/15 D. D. & L. A.D.S.S./Forms/C. 2118.

Army Form C. 2118.

Instructions regarding War Diaries and Intelligence Summaries are contained in F. S. Regs., Part II. and the Staff Manual respectively. Title pages will be prepared in manuscript.

WAR DIARY
or
INTELLIGENCE SUMMARY.
(Erase heading not required.)

Place	Date	Hour	Summary of Events and Information	Remarks and references to Appendices
CHUIGNOLLES	15.3.17		Visited water points in Forward Area in morning – viz Grand Bois, Petit Bois, Bois Est & Assevillers Soup Kitchen & Prisoners Cage at DOMPIERRE and billets of 1st L.N.Lancs with A.D.M.S.	
			Fatigue party of 20 from 1st D.A.C. cleaning up No 6 Camp. i/c N.C.O. of Section.	
			Weather fine slight frost at night – CUISINES party returned, having erected combined drying room & incinerator.	
	16.3.17		Inspected billets at CHUIGNOLLES and CHUIGNES – 1st Northants, 2nd K.R.R.C. and 2 R Sussex with A.D.M.S	
			Fatigue party of 20 from 1st D.A.C. cleaning up No 6 Camp. i/c N.C.O. of Section.	
	17.3.17		Visited ASSEVILLERS with A.D.M.S. – Sample of water from well at BARLEUX, received from Capt POWELL – 409th (Lowland) Field Coy R.E. – found to contain ARSENIC – A.A. & Q.M.G – ADMS – and C.R.E. notified and ~~~~ notice POISONED WATER placed on well –	
			Pte CALVERLEY joined Subsection at CHUIGNES – weather fine –	
	18.3.17		Visited BARLEUX and ETERPIGNEY with A.D.M.S. – weather fine –	
	19.3.17		Visited BARLEUX and ETERPIGNEY. and took samples of water which were handed over to Mobile Laboratory –	
	20.3.17		Visited VILLERS CARBONELL, BRIE, and ETERPIGNEY – collected samples of water –	
			17 men of Sanitary Section inoculated with T.A.B	
			weather unsettled & showery –	
	21.3.17		Report on samples of water collected yesterday sent to G and Q – A.D.M.S. and C.R.E. and copies of same circulated throughout the Division (1st Div No 6865/2 of 22.3.17)	
			Visited Divisional Soup Kitchen at DOMPIERRE in morning – In afternoon visited Div. Baths at CHUIGNES and incinerators &c in CHUIGNOLLES with S.O. 42nd Division –	
			weather unsettled slight snow –	[initials]

2353 Wt. W2544/1454 700,000 5/15 D. D. & L. A.D.S.S./Forms/C. 2118.

Instructions regarding War Diaries and Intelligence Summaries are contained in F. S. Regs., Part II. and the Staff Manual respectively. Title pages will be prepared in manuscript.

Army Form C. 2118.

WAR DIARY
or
INTELLIGENCE SUMMARY.
(Erase heading not required.)

Place	Date	Hour	Summary of Events and Information	Remarks and references to Appendices
CHUIGNOLLES	22/3/17		Routine work. Weather fine but cold N.C.O. of Section fixed notice boards to wells & Water Points at VILLERS CARBONEL and BRIE	
	23/3/17		do. do.	
	24/3/17		do. do. Summer time commenced from 11 p.m.	
	25/3/17		Visited DOMPIERRE and BECQUINCOURT. met by appointment S.O. 50th Div. at MERICOURT. Sub section at CHUIGNES returned to Section Headquarters. Weather fine.	
	26/3/17		Routine work. Subsection returned to CHUIGNES. order re move having been cancelled. Rain nearly all day	
	27/3/17		New P.H.G. smoke helmets issued to men in exchange for old ones returned to ordnance. Fire orders re read out on parade. Weather showery.	
	28/3/17		N.C.O. of Section fixed notice boards re chlorination &c to wells at DOMPIERRE, BECQUINCOURT and vicinity. Weather fine. Capt Torswill left for England on leave.	
	29/3/17		Capt W. T MUNRO. RAMC. assumed temporary command of Section vice Capt Torswill on leave S O 50th Division advised that his Sub sections in new area, would be withdrawn today. F. A & M. S proceeded to MERICOURT in morning and arranged to take over billets, but order was cancelled at one p.m. Billet &c at advanced Div. Hq disinfected after case of Measles. Weather showery.	
	30/3/17		Visited and inspected Water Points at CHUIGNES with reference to epidemic of diarrhoea in 2nd Welsh. and sent sample of water to Mobile Laboratory for bact. exam examination. Visited and inspected water points in back area. Weather showery.	W.T.M.

2353 Wt. W2544/1454 700,000 5/15 D. D. & L. A.D.S.S./Forms/C. 2118.

Instructions regarding War Diaries and Intelligence Summaries are contained in F. S. Regs., Part II. and the Staff Manual respectively. Title pages will be prepared in manuscript.

Army Form C. 2118.

WAR DIARY
or
INTELLIGENCE SUMMARY.
(Erase heading not required.)

Place	Date	Hour	Summary of Events and Information	Remarks and references to Appendices
CHUIGNOLLES	31/3/17		Completed inspection of wells in Back Area, fixed notices to same where necessary and reported on same to A.D.M.S. 1st Division. Section employed on routine work, making stock of latrine boxes and urinals &c. Weather showery and unsettled.	
			Wm. T. Munro Capt. R.A.M.C. Acting O.C. 1B San. Section, 1st Division.	

2353 Wt. W2544/1454 700,000 5/15 D. D. & L. A.D.S.S./Forms/C. 2118.

www.ingramcontent.com/pod-product-compliance
Lightning Source LLC
Chambersburg PA
CBHW080847230426
43662CB00013B/2043